THE
UK RES
WINE LISTS

NEVILLE BLECH

edited by Philip Williamson and David Moore
Authors of the acclaimed *Wine behind the label*

Williamson Moore Publishing Limited
www.winebehindthelabel.com

First published in 2005 by Williamson Moore
13 Rances Way Winchester Hampshire SO22 4PN United Kingdom
Tel/Fax +44 (0)1962 625 539
E-mail: info@williamson-moore.co.uk

A catalogue record for this book is available from the British Library.

ISBN 0-9544097-2-8

Editorial assistance from Bill Evans and Ed Francis

Designed by Davis Wadicci

Printed and bound in Great Britain by Ashford Colour Press Ltd, Fareham, Hants

Whilst every care has been taken in the preparation of this guide, the publishers and authors cannot accept responsibility of any kind for consequences arising from reliance upon information contained in it.

ABOUT THE AUTHOR

After qualifying as a Chartered Accountant, Neville Blech spent two years broaching his wine knowledge in Italy. On his return to England he spent some years as a partner in an accountancy practice whilst continuing to broaden his wine knowledge in both theory and practice.

In 1974, he and his talented wife Sonia, opened a 'restaurant with rooms' in the Wye Valley, which also became the first Michelin starred restaurant in Wales with Sonia being the first woman chef to gain a Michelin star in the UK. On returning to London in 1980, they opened the highly acclaimed Mijanou Restaurant in Ebury Street, where Neville became the first winner of the Wine List of the Year competition, sponsored by Wines of Spain, in 1988.

In 1996 they were made "an offer they couldn't refuse" for the restaurant and Neville then continued to build up his wine importing business, The Wine Treasury, which specialised in wines from California and Italy. This was sold in 2002 and he now concentrates on developing www.bacchusandcomus.co.uk - a website for the gastronomically washed - writing, consulting and organising wine tours and dinners.

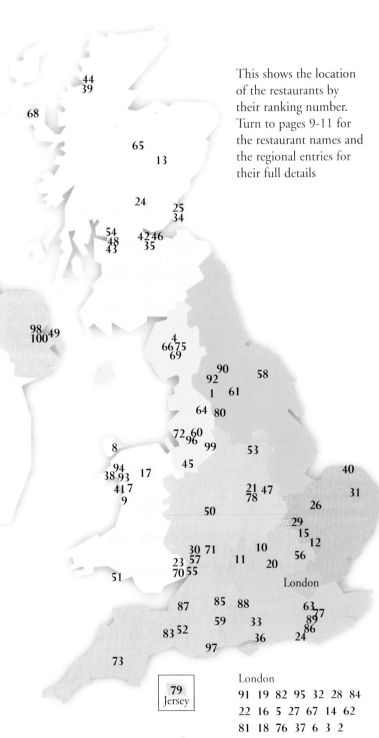

This shows the location of the restaurants by their ranking number. Turn to pages 9-11 for the restaurant names and the regional entries for their full details

London

91 19 82 95 32 28 84
22 16 5 27 67 14 62
81 18 76 37 6 3 2

79 Jersey

4

CONTENTS

INTRODUCTION

Imagine this situation. You are hosting a lunch or dinner at a well-known restaurant in the area and you are confronted with the wine list. You want to get on with enjoying your time, be it with family, friends or business colleagues, and you find the you may have to plough through a hundred, two hundred, three hundred or even more wines (sometimes many more). You desperately need to make a quick decision on your wine choices – so do you (a) go for the cheapest House wine, even if you know that it's going to taste like you've licked the backs of a thousand envelopes, (b) ask the sommelier for advice (assuming there is one) and hope that he or she is not going to recommend something which is way beyond your budget, (c) go for something safe like Sancerre or a well known claret that you can either afford, or if the company's paying, something that will suitably impress, or (d) try to go it alone and choose something that you think will be interesting and good value?

What should you be looking for? Well, unless you are on a strict budget, the first thing you should be looking for is quality. Does this restaurant have a good selection of quality wines? And if so, are there any such wines that demand attention as being value for money? Apart from the obvious top clarets and Burgundies there are many places in the world today where great wine is produced and we look to the enterprising restaurateur for a list which is quality driven all round, innovative and exciting. Does the restaurant have an interesting selection of half-bottles? If so, I, for one, would be delighted to forego a bottle of wine with the meal for three halves! Does the restaurant have an interesting selection of dry wines by the glass to allow me to experiment? (And I don't mean the cheapest House red and white the proprietor can lay his hands on). Is the list an easy read, with helpful tasting notes (geared to the cuisine and not to some wine merchant's blather), or is there a helpful and knowledgeable sommelier to guide you through it?

The best wine choices happen when an interested and knowledgeable customer and an experienced sommelier work together – rather than in a competition to outsmart each other – to find inspired matches for the group of people, the food they are ordering and their budget. But not all restaurants have a sommelier, so prior knowledge of the list is a huge bonus in this situation, as well as in the sadly more common scenario where you feel you just have to go it alone. And that's where this book comes in.

In our quest to find some wine list paradigms, we took all of the top UK wine lists submitted to us and put them under the microscope to see if they meet up to our expectations. Wine quality was determined from the star rating system in

INTRODUCTION

Wine behind the Label – the only global reference with sufficient scope and depth for the task in hand. The criteria used to select, then rate the Top 100 is somewhat complicated, based on (a) the percentage of wines on the list rated at 4, 5 or super 5 stars in *Wine Behind The Label*; (b) the percentage of 3-star wines on the list (with a coefficient factor); (c) the percentage of 3-, 4- and 5-star wines listed at under £30, £40 and £50 (again with a coefficient factor); (d) the proportion of the total number of half-bottles and wines by the glass on the list (with an adjustment for dessert wines); (e) the percentage of 3-, 4- and 5-star half-bottles and wines by the glass on the list and (f) an overall impression of the list generally. The score is then tallied and the lists are set out in the following pages in their order of merit. Note that it is not within the province of this book to comment on any wine that does not merit at least 3 stars in *Wine Behind the Label* unless they are of exceptional value.

Our research turned up some interesting findings which you can uncover on these pages. It also is interesting to observe that although the emphasis is on overall quality in the list, those establishments that can list quality at very low prices have scored heavily, even though they may not have as many quality wines as some of the more expensive ones. Thus there are 8 London establishments in the top 20 and 4 from rural Wales.

Caveats
1. This list has been compiled from wine lists submitted to us between March and June 2005. Some establishments did not submit their list, so if you do not find your favourite wine list here, it could be that we did not see it and you should not therefore assume that it wasn't good enough to make the Top 100. Obviously, we cannot make a judgement on what we haven't seen, so if you think that there is a glaring omission, please persuade the restaurant to submit their wine list for next year's edition. After all, it doesn't cost them anything – there is absolutely no charge for admission.

2. This review is solely on the wine list. It does not take into account the quality or price of the food (although many of the restaurants listed are highly rated for it – you will have to look at other guides for that), nor the quality of the wine service, since we have not visited most of these establishments, although, again, you will find comments on this in other guides.

HOW TO USE THIS BOOK

This book will take the heartache out of making difficult wine decisions. By doing just a little homework before you arrive at the restaurant, you will be able to narrow down the choices to just a handful of wines which you know are going to be good value for money (in the context of the list and your budget) or simply outstandingly good. From these you can make a final selection according to which dishes you order – either go it alone or discuss the options with the friendly staff, who no doubt will be most impressed with your knowledgeable grasp of their list. So, this is what to do, step by step:

1. Choose a restaurant – you will find that all of them are featured in one food guide or another and all have a good local reputation, so there shouldn't be any problem about the food. The restaurants are grouped regionally and there is also an index at the back of the book. However, if the wine is more important than the food for you, then simply go by the order of merit in this book.

2. Get a general idea of the pricing level to expect and select half a dozen or so of the wines featured in the book as being good value for the quality and write them down on a piece of paper to take with you to the restaurant.

3. When you get the wine list, quickly check that the wines are still on the list (with the use of computers these days, lists tend to change more frequently than they used to). The likelihood is that there will be vintage changes and more probably price changes, but hopefully not too many de-listings.

4. When your guests have chosen their food, you can confidently make your choice from the wines you have written down, which should considerably shorten the time you have to spend ignoring your guests.

5. Confirm your choices with the sommelier or chief order-taker, relax and enjoy the occasion.

Even if you are visiting restaurants that are not in this book, I hope that you will be able to glean sufficient knowledge to make informed wine choices every time you eat out.

Happy wining and dining

RANKINGS

Top 100 OVERALL

1	DEVONSHIRE ARMS - BURLINGTON RESTAURANT	190.35
2	TATE RESTAURANT	177.36
3	RSJ	171.35
4	SHARROW BAY	163.38
5	GORDON RAMSAY	161.97
6	RANSOME'S DOCK	156.42
7	DYLANWAD DA	155.25
8	YE OLDE BULL'S HEAD	154.95
9	PENHELIG ARMS	153.14
10	CROOKED BILLET	152.69
11	CHERWELL BOATHOUSE	151.67
12	SYCAMORE HOUSE	149.96
13	DARROCH LEARG	145.87
14	LA TROMPETTE	144.52
15	OLD BRIDGE AT HUNTINGDON	141.64
16	THE GLASSHOUSE	140.61
17	TYDDYN LLAN	139.46
18	LOCANDA LOCATELLI	137.83
19	BENTLEY KEMPINSKI 1880	135.52
20	SIR CHARLES NAPIER	131.58
21	OPERA HOUSE, LEICESTER	131.14
22	FIFTH FLOOR HARVEY NICHOLS	130.70
23	THE BELL AT SKENFRITH	130.58
24	KILLIECRANKIE HOUSE	130.49
25	THE PEAT INN	129.78
26	OLD FIRE ENGINE HOUSE	128.21
27	GREAT EASTERN HOTEL - AURORA	126.01
28	ENOTECA TURI	125.78
29	GRANGE HOTEL, BRAMPTON	124.53
30	LUMIÈRE	124.39
31	THE WILDEBEEST ARMS	123.39
32	THE DON	120.91
33	JSW	120.78
34	SANGSTER'S	118.49
35	WITCHERY BY THE CASTLE	117.70
36	36 ON THE QUAY	117.41
37	OXO TOWER	117.30
38	PLAS BODEGROES	114.06
39	SUMMER ISLES HOTEL	113.94
40	MORSTON HALL	112.06
41	PENMAENUCHAF HALL	111.87
42	CHAMPANY INN	111.45

43	UBIQUITOUS CHIP	111.40
44	THE ALBANNACH	111.23
45	CHESTER GROSVENOR – ARKLE RESTAURANT	111.13
46	FISHERS IN THE CITY	111.00
47	HAMBLETON HALL	110.78
48	BRIAN MAULE	110.55
49	SHANKS	110.34
50	HOTEL DU VIN, BIRMINGHAM	109.58
51	FAIRYHILL	109.40
52	LITTLE BARWICK HOUSE	108.23
53	THE OLD VICARAGE	107.56
54	ÉTAIN	105.98
55	CORSE LAWN	104.89
56	NOVELLI AT AUBERGE DU LAC	103.41
57	CHAMPIGNON SAUVAGE	103.26
58	THE STAR INN, HAROME	101.11
59	LES MIRABELLES	101.02
60	THE LIME TREE	100.82
61	HOTEL DU VIN, HARROGATE	97.92
62	LE CAFÉ DU JARDIN	96.85
63	GRAVETYE MANOR	96.37
64	NORTHCOTE MANOR	95.97
65	THE CROSS, KINGUSSIE	95.89
66	WHITE MOSS HOUSE	95.03
67	KENSINGTON PLACE	94.64
68	THE THREE CHIMNEYS	93.96
69	HOLBECK GHYLL	92.79
70	CROWN AT WHITEBROOK	92.51
71	COTSWOLD HOUSE	91.95
72	60 HOPE STREET	91.05
73	LEWTRENCHARD MANOR	89.92
74	HOTEL DU VIN, BRIGHTON	88.28
75	LINTHWAITE HOUSE HOTEL	85.59
76	MC CLEMENTS	83.79
77	HOTEL DU VIN, TUNBRIDGE WELLS	83.05
78	FIRENZE	82.11
79	LONGUEVILLE MANOR	81.82
80	THE WEAVERS SHED	81.26
81	LE DEUXIÈME	80.37
82	BLEEDING HEART	78.55
83	COMBE HOUSE	78.13
84	EYRE BROTHERS	77.68
85	THE WINDMILL	76.79
86	THE JOLLY SPORTSMAN	76.38

RANKINGS

87	CHARLTON HOUSE - THE MULBERRY RESTAURANT	75.19
88	GREYHOUND INN	75.11
89	THE GRIFFIN INN, FLETCHING	74.97
90	SWINTON PARK	73.55
91	AL DUCA	73.07
92	THE YORKE ARMS, RAMSGILL	71.92
93	MAES-Y-NEUADD	68.03
94	PORTMEIRION HOTEL	67.20
95	BRADLEYS	65.39
96	THE LOWRY HOTEL	60.92
97	THE MANSION HOUSE POOLE	60.80
98	CAYENNE	59.11
99	THYME RESTAURANT	56.72
100	ROSCOFF	55.36

Top 100 by QUALITY

1	GORDON RAMSAY	140.30
2	DEVONSHIRE ARMS - BURLINGTON RESTAURANT	135.84
3	TATE GALLERY	121.05
4	LOCANDA LOCATELLI	117.72
5	BENTLEY KEMPINSKI 1880	109.12
6	RANSOME'S DOCK	109.05
7	SHARROW BAY	107.74
8	GREAT EASTERN HOTEL - AURORA	103.36
9	LA TROMPETTE	102.03
10	THE GLASSHOUSE	98.89
11	THE DON	96.01
12	CHERWELL BOATHOUSE	95.33
13	36 ON THE QUAY	93.90
14	JSW	90.31
15	ENOTECA TURI	90.24
16	CHESTER GROSVENOR – ARKLE RESTAURANT	87.98
17	HOTEL DU VIN, BIRMINGHAM	86.58
18	NOVELLI AT AUBERGE DU LAC	85.79
19	THE PEAT INN	85.70
20	OXO TOWER	85.34
21	HAMBLETON HALL	84.45
22	SIR CHARLES NAPIER	83.94
23	CHAMPANY INN	83.52
24	FIFTH FLOOR HARVEY NICHOLS	82.63
25	OLD BRIDGE AT HUNTINGDON	78.60
26	WITCHERY BY THE CASTLE	78.23
27	ÉTAIN	76.99

28	SUMMER ISLES HOTEL	76.76
29	THE OLD VICARAGE	74.63
30	OPERA HOUSE, LEICESTER	74.33
31	LES MIRABELLES	73.45
32	TYDDYN LLAN	72.33
33	NORTHCOTE MANOR	72.19
34	UBIQUITOUS CHIP	71.95
35	FAIRYHILL	71.12
36	LITTLE BARWICK HOUSE	71.07
37	OLD FIRE ENGINE HOUSE	70.53
38	SHANKS	69.20
39	THE BELL AT SKENFRITH	68.69
40	YE OLDE BULL'S HEAD	68.64
41	MC CLEMENTS	68.58
42	CROOKED BILLET	67.85
43	RSJ	67.30
44	BRIAN MAULE	66.77
45	GRAVETYE MANOR	66.29
46	COTSWOLD HOUSE	61.75
47	HOLBECK GHYLL	60.76
48	HOTEL DU VIN, HARROGATE	59.91
49	THE THREE CHIMNEYS	58.69
50	LUMIÈRE	58.39
51	KENSINGTON PLACE	57.81
52	LONGUEVILLE MANOR	57.50
53	THE CROSS, KINGUSSIE	56.80
54	BLEEDING HEART	56.27
55	AL DUCA	56.08
56	PLAS BODEGROES	56.07
57	MORSTON HALL	54.12
58	THE ALBANNACH	51.90
59	CORSE LAWN	50.74
60	HOTEL DU VIN, BRIGHTON	50.71
61	HOTEL DU VIN, TUNBRIDGE WELLS	49.53
62	DARROCH LEARG	48.14
63	THE YORKE ARMS, RAMSGILL	47.86
64	THE WINDMILL	47.01
65	EYRE BROTHERS	46.18
66	CHAMPIGNON SAUVAGE	45.35
67	FISHERS IN THE CITY	44.77
68	60 HOPE STREET	44.22
69	COMBE HOUSE	43.32
70	PENHELIG ARMS	42.77
71	SWINTON PARK	42.73

RANKINGS

72	LINTHWAITE HOUSE HOTEL	42.66
73	CHARLTON HOUSE - THE MULBERRY RESTAURANT	41.10
74	KILLIECRANKIE HOUSE	40.22
75	WHITE MOSS HOUSE	40.17
76	THE LOWRY HOTEL	40.03
77	THE JOLLY SPORTSMAN	39.91
78	GREYHOUND INN, STOCKBRIDGE	39.64
79	PENMAENUCHAF HALL	39.21
80	THE STAR INN, HAROME	38.82
81	LEWTRENCHARD MANOR	38.61
82	THE LIME TREE	37.08
83	SYCAMORE HOUSE LITTLE SHELFORD	36.12
84	MAES-Y-NEUADD	35.15
85	DYLANWAD DA	35.08
86	THE GRANGE BRAMPTON	33.55
87	ROSCOFF	32.87
88	PORTMEIRION HOTEL	30.81
89	LE DEUXIÈME	30.80
90	THE GRIFFIN INN, FLETCHING	30.44
91	SANGSTER'S	29.82
92	CAYENNE	26.09
93	LE CAFÉ DU JARDIN	24.80
94	THYME RESTAURANT	24.65
95	BRADLEYS	23.91
96	THE MANSION HOUSE POOLE	23.09
97	THE WILDEBEEST ARMS	20.94
98	THE WEAVERS SHED	20.59
99	FIRENZE	20.35
100	CROWN AT WHITEBROOK	19.26

Top 100 for VALUE

1	SYCAMORE HOUSE LITTLE SHELFORD	105.83
2	DYLANWAD DA	104.17
3	PENHELIG ARMS	90.37
4	RSJ	84.05
5	THE WILDEBEEST ARMS	82.45
6	THE GRANGE BRAMPTON	76.98
7	SANGSTER'S	76.67
8	DARROCH LEARG	73.73
9	YE OLDE BULL'S HEAD	72.32
10	KILLIECRANKIE HOUSE	71.27
11	LE CAFÉ DU JARDIN	57.05
12	CROWN AT WHITEBROOK	56.25

RANKINGS

RANKINGS

57	PORTMEIRION HOTEL	17.39
58	SUMMER ISLES HOTEL	17.18
59	HOLBECK GHYLL	17.03
60	THYME RESTAURANT	16.07
61	LINTHWAITE HOUSE HOTEL	15.93
62	MAES-Y-NEUADD	15.88
63	THE MANSION HOUSE POOLE	15.71
64	WITCHERY BY THE CASTLE	15.47
65	CHARLTON HOUSE - THE MULBERRY RESTAURANT	15.09
66	SWINTON PARK	14.82
67	HOTEL DU VIN, TUNBRIDGE WELLS	14.73
68	ENOTECA TURI	14.54
69	CHAMPANY INN	13.93
70	THE LOWRY HOTEL	13.89
71	COMBE HOUSE	13.81
72	OXO TOWER	12.96
73	EYRE BROTHERS	12.50
74	HAMBLETON HALL	12.33
75	LES MIRABELLES	11.57
76	THE YORKE ARMS, RAMSGILL	11.06
77	FAIRYHILL	11.02
78	DEVONSHIRE ARMS - BURLINGTON RESTAURANT	10.51
79	ROSCOFF	10.22
80	JSW	10.20
81	THE OLD VICARAGE	9.93
82	THE WINDMILL	9.78
83	BLEEDING HEART	9.28
84	THE THREE CHIMNEYS	9.27
85	36 ON THE QUAY	8.51
86	COTSWOLD HOUSE	8.20
87	HOTEL DU VIN, BIRMINGHAM	8.00
88	AL DUCA	7.99
89	MC CLEMENTS	6.22
90	THE DON	5.82
91	NORTHCOTE MANOR	5.78
92	GREAT EASTERN HOTEL - AURORA	5.65
93	LOCANDA LOCATELLI	5.11
94	GRAVETYE MANOR	5.08
95	BENTLEY KEMPINSKI 1880	4.40
96	LONGUEVILLE MANOR	4.32
97	CHESTER GROSVENOR – ARKLE RESTAURANT	4.15
98	CROOKED BILLET	3.84
99	NOVELLI AT AUBERGE DU LAC	2.62
100	GORDON RAMSAY	0.67

BEST OF THE BEST BUYS

The best of the Best Buys are the most outstanding of those wines chosen as Neville's Best Buy for each establishment and represent exceptionally good value for what the wine is. Whilst most of these would be from some of the restaurants with the smallest mark ups there are a number from some of the more expensive restaurants which, for one reason or another, possibly because they have been in stock a long time and have been purchased some years ago, or perhaps some error of calculation in the customer's favour, are exceptional value at whatever the quality level. Kistler Sonoma Coast Chardonnay 1988 from The Old Bridge at £55 and Domaine du Vieux-Télégraphe 2000 from The Bell at Skenfrith at £19, are but two examples.

7 DYLANWAD DA (Wales)
Huët Vouvray Le Mont Demi-Sec 2000 at £19.20

8 YE OLDE BULL'S HEAD (Wales)
Joseph Phelps Napa Valley Syrah 1995 at £28.50

9 PENHELIG ARMS (Wales)
Quinta do Vale Doña Maria 2000 from the Douro in Portugal at £16

11 CHERWELL BOATHOUSE (South East)
Morris and Verdin's own vineyard Beaune Les Pertuisots 2001
at £7.50 the glass, £25 the bottle

12 SYCAMORE HOUSE (East Anglia)
Ridge Geyserville Zinfandel 2001, 5 star quality at £29.50

15 OLD BRIDGE, HUNTINGDON (East Anglia)
Kistler Sonoma Coast Chardonnay 1998 at £55

20 SIR CHARLES NAPIER (South East)
Jade Mountain Côtes du Soleil Mourvèdre/Syrah 1997 from California at £18.50

23 THE BELL AT SKENFRITH (Wales)
Châteauneuf-du-Pape 2000 from Domaine du Vieux-Télégraphe at £19

31 THE WILDEBEEST ARMS (East Anglia)
2002 Chardonnay from Howard Park in Western Australia at £22.95

BEST OF THE BEST BUYS

34 SANGSTER'S (Scotland)
Lucien Crochet's "Le Chêne Marchand" Sancerre 2003 at £19.95

50 HOTEL DU VIN BIRMINGHAM (Midlands)
Costières de Nîmes 2002 from Château Mas Neuf, at £17.50

51 FAIRY HILL (Wales)
Vouvray Moelleux Clos de Bourg from Huët in the excellent
1989 vintage at £45

58 THE STAR INN HAROME (North East)
Nyetimber Classic Cuvée 1996 at £21.50

59 LES MIRABELLES (South West)
Tokay Pinot Gris Grand Cru Steinert 1999 from Domaine Rieflé at £25.30

61 HOTEL DU VIN HARROGATE (North East)
Dão Colheita Seleccionada 2000 from Quinta de Cabriz in Portugal, at £14

63 GRAVETYE MANOR (South East)
Bollinger RD 1985, at £75

66 WHITE MOSS HOUSE (North West)
Cape Mentelle Cabernet Sauvignon 2000 from Western Australia at £20.50

74 HOTEL DU VIN BRIGHTON (South East)
Rueda Basa 2004 from Telmo Rodríguez in Spain at £18

77 HOTEL DU VIN TUNBRIDGE WELLS (South East)
Dom Pérignon 1996 at £79.50

80 THE WEAVERS SHED (North East)
Morellino di Scansano Bellamarsilia 2003 from Poggio Argentiera,
in Tuscany, at £15.95

94 PORTMEIRION HOTEL (Wales)
Château Roc de Cambes 1996, Côtes de Bourg at £34

LA CRÈME DE LA CRÈME

Overall Best Restaurant Wine list

Devonshire Arms – Burlington Restaurant

Best Restaurant Wine list for Quality

Gordon Ramsay

Best Restaurant Wine list for Value

Sycamore House (Little Shelford)

Best list for Wines by the glass

Crooked Billet

Best list for Wines by the half bottle

The Bell at Skenfrith

Picture: The Three Chimneys, Isle of Skye

Symbols at end of entry

 A strong showing in quality half-bottles

 A good selection of quality wines by the glass

91st

AL DUCA

4-5 Duke of York Street, SW1Y 6LA

020 7839 3090

This is a very fine all-Italian list (except for Champagnes, of course) and well over half of the 130-odd wines are of 3-star quality or above. On the other side of the coin, prices are pretty steep, with less than 10% of those quality wines qualifying for value. There are no half-bottles listed and while there are 14 wines by the glass, only two are of 3-star quality or above, the 3-star Franciacorta Millesimato Brut Bellavista 1999 sparkler at £7.50 a glass (£34 a bottle) and the 4-star Barolo 2000 from Elvio Cogno at £12 a glass (£52 the bottle). The wines on the main body of the list are arranged by style, but there are no tasting notes, so you will have to rely on the front-of-house staff for guidance.

In the 'Light and aromatic white wines' section there is some good value to be found in the Terlaner Classico 2003 (Pinot Bianco, Sauvignon and Chardonnay) from the excellent Terlano co-operative at £25, as well as the Chardonnay 2003 from Pojer & Sandri in the Trentino, also at £25. Value is less apparent in the 'Rich, full bodied and barrel fermented white wines', where the **Colli Orientali del Fruili Chardonnay 2002** from Ronco del Gnemiz comes in just off the cusp at £32.

'Fruit driven and medium bodied red wines' has the **Carmignano Villa di Capezzana 2001** from Tuscany at £40 and the Merlot 2001 Ignaz Niedrist in the Alto Adige at £46. 'Full bodied and spicy red wines' fall short on price/quality ratio, as do 'Fine and mature reds', but at least here you can get into some of the superstars (at a price) such as the Barolo 1999 from Bartolo Mascarello at £115 and the **Barbaresco Rabajà 1999** from Bruno Rocca at £150 – both 5-star wines. At the end of the list is a page of fine wines – pretty much some of the best wines you can find from Italy – but there's little under £100. In this case you might as well go for the best at the most reasonable price that you can find, which looks like the super 5-star Brunello di Montalcino La Casa 1998 from Caparzo at £150, or you could go for the 1997 at £220, which is probably the vintage of the decade. There are other super 5-star wines on the page, but these start at £300 and are really geared to the international jet set, rather than serious drinkers. Finally, there is a page called 'Wine producers of the month' and in the list that we were sent, the best price/quality ratio came from the **2002 Cusumano Benuara** Nero d'Avola/Syrah at £22, which is also the Best Buy.

Neville's Best Buy: **Cusumano's** Benuara Nero d'Avola/Syrah blend 2002 at £22

Score: *Quality* 56.08 *Value* 7.99 *Impression* 9.00 *Total* **73.07**

Ranking: *Quality* 55 *Value* 88 *Impression* 97 = *Overall* **91st**

Recommendations:
NB: 1999 **Bruno Rocca** Barbaresco Rabajà at £150
DM: 2002 **Ronco del Gnemiz** Colli Orientali del Fruili Chardonnay at £32
PW: 2001 **Capezzana** Carmignano Villa di Capezzana at £40

Find out more about wine and wine producers at *www.winebehindthelabel.com*

19th

THE BENTLEY KEMPINSKI 1880

27-33 Harrington Gardens, SW7 4JX
020 7244 5555

This list has been created for the upmarket restaurant of this relatively new hotel by head sommelier Deborah Kemp. The emphasis is on providing a range of different grape varieties as well as a large selection of wines by the glass, currently 43, of which 25 are of 3-star quality or more. The list is conventionally arranged by country and region and of the 262 bins on the list, over 70% meet our quality criteria, but alas, only 7 wines of the 262 meet our value criteria. Nevertheless, this is a very good list and as long as you are not too worried about price, you should have an enjoyable time with it.

As often, the list starts of with a selection of Champagnes, with Taittinger Brut Réserve NV the entry-level wine at £49, which certainly isn't cheap. Dom Pérignon 1996 at £145 is about par for London, but most other Champagnes are pretty stiffly priced. French white wines follow and in the Alsace section Bruno Sorg's Muscat 2002 at £29 represents the best value and similarly, in the Loire section, **Domaine de Chatenoy Ménétou-Salon 2004** at £29.50 is the only quality wine under £30. As always, in the white Burgundies, the Chablis prove to be better value than the wines from the Côte d'Or, the cheapest 3-star wine being 1er Cru Les Fourneaux 2002 from Jean-Pierre Grossot at £40, which is no bargain either. At the top end, the super 5-star Corton Charlemagne from Bonneau du Martray is a whopping £285 for the 1987 vintage – quite mature, but then Bonneau du Martray's wines have a reputation for longevity. Italian whites have the 4-star 'Dreams' 2001 from Jermann at £85, but nothing really at the entry level end unless you would be happy with the 2-star Est! Est!! Est!!! 2002 from Falesco at £19.50. Spain has Cal Pla Blanco 2002 from Mas d'en Comte in Priorat at £28 and Austria has the Alte Reben Grüner Veltliner 2003 from Schloss Gobelsburg at £48.50, both 3-star wines, as is the Riesling Spätlese Norheimer Kirschneck 1999 at £45 from Dönnhoff in the Nahe in Germany. USA chips in with the Ibarra Young Vineyard Marsanne 2002 from Qupé in Santa Barbara, also at £45, but De Trafford's 2003 Chenin Blanc from Stellenbosch in South Africa is better value at £34. Gravitas Sauvignon Blanc 2003 at £34 is the best shot in the New Zealand whites, whilst in Australia Moss Wood Margaret River Semillon/Sauvignon 2004 is also 3-star quality at £32, but the best value in this section is undoubtedly the Petaluma Clare Valley Riesling 2002 at £39.

The reds start off with a nice selection from the Loire Valley, with Chinon Cuvée Terroir 2002 from Charles Joguet looking reasonable at £32, but there is nothing of great value on the entry-level side of the red Rhônes. Instead, there is a collection of some superb super 5-star wines, including Châteauneuf-du-Pape 1996 from Domaine du Vieux Télégraphe at £125 and Hermitage Les Bessards 1999 from Délas Frères at £130, but compare those prices with the £28 charged for the 1999 Vieux-Télégraphe and the £32 charged for the Bessards 1994, by Darroch Learg in Ballater (qv), to get some idea of the different pricing policies. In the South-West France section, Madiran Chapelle l'Enclos 1996 from Domaine Patrick Ducournau is priced at £29.50. There are some heavyweights in the red Burgundy section, many at 3-figure prices, but probably the best value here would be the Chambolle-Musigny 1999 from Domaine Magnien at £57. There are also some very fine clarets on the list in mature (and good drinking) vintages, again at pretty stiff prices, so it's probably as well to go for Château Fleur Cardinale 1999 at £56, just about ready to drink. Italian reds bristle with wines of 4-star quality or more and the **Il Poggione Brunello di Montalcino 1999** at £68 looks to be the best quality/price ratio. Spain, too, has some big hitters, but here the value is to be found in **Pagos de Posada Reserva Tilenus 2000** from Bodegas Estafania at £65, a beautifully hand-crafted wine from a tiny vineyard, although it may be a little too young to drink. The USA section has the super 5-star Shafer Hillside Select Cabernet Sauvignon 1998, but at £280 it is priced way over the top. There is little we can recommend as value in the other sections from around the world, but the Vergelegen Merlot 2001 from Stellenbosch in South Africa at £35 just about squeezes in. There's little of real value, too, in the dessert wines section, but there is, of course, plenty of good quality – Riesling Cuvée Frédéric Émile VT from the wonderful 1983 vintage is on at £190 and Château d'Yquem 1990 is on at £320, but the sweet-toothed value-seeker would probably plump for a bottle of **Moscato d'Asti Bricco Quaglia 2003** from La Spinetta at £30, one of the most more-ish wines on the planet.

A number of the wines mentioned above feature in the wines by the glass programme, and it may be that this is the way to proceed here, although a certain amount of abstemiousness may be necessary to keep the outlay within limits. It's a pity, really, because the list is full of quality wines, but it's like treading over eggshells to carefully root out the value.

Neville's Best Buy: Pagos de Posada Reserva Tilenus 2000 from **Bodegas Estefania** at £65

Score: *Quality* 109.12   *Value* 4.40   *Impression* 22.00   *Total* **135.52**

Ranking: *Quality* 5   *Value* 95   *Impression* 21 =   *Overall* **19th**

Recommendations:
NB: 2003 **La Spinetta** Moscato d'Asti 'Bricco Quaglia' at £30
DM: 2004 **Domaine de Chatenoy** Ménétou-Salon at £29.50
PW: 1999 **Il Poggione** Brunello di Montalcino at £68

82nd

BLEEDING HEART

The Cellars, Bleeding Heart Yard, Greville Street, EC1N 8SJ
020 7242 8238

The Wilsons' cosy establishment sports a comprehensive wine list. Over 400 bins cover a lot of ground, with particular emphasis on France and New Zealand. The New Zealand selection is impressive, France less so, but the Rhône section, with its selection of vintages of Jaboulet's Hermitage La Chapelle and wines from other top flight producers, stands out. Choice, of course, is abundant, at all prices, although the mark ups are pretty par for the course for London, so you won't find any bargains here. There is a small percentage of half-bottles, but the selection of larger formats is more than usual. The list is conventionally arranged by country and France is divided into the usual regions. Good quality wines are to found under all sections, but tend to be more of 3-star quality than 4 or 5.

Champagne is comprehensively covered and the best value appears to be in the vintage section. **Laurent-Perrier 1996** at £45 is cheaper than some of the NV Champagnes on the list and a Dom Pérignon magnum at £250 seems reasonable for the quality. White Loires are pretty straightforward and the choice of only one white Bordeaux is disappointing. The ante is upped in the white Burgundies with a good selection, although there are a few producers who are resting on their (past) reputations. The Meursault 1er Cru Perrières 2000 from Coche-Dury is a stunning super 5-star wine, but at £199 you might have to think twice about buying it. In Alsace, Hugel's Pinot Gris SGN 1990 at £99.95 is another super 5-star wine. In Australian whites, Petaluma's Riesling at £28.95 is looking good, too. In California, Ramey's Hyde Vineyard Chardonnay is a great wine, but again at £110 the pricing becomes a little steep. There's a big choice of New Zealand whites, with Kumeu River Chardonnay, £37.95, seeming to be the best value on the list.

In reds, an extensive list of Bordeaux wines range from Château La Gasparde, Côtes de Castillon at £21.95 to £995 for Petrus 1995, but unfortunately most of the wines and the vintages are second division. Red Rhônes are much more exciting with wines from Graillot (St-Joseph £35.50), Guigal, Lionnat and Jaboulet. There's an impressive run of La Chapelle in vintages ranging from 1982 to 2000 at prices between £99.95 and £175. La Turque (1996) and La Mouline (1997) from Guigal at £280 and £290 respectively do not seem out of line for a London restaurant. Red Burgundy is well represented, too, and if anything has more overall quality than the clarets. Henri Gouges' Nuits-Saint-Georges Clos des Porrets 1999 at £89 is one of the better quality/price ratio wines but still expensive. In southern France, **Château Val Joanis Reserve les Griottes 2001** comes in well at £26.75. Portugal, Spain and Italy are there, but not in great depth: Chryseia 2001 from Bruno Prats and the Symington family, is one of the new wave dry wines from the Douro, not cheap at £75, but good wine; **Les Terrasses**, from Alvaro Palacios in Priorat is not far behind at £36; and the **Sette Ponti Crognolo** is a good example of non-DOCG Sangiovese from Tuscany at

£38.75. There are lots of sexy Pinot Noirs from New Zealand on the list, including old favourite Ata Rangi at £59.95. The Wilsons' own Trinity Hill Vineyard Syrah at £29.50 is also a good buy. There's a fair choice of Australian reds with Howard Park Cabernet/Merlot at £45 taking precedence on the Bordeaux blends, while in the big Aussie Shiraz types, The Armagh (£125) clearly takes precedence over Hill of Grace (£240). California has a fair bit of second division stuff, but the offerings from Ridge (Lytton Springs Zinfandel/Petite Sirah/Carignane) at £57.50 and the Saintsbury entry-level Pinot Noir at £45.50 would seem to be the ones to go for. Argentina, Chile and South Africa are barely represented, with Catena's Alta Cabernet Sauvignon, £66, being the only wine of real class from these regions. This is a lengthy list, with some good choices, but it is fairly conservative with only a modicum of innovative excitement about it.

Neville's Best Buy: **Laurent-Perrier** 1996 Champagne at £45

Score: *Quality* 56.27   *Value* 9.28   *Impression* 13.00   *Total* **78.55**

Ranking: *Quality* 54   *Value* 83   *Impression* 87 =   *Overall* **82nd**

Recommendations:
NB: 2001 **Château Val Joanis** Reserve Les Griottes at £26.75
DM: 2002 **Alvaro Palacios** Priorat Les Terrasses at £36
PW: 2001 **Sette Ponti** Crognolo at £38.75

Find out more about wine and wine producers at *www.winebehindthelabel.com*

95th

BRADLEYS

25 Winchester Road NW3 3NR
020 7722 3457

Simon Bradley's cosy neighbourhood restaurant in North London has a good wine list arranged by style and with a useful tasting note for each wine, making this a very user-friendly list. There are around 130 wines in all, of which over 20% are of 3-star quality or more, and of these, just over a quarter qualify for our price criteria as well. There are some 20 half-bottles of dry wines listed and 11 wines by the glass, but these are aimed at the budget spenders, although there are some good 2- and 3-star wines among them.

There is no great value in Champagne, although there is undoubted quality in the Dom Pérignon 1996 at £120 and the Krug NV at £130, but they are a little bit on the pricey side. In the 'Clean and fresh' white wine section, the Cornell Colterenzio Pinot Grigio 2003 from the Alto Adige in Italy is good value at £21 (£5 a 175ml glass) and in the 'Aromatic' section, the **Plantagenet Mount Barker Riesling 2003** from Western Australia at £21.50 is 3-star value, too. 'Medium weight' white wines has the **Cuvée des Conti Bergerac Blanc 2003** excellently priced at £20 and the **Thelema Chardonnay 2002** from South Africa at £29. There is nothing to match our desired price/quality ratio in the 'Full bodied' white wines from fairly uninspiring choices, but there are interesting reds in the 'Medium weight' section. Here you have the Morgon Prestige Beaujolais 2002 from Georges Duboeuf at £26.50 and the Yering Station Pinot Noir 2001 from the Yarra Valley in Australia at £30. There are many good 2-star wines in the 'Heavy weight' section, but the 3-star wines there are not outstanding for the price. However, in 'Blockbusters', the Plantagenet Cabernet Sauvignon 2001 is not a bad price at £33. Finally in 'The old ones' the super 5-star Château Léoville-las-Cases 1970 is certainly worth a look at £150.

Neville's Best Buy: **Château Tour des Gendres** Cuvée des Conti Bergerac Blanc 2003 at £20

Score: *Quality* 23.91 *Value* 18.48 *Impression* 23.00 *Total* **65.39**

Ranking: *Quality* 95 *Value* 52 *Impression* 18 = *Overall* **95th**

Recommendations:
NB: 1970 **Château Léoville-las-Cases** at £150
DM: 2002 **Thelema** Chardonnay at £29
PW: 2003 **Plantagenet** Mount Barker Riesling at £21.50

Find out more about wine and wine producers at *www.winebehindthelabel.com*

London restaurants

32nd

THE DON

The Courtyard 20 St Swithun's Lane EC4N 8AD
020 7626 2616

The Don, like its sister restaurant, the Bleeding Heart (qv), has a very comprehensive wine list. There are nearly 500 bins, of which over 100 are of 3-star quality and nearly 200 of 4- or 5-star quality. Of course, being a London City restaurant, prices are pretty high which explains its position several pegs down the order of merit. Nevertheless, if you are prepared to pay the piper, there are some very sweet tunes coming out of this list. It is conventionally arranged by country and region separately for red and white wines, as are the pages for half-bottles and dessert wines. This is preceded by a page of sherries, a page of 'Vins du patron' (the owners, Robert and Robyn Wilson are partners in the Trinity Hill vineyard in New Zealand, so all their wines are listed here), a page of wines by the glass and two pages of Champagnes with fortified wines and digestifs at the end.

The two best wines from Trinity Hill are the Cabernet Sauvignon/Merlot 1998 at £28.95 the bottle (£58 the magnum and £7.25 the glass) and the Syrah 2000 at £29.50 the bottle, £7.30 the glass. Other wines by the glass are not that interesting. In Champagnes, Roederer's Brut Premier NV is not badly priced at £52, nor is the 1997 Cristal at £170 for super-5 star quality. Loire whites include the Jasnières Cuvée Clos Saint-Jacques 1999 from Joël Gigou at £33.50 – an intense and crisp wine from one of the most northerly appellations of the Loire Valley. Bordeaux whites are impressive, with Ygrec 2002 (the dry white of Château d'Yquem) at £157, but you could well be satisfied with the 3-star Vieux Château Gaubert 2001 at £28.50. A rarity is **Arbois Vin Jaune 1995** from Domaine Rolet in the Jura at £50. In the Alsace section there area couple of SGNs from the 1989 vintage – Tokay-Pinot Gris Hengst from Josmeyer at £110 and Gewurztraminer from Hugel at £145, but you can also pitch in with Pinot Gris Lerchenberg 2002 from Marc Kreydenweiss at £35. There are, of course, some really big hitters from Burgundy with Chablis generally being better value: the super 5-star Grand Cru Les Clos 2001 from Dauvissat at £89 is perhaps more acceptable than the super 5-star Le Montrachet 1999 from Ramonet at £600. The white Rhône selection includes another super 5-star wine – Jean-Louis Chave's white Hermitage 1997 at £145. From the far south of France **Mas de Daumas Gassac Blanc 2004** at £49 is one of the few 5-star wines under £50 on the list, so this could be well worth going for. The choice of Italian whites doesn't reach any higher than 3 stars, so it's best to go with the least expensive, which looks extraordinarily good value (at least, for this list), the Chardonnay Al Poggio 2001 from Castello di Ama at £29.50. The best shot in Spanish and Portuguese whites is Redoma Branco 2000 from Dirk Niepoort at £36.50, whilst from South Africa, the Meerlust Chardonnay 1999 is 3-star quality at £38.50. Australian whites don't fascinate, but the Chardonnay/Roussanne 2001 from Giaconda in Victoria at £55 could be interesting. A much better bet is the selection from California with the pick of the bunch being another 4-star wine under £50, the Alban Viognier 2001 at £48. New Zealand wines, of course, are dominated by Trinity Hill, but Gravitas Sauvignon Blanc 2003 at £29.50 is worth a look.

The reds start off with a long list of clarets – Château Cambon la Pelouse 1999 from the Haut-Médoc is entry-level quality at £36.50 and should please, but those looking for grander offerings have plenty of choice in mature vintages with Château Pichon Lalande 1990 seeming to have the best price/quality ratio at £190, but there are plenty of goodies to choose from. There are tougher choices in the red Burgundies, especially at the lower end, so maybe you should plump for Armand Rousseau's Grand Cru Clos de la Roche 1997 at £130, or if you really want to spoil yourself, La Tâche 1993 from Domaine Romanée-Conti at £795 – it should just about be ready to drink. Red Rhônes have some top quality wines with Jasmin's Côte-Rôtie 1996 at a reasonable £69, and Jean-Louis Chave's Hermitage 1988, which should be drinking beautifully now at a mere £275. Further south, Château de Pibarnon Bandol 2000 is reasonably priced at £43, if not yet ready to drink. In Italy, the Cabernet Sauvignon/Cabernet Franc/Merlot blend Vallagarina 1996 from San Leonardo in the Trentino at £48 is another 4-star wine under £50 but you could go for a bottle of Solaia 1990 at £395. The Spanish selection continues with a number of wines of great quality – best value is Bodega Alion 1999 at £65, although you might try **Chryseia 2001** from the Douro in Portugal at £55. The top Argentinian wines are really too pricey to consider, despite their undoubted quality, but there are some good offerings from Australia with Pike's Polish Hill Shiraz 2001 from Clare Valley reasonable value at £29.50. Of course, you can always go for the big guns – Henschke's Hill of Grace 1996 is £250 and Penfold's Grange 1981 is £395. There's a strong showing of Californian reds, from **Jade Mountain Syrah 1996**, which is 4-star quality at £44.50, to one of the cult wines from Manfred Krankel – The Ventriloquist 2001, a hedonistic blend of Rhône varietals at £155. The list comes into its own in New Zealand where, apart from the 'Vins du patron' at Trinity Hill, there are excellent Pinot Noirs from Ata Rangi in Marlborough, the 2001 vintage being at £58, and from Mount Edwards in Central Otago, where the 2002 vintage is on offer at £54, not forgetting the top Cabernet, Stonyridge Larose 1998 from Waiheke Island at £120.

There are half-bottles galore at all prices – Ridge Geyserville Zinfandel 2000 is 5-star quality and looks to be good value at £31.50. More traditional drinkers might prefer Château Margaux 1988 at £215. There's a page of magnums, too. Trinity Hill Cabernet Sauvignon/Merlot 1999 is well priced at £58, and a magnum of Camartina 1997 – a great blend of Sangiovese and Cabernet Sauvignon with a little Merlot and Syrah from Querciabella in Tuscany – is impressive 5-star quality at £180. There are a few wines in even bigger formats, too, and we are sure that you would make Le Patron very happy if you indulged in a Balthasar (12 litres) of his Trinity Hill Cabernet Sauvignon/Merlot 1998 at £460.

Dessert wines are impressive but pricey – a bottle of Château d'Yquem 1990 is £560, around twice the price you could find it in many places elsewhere, so probably the best choice in this section would be to go for a half-bottle of Riesling Vendanges Tardives 1989 from Hugel at £44. There is a stunning selection of Madeiras and ports, from 5-year-old Sercial from Cossart Gordon at £35 a bottle, £3.75 a glass, through Sandeman's Vau Vintage 1997 at £59 a bottle, £6.50 a glass, Blandy's Sercial 1940 at

£250 a bottle, Dow's 1955 Vintage Port at £360 a bottle, right up to Barbeito Malvasia 1900 at £480 a bottle, and Cockburn's 1927 Port at £900. There is also an enormous selection of digestifs but that is not within the scope of this book. This is certainly the place to impress your Japanese banker friends, providing they are paying the bill!

Neville's Best Buy: **Mas de Daumas Gassac** Blanc 2004 at £49

Score: *Quality* 96.01 *Value* 5.82 *Impression* 19.08 *Total* **120.91**

Ranking: *Quality* 11 *Value* 90 *Impression* 42 = *Overall* **32nd**

Recommendations:
NB: 1995 **Domaine Rolet** Arbois Vin Jaune at £50
DM: 1996 **Jade Mountain** Syrah at £44.50
PW: 2001 **Prats & Symington** Douro Chryseia at £55

Find out more about wine and wine producers at *www.winebehindthelabel.com*

London restaurants

ENOTECA TURI

28 Putney High Street SW15 1SQ
020 8785 4449

G iuseppe Turi's passion for wine is reflected in the name of his restaurant, since the word *enoteca* means wine library in Italian. So we suppose that in his restaurant you need to match the food with the wine, and not vice versa. It's an Italian restaurant, of course, but what is rather refreshing is that the list is by no means confined to Italian wines and as a true connoisseur, Giuseppe knows that quality knows no bounds. Over half the wines on the list are of 3-star quality or above and although the prices are a little on the high side by national standards, they are not over the top as far as London is concerned. Another great plus for this list is the comprehensive and detailed notes given for most of the wines together with some useful general notes for each section. Effectively, the list is divided into two sections – Italy and the rest of the world – but as is common, there are separate sections for Champagnes and sparkling wines, and for dessert wines, which cover the whole world. There are few half-bottles on the list, but there is a reasonable selection of wines by the glass, which are linked as recommendations to the various dishes on the menu.

A number of high class Italian sparkling wines appear in the sparkling wines and Champagnes section, but the best value would appear to be the very fine Champagne from Beaumont des Crayères at £35. There are a number of inexpensive Italian whites, but the quality doesn't really kick in until you reach Franz Haas's Manna Cru 2002 from the Alto Adige at £30. Cervaro della Sala 2002, a mostly Chardonnay wine from one of Antinori's major outposts in Umbria, is good 4-star value at £47. 'Popular reds' has some excellent value wines such as Barbera d'Alba 1998 from Gabutti at £19.50 and Teroldego Rotaliano 2002 from Elisabetta Foradori in the Trentino at £20. In the 'Central and South' section, the **2000 D'Angelo Canneto** from old vine Aglianico is outstanding value at £28.50. Mauro Vannucci's (Piaggia) Carmignano Riserva 1999 from Tuscany is another top quality wine at £49. In the Chianti section, Querciabella 2002 is good value at £28 for 3-star quality as is the Vino Nobile di Montepulciano 2001 from Dei at £29.50. Super Tuscans abound, from Luigi d'Alessandro's Il Bosco Syrah 1999 at £46 right up to Masseto 1997 at £295. North-East Italy has Moschioni's Rosso Moschioni 2002 at £26 from the Colli Orientali as good value and if you really want to splash out, Romano Dal Forno's Amarone della Valpolicella Monte Lodoletta 1995 is on at £250. If you want the 1996, you will need to fork out £300. On the other hand, Tenuta San Leonardo's estate wine from 1996 is 4-star quality at £44. There are some good value Dolcettos from Piedmont – Dolcetto d'Alba Barturot 2001 from Ca' Viola looking best at £25 – but there are also a number of more expensive wines such as Barbera d'Alba Bricco Marun 1999 from Correggia at £48. The best value Barbaresco on the list is the Vanotu 1996 from Giorgio Pelissero at £49, but you can choose lots of other high quality Barbarescos going right up to Gaja Tildin 1998, super 5 stars at £350 (or £700 a magnum, if you are so inclined). Barolos, too, are represented in a wide range of prices, from the 4-star **Barolo**

Pernanno 1997 from Bongiovanni at £46, to the much sought after super 5-star Barolo Falletto di Serralunga Riserva 1996 from Bruno Giacosa at £245.

The substantial 'Rest of the world' section kicks off with some impressive offerings from Burgundy – the Chassagne-Montrachet 1er Cru Morgeots 1999 from Domaine Laurent Pillot looking the best value at £48. New World Chardonnays has Sanford Winery Barrel Select Chardonnay 1998 the best buy at £51. The rest of the white wines are all French, with Les Cul de Beaujeu Sancerre 2002 from François Cotat at £33 looking good value. There is also their exceptional, late harvest Sancerre, made only in the best years – **La Grande Côte Cuvée Speciale 1995** (which was only released in 2004) at £58. The white Rhône selections include the super 5-star Hermitage Blanc 1999 from Jean-Louis Chave at £135. There's nothing of outstanding value in the red Burgundies, but Gevrey-Chambertin 1er Cru Clos Saint-Jacques 1999 from Louis Jadot at £98 is super 5-star quality, if a little too young to drink. There are some great first growth properties in the Bordeaux section, although not in their finest vintages – it's probably better to go for the 5-star Château Angélus 1995 at £125, being around half the price of the super 5-star first growths on offer. Some good 4-star wines crop up in 'New World Cabernet and Merlot blends', with Cain Cellars' Cain Five 1995 at £62 looking best, but there are no bargains in this section. Amongst a really good selection from the Northern Rhône, René Rostaing's super 5-star Côte-Rôtie Côte Blonde 1998 at £125 is a far better bet than Guigal's La Turque 1998 at £325, while in the Southern Rhône, there is even better value with the **Châteauneuf-du-Pape 1999** from Domaine du Vieux-Télégraphe at £59. The Spanish red selection is high quality but pricey, whilst the only offering from Australia, Clarendon Hills' Australis 1998, is pretty outrageously priced at £180 – not Giuseppe's fault, we hasten to add, but the producer's.

In the dessert wine section, a 50cl bottle of Côteaux du Layon 2001 from Château Pierre-Bise at £28 looks to be the best value, but there are wines of extraordinary quality including Patrick Baudouin's Côteaux du Layon Aprés Minuit 1997 at £150 for a 50 cl bottle and Château Tirecul-La-Gravière Cuvée Madame 1995 for the same size bottle at £160, although with these you are well and truly paying for scarcity value. All in all, this is a very fine list and the fact that they cellar a number of fine wines until they reach drinking maturity ensures that the prices will not be too steep when they eventually hit the list.

Neville's Best Buy: **D'Angelo's** Canneto from old vine Aglianico at £28.50

Score: *Quality* 90.24   *Value* 14.54   *Impression* 21.00   *Total* **125.78**

Ranking: *Quality* 15   *Value* 68   *Impression* 33 =   *Overall* **28th**

Recommendations:
NB: **Cotat** Sancerre La Grande Côte Cuvée Speciale at £58
DM: 1999 **Domaine du Vieux Télégraphe** Châteauneuf-du-Pape at £59
PW: 1997 **Bongiovanni** Barolo Pernanno at £46

Find out more about wine and wine producers at *www.winebehindthelabel.com*

84th

EYRE BROTHERS

70 Leonard Street EC2A 4QX
020 7613 5346

The short wine list in this restaurant for city slickers has an Iberian slant and whilst there are not so many 3-star and higher quality bargains, the overall quality is reasonable, with many 2-star wines on the list. The list has some 70 wines overall, of which around a quarter are of 3-star quality or above. It is arranged simply by dividing the list into white, rosé and red wines, with the wines listed in ascending price order and mostly accompanied by a short tasting note. Some 14 dry wines come by the glass but half-bottles are scant

In the white wine section, the 4-star **Chablis 1er Cru Vaillons 2002** from Billaud-Simon is good value at £44.10 (£26 for a half) and the 2001 Meursault from Henri Germain is in at £53 but a fine cheaper option, if no bargain, is the **2003 Saint-Véran Les Rochats** from Domaine de la Croix Senaillet at £32. Red wines include the 5-star **Ridge Geyserville Zinfandel 2001**, well priced at £45.50. There are some real heavyweights (at a price) on the list, too, with Tirant 1999 – a blend of Grenache, Carignan and Cabernet Sauvignon from Rotllán I Torra in Priorat in Spain – at £70 taking precedence over the Barca Velha 1995 from the Douro in Portugal at £192 and Château Mouton-Rothschild 1990 at £198.

In dessert wines **Château Rabaud-Promis** Sauternes 1996 is £34 a half-bottle (£8.50 a glass) and in the list of ports, Croft 1977 is £108.

Neville's Best Buy: **Billaud-Simon** Chablis 1er Cru Vaillons 2002 at £44.10

Score: *Quality* 46.18   *Value* 12.50   *Impression* 19.00   *Total* **77.68**

Ranking: *Quality* 65   *Value* 73   *Impression* 43 =   *Overall* **84th**

Recommendations:
NB: 2001 **Ridge** Geyserville Zinfandel at £45.50
DM: 1996 **Ch. Rabaud-Promis** Sauternes (half-bottle) at £34
PW: 2003 **Domaine de la Croix Senaillet** Saint-Véran Les Rochats at £32

22nd

HARVEY NICHOLS FIFTH FLOOR

Harvey Nichols 109-125 Knightsbridge SW1X 7RJ
020 7235 5250

This list of nearly 800 wines is thoughtfully laid out by style and is preceded by a useful 'short' selection by the head sommelier, again laid out by style, some of which are available by the glass in special flights of tasters, as well as other wines normally available by the glass. This does allow one to experiment, although the lack of detailed tasting notes means that you have to keep asking someone for advice. Nevertheless, this is a superb list with over half the entries being of 3-star quality or more. It does fall down a little on the pricing, but what should you expect in such a prestigious location? However, a pricing plus point is that on Monday nights, a selection of wines are available in the restaurant at wine shop prices, so armed with this knowledge, you should be able to pick your way through some of the selections without breaking the bank

The wine list proper, called 'The big selection', kicks off with a whole page of sparkling wines and Champagnes, with the **Croser Brut 2001** from South Australia at £36 the best of the entry-level sparklers. Champagnes run from Pol Roger White Foil NV at £50 right up to Krug Clos du Mesnil 1990 at £710, although Dom Pérignon Cuvée Œnothèque 1976 at £680 is not far behind. In Whites the 'New World, general aromatics' section has John Alban's 2001 Central Coast Viognier from California at £43, whilst the fine Riesling section has Jeffrey Grosset's Watervale Clare Valley Riesling 2003 at £32.50, another 4-star wine quite correctly bottled with a Stelvin closure. 'Sauvignon, Semillon and blends' has the New Zealand Isabel Estate Sauvignon Blanc 2004 at a fairly hefty £28.50 and the long list of New World Chardonnays has Au Bon Climat Wild Boy Chardonnay 2001 from California at £32.50 for 3-star quality and Kistler's Dutton Ranch or McCrea Vineyard 2002 at £185 for 5-star bottles.

'Old World whites' starts off with a short selection of German and Austrian wines, with the elegant Brauneberger Juffer-Sonnenuhr Riesling Spätlese 2002 from Willi Haag at £33 looking to be a good pick. Spanish whites are reasonably represented – look out for the aromatic Rías Baixas 2003 from Pazo de Señoráns at £31. There are Italian whites aplenty, with some good wines at fairly stiff prices, but Nicola Bergaglio's Gavi di Gavi 2003 at £26 is one of the best examples from this sometimes overrated appellation. On to France, where the Alsace section is dominated by wines from Josmeyer, which is no bad thing, with the sumptuous Tokay-Pinot Gris Vieilles Vignes Foundation 1999 being the pick of the bunch at £45. Regional French whites include the rare and stratospherically priced Clos Nardian from Château Teyssier in Bordeaux – the 2000 vintage is in at £110 – but the St-Péray 2001 from Bernard Gripa at £38 is a more down-to-earth proposition. It's also nice to see a wine from this appellation on a list – it doesn't often happen. Loire whites are pretty straightforward, but white Burgundies contain a number of real heavyweights with Ramonet's super 5-star Bâtard-Montrachet 2000 at £265 being the best price of several others of that ilk.

Anyone looking for more affordable white Burgundy could well go for Pillot's Chassagne-Montrachet 1er Cru Morgeots 2000 at £58.

'New World reds' starts off with a fine selection of Pinot Noirs, with the almost unobtainable **Kistler Sonoma Coast Pinot Noir 2002** coming in at £185, but the 2001 Kooyong Pinot from the Mornington Peninsular in Victoria, Australia at £43 is worth a try. A long list of 'New World Bordeaux blends' follows, with 3-star Howard Park Cabernet Sauvignon 2001 from Western Australia looking good value at £30 and 5-star Cullen Diana Madeleine Cabernet Sauvignon/Merlot 2001, also from Western Australia, at a very fair £70. Certainly the Bordeaux blends from the best producers in Western Australia are proving to be the best value for money wines in any list. In 'Exotic blends', Ben Glaetzer's The Wallace 2001, a blend of Shiraz, Cabernet and Grenache, sits well at £27.50, and if you want something with a bit more finesse, then Joseph Phelps's Châteauneuf-du-Pape clone Le Mistral 2001 (too many grape varietals to mention here, but they are all on the back label) at £50 looks reasonable for the establishment, too. There is a small selection of Zinfandels, with Larry Turley's **Dogtown Vineyard Zinfandel 2002** from the Napa Valley at £72 being the pick of the bunch.

'Old World reds' starts with wines from the Iberian peninsular, with the usual suspects of Vega Sicilia, Pingus and l'Ermita there at very high prices, but Alion Reserva 1999 at £60 (still highly priced) is probably the best value in the section. There is a big selection of top quality Italian reds, but nothing of reasonable bottle age – let alone price. However, two Barolos from Massolino, Parafada 1999 at £69 and Vigna Rionda 2000 at £50, look intriguing, but is this infanticide? A small selection of good Greek red wines are also on the list. France next, kicking off with some regional wines, the most interesting being the **Collioure Les Junquets 1999** from the Estate of the late Dr Parcé, Domaine du Mas Blanc, at £45. There is a good spread of red Rhônes, mainly from the south, the reliable Domaine Pallières Gigondas 2001 at £29.50 helping to increase the value rating here and Château Rayas Châteauneuf-du-Pape 2001 at £190 not, as well as being far too young to drink. What should be drinking well is the Hermitage La Chapelle 1990, but at £525 the bottle it jolly well ought to. Red Burgundies abound, ranging from François Raquillet's Mercurey 1er Cru Les Naugues 2001 at £32 to Henri Jayer's Vosne-Romanée 1er Cru Les Brulées 1983 at £2,200. There are some *grand cru* wines of recent vintages ranging between £142 and £300, but the wine to drink in this section is probably Comtes Lafon's Volnay 1er Cru Santenots du Milieu 2001 at £82. Among the many clarets is a good selection of wines with bottle age, at all prices, going up to Pétrus 1982 at £4,200. Compared with that, Margaux 1982 at £1,000 looks a positive bargain. Under £100 from such an impressive list, we would probably go for Clos de l'Oratoire 1998 St-Émilion Grand Cru at just on the £100 button for a fine wine from a good vintage on the Right Bank.

Stickies are well represented from all over the globe – of course, there's some Yquem and a half-bottle of the very good 1996 vintage will set you back £160, but Alois Kracher's Chardonnay No 3. Trockenbeerenauslese 2000 at £50 the half-bottle is also super 5-star quality at less than half the price. There are some good ports and sherries by the bottle and the glass, with the sherries in particular being reasonably priced. You can actually have a flight of four sherry tasters for £12.95. If port is a bit on the heavy side for you, try the Banyuls Cuvée St. Martin 1985 from Domaine de Mas Blanc at £65 as an alternative. Finally, there is a selection of halves and magnums. There are not a lot of dry halves in relation to the overall size of the list, but the magnums fare better. It is also nice to see dry white wines in magnums, with Joseph Phelps's Ovation Chardonnay 1997 at £130 standing out. The reds, unfortunately, suffer from youthfulness, with the two Zinfandels from Ridge, vintage 2000, probably being forward enough to enjoy at £95 and £100 respectively. Otherwise, it's Château Lafite 1990 at £1,150!

All in all, this is a very interesting list – well thought out, but perhaps lacking bottle age in some of the finer reds. There are not a lot of half-bottles in proportion to the list, but there is enough by the glass to satisfy a drinker on a moderate budget.

Neville's Best Buy: **Turley** Dogtown Vineyard Zinfandel 2002 at £72

Score: *Quality* 82.63   *Value* 18.07   *Impression* 30.00   *Total* **130.70**

Ranking: *Quality* 24   *Value* 54   *Impression* 6 =   *Overall* **22nd**

Recommendations:
NB: 2002 **Kistler** Sonoma Coast Pinot Noir at £185
DM: 1999 **Domaine du Mas Blanc** Collioure Les Junquets at £45
PW: 2001 (Petaluma) **Croser** Brut at £36

 Find out more about wine and wine producers at *www.winebehindthelabel.com*

16th

THE GLASSHOUSE

14 Station Parade Kew TW9 3PZ
020 8940 6777

This is not quite what you would expect from a local restaurant in Kew, but then all of the restaurants that Nigel Platts-Martin ever had a hand in were out of the ordinary. Wine has been important in all his restaurants and this one is no exception. There are nearly 600 bins here, of which around two-thirds are of 3-star quality or above. Prices are of course the issue, although they are not overtly excessive for London, but expect to pay around half as much again for the same bottle you would at the Penhelig Arms in Aberdovey (qv).

The list starts with a short selection of wines by the glass, but there is nothing special there – better to go straight on to the main list. The list of halves, however, has some worthwhile entries such as the Al Poggio Chardonnay 2002 from Castello di Ama in Tuscany at £17.50 and 1999 Vieux-Télégraphe at £27.50. The House Champagne (if you could call it that) is from Larmandier-Bernier, a small high class grower, at £35 a bottle for the NV and £43.50 for the Blanc de Blancs, which impressively sets the tone for the whole list. At the top end of the scale Henri Giraud's Ay Grand Cru Fût de Chêne 1993 at £130 shows an eye for contrarian choices. There are more conventional choices in the list of white Burgundies with Henri Germain's Chassagne-Montrachet 1er cru Morgeot 2000 at £60, good 4-star value. You could up the ante and go for the super 5-star Bâtard-Montrachet 1997 from Domaine Leflaive, but that would set you back £160. White Loires are of good quality, too, with the Jasnières Cuvée Clos Saint-Jacques Vieilles Vignes 1999 from Domaine de la Charrière at £26.50 worth drinking. Alsace shines with good choices again – Trimbach's Riesling Clos Sainte-Hune 1999 is super 5-stars at £79.50 – a good price for London. Southern French whites are a bit of a mixed bag, but if you want something special, try the richly flavoured **2002 Blanc de Blancs** from Domaine Hauvette, somewhat incongruously classified as a Vin de Pays des Bouches-du-Rhône, a stunner at £45. Jura and Savoie are well represented with Quenard's Roussette de Savoie 2003 at £22.50 and Rolet's Arbois Vin Jaune 1995 at £57.50. White Rhônes are exclusively from the north, with the best being André Perret's Saint-Joseph Blanc 2001 at £24.50 and his Condrieu Côteaux du Chéry 2002 at £55. Italian whites have Jermann's 2002 Vintage Tunina at £49.50, whilst Spain and Portugal weigh in with René Barbier's Clos Nelin 2002 at £30 and Dirk Niepoort's Redoma white from the Douro at £35. Austria has 4 different Grüner Veltliners with Franz Hirtzberger's Axpoint Smaragd 2003 showing 4-star quality at £32, but the selection of German wines does not quite match the quality of the Austrians. Australia again has plenty of quality whites to choose from, with Jeffrey Grosset's Polish Hill Riesling 2000 at £35 looking good. There's not much to shout about in South African whites, but as usual, New Zealand whites shine with the 2004 Isabel Sauvignon Blanc at £29.50 and the 2002 Kumeu River Chardonnay at £40 worth drinking, if a little expensive. The choice of California whites is very high class, with the 2000 Kistler Vineyard Chardonnay at £95 well worth the extra tenner over the Les Noisetieres 2002. At the entry level, Rosenblum Cellars Dry Creek Valley Marsanne 2001 at £29.50 sits well among its peers.

The page of Bordeaux wines exudes quality, with most bottles being of drinkable vintages. There is nothing really outlandish or extravagant, the most expensive wine being Château Pétrus 1994 at £450, but if you are going to spend that sort of money, you might as well go for the Pichon Lalande 1982 at £325. More down to earth spenders, however, might consider Château l'Enclos 1998 Pomerol at £52.50 – a good vintage for Right Bank wines that should just about be beginning to drink. Red Burgundies, too, have much to commend, with Robert Chevillon's Nuits-Saint-Georges 1er Cru Les Saint-Georges 2000 at £65 taking the mid-price honours in the Côte de Nuits and Jean-Marc Boillot's Volnay Ronceret 1er Cru 2000 doing the same thing at the same price in the Côte de Beaune. There is only one entry in the Loire red section, but it is quite a wine – Pierre-Jacques Druet's Bourgueil Cuvée Vaumoreau 1988, only made in the best years, and you are, of course, having to pay £55 for the scarcity value. Nevertheless, it is very good. Red Rhônes are pretty much evenly spread between north and south, but the outstanding value for money wine here is Lirac Cuvée de la Reine des Bois 1999 from Domaine de la Mordorée at £27.50. Red wines from the rest of southern France include some heavyweights such as Alain Brumont's 1995 Madiran Château Montus XL at £85, but again, great drinking value can be found with the **2001 Domaine Piétri-Géraud Collioure** at £22.50. There are some reasonable red wine choices from Austria, Germany and Lebanon, but nothing outstanding, Spain produces better quality with the ubiquitous Alion Reserva 1999 at £55 (about par for the course in London) and 1987 Vega Sicilia Unico at £135. In Portugal, Quinta do Vale Doña Maria 2001 at £39.50 is also good, if a little expensive at this price. There are 2 pages of Italian reds, including some great names, with **Roberto Voerzio's Barolo Cerequio 1998** at £95 being exceptionally good value considering that it retails for about £70. There are also some interesting and unusual offerings such as Il Bosco Syrah 2000 from Luigi d'Alessandro in eastern Tuscany at £47.50 and the **Terre Brune Carignano del Sulcis Superiore** from the Santadi co-operative in Sardinia at £45. California boasts a huge swathe of quality wines, ranging from Cline's Ancient Vines Mourvèdre 2002 at £32.50 to Harlan Estate 1996 at £220. There's also plenty of good stuff between those prices. New Zealand reds include the rare cult wine, **Dry River Amaranth Pinot Noir 2001**, from a tiny estate in Martinborough. This is something to be tried, even if it is £65 a bottle. The Argentinian section has Michel Rolland's little plaything, Yacochuya Malbec 1999, at £75 a bottle; maybe it's better to go for the Clos de los Siete Malbec/Cabernet/Merlot blend 2003 at £29.50. There is a full page of Australian reds, with Penfold's Grange 1998 and Henschke's Hill of Grace 1991, sharing top honours at £250 a pop, but notwithstanding good Bordeaux blends from some producers in Western Australia, try the Diamond Valley Close Planted Pinot Noir 2000 from the Yarra Valley at £48.50.

Before you get on to the stickies, there is a page of magnums. 1997 Riesling Cuvée de Cinquantenaire from Albert Mann in Alsace at £90 looks intriguing, whilst 1982 Haut-Brion at £550 looks positively sumptuous. There are a lot of excellent dessert wines with a veritable lotto of Trockenbeerenauslese numbers from Alois Kracher between £45 and £65 the half – and you can even get a glass of his Beerenauslese for

£4.25, but the range is well spread around the world, with 14 others available by the glass.

This list has been very well thought out, with an eye to quality – it is very long and it is not a run-of-the-mill list, but the absence of tasting notes makes it hard for the customer to make decisions, so reliance on the sommeliers is essential. Nevertheless, it is certainly worth the voyage for the wine list alone and if you choose carefully, you won't come away too light in the pocket.

Neville's Best Buy: **Roberto Voerzio's** Barolo Cerequio 1998 at £95!! For a more affordable alternative go for: 2001 **Domaine Piétri-Géraud** Collioure at £22.50

Score: *Quality* 98.89   *Value* 19.72   *Impression* 22.00   *Total* **140.61**

Ranking: *Quality* 10   *Value* 50   *Impression* 21 =   *Overall* **16th**

Recommendations:
NB: 2001 **Dry River** Amaranth Pinot Noir at £65
DM: 2002 **Domaine Hauvette** Blanc de Blancs at £45
PW: 1999 **Santadi** Carignano del Sulcis Superiore Terre Brune at £45

Find out more about wine and wine producers at *www.winebehindthelabel.com*

5th

GORDON RAMSAY

68-69 Royal Hospital Road SW3 4HP
020 7352 4441

This is a wine list of the highest quality, as befits a restaurant with 3 Michelin stars. There are over 900 wines to choose from, with around a quarter of them rated 3 stars or above, and a further half rated 4 stars or higher. As a model quality wine list this rates second to none in the UK, but of course there is a hefty price to pay for this. Only 6 wines rated 4 stars or above sell for £50 or less and only 9 of the 3-star wines are £30 or under. For example, Leeuwin Estate Prelude Chardonnay is £42 a bottle here, but at Sycamore House (qv) it is a mere £21. But you may feel it's worth the splash to find a great rare wine, and there are plenty of those, whatever the price.

The list runs to 31 pages of closely spaced entries without any tasting notes, and that is without the separate Champagne and Digestif list! Most interesting among the Champagnes are the vintages of Dom Pérignon Cuvée Œnothèque, 1962, 1973, 1980, 1985, 1988. This is a library of rare old vintages that illustrates the various stages of ageing that Dom Pérignon undergoes. All the bottles were disgorged together in 1999. The bottle prices vary from £240 to £490 and if you wanted to try all 5 (and why shouldn't you?) it would set you back a mere £1,960. You could, however, be a little more down-to-earth, and go for the Nyetimber Classic Cuvée at £36, which is a very reasonable price for this establishment.

The main wine list kicks off with a page of wines available by the glass. This is far from basic fare and it's nice to see such offerings by the glass as Gewürztraminer Grand Cru Furstentum 2001 from Bott-Geyl and Asinone Vino Nobile di Montepulciano from Poliziano, both 4-star wines and both at £13.50 for 175ml. Bottles start with some French regional whites including Roussette de Savoie 2002 from André et Michel Quénard at £28. Alsace follows, with the best bet being the Pinot Gris Cuvée Sainte-Catherine 1998 from Domaine Weinbach at £75. There is not a lot of value in the Rhône whites, but there is top quality, with Chave's Hermitage Blanc 1998 at £180 and 1997 at £190. White Bordeaux doesn't thrill until you get into the 2 vintages of Château Haut-Brion Blanc with the 1981 at £240 taking the honours over the 1997 at £280. There are some top names in the Loire whites, but the Savennières Cuvée d'Avant 2000 from Pierre Soulez at £39 looks best value. A host of great white Burgundies includes a long list of *grands crus* from Corton-Charlemagne to Montrachet, but if we were looking for value, we would plump for Gérard Chavy's Puligny-Montrachet 1er Cru Les Folatières 1999 at £68. Ditto for red Burgundies, but René Engel's Vosne-Romanée 1er Cru Les Brulées 2001 at £85 is 5-star quality – so is his Clos de Vougeot 1994 at twice the price. Red wines from the Côtes de Nuits are almost encyclopaedic, but those from the Côtes de Beaune are less impressive. There are no real bargains in the Northern Rhône red selections, even if every wine listed is of at least 3-star quality. Auguste Clape's Cornas 1999 is 5-star quality in a good vintage at £92, but you could go the whole hog and indulge in the super 5-star **Jean-Louis Chave Hermitage 1997** at £195, or even the 1983 vintage at £349 – or if you really want to push the boat out, you could go for his Ermitage Cuvée Cathelin 1998 at £900. Southern Rhône selections are a little more down-to-earth and super 5-star quality can be found with Domaine Pegaü's Châteauneuf-du-Pape Cuvée da Capo 2000 at only £280. There is better value for money in the French regional section with Saint-Chinian Domaine Rimbert Mas au Schiste 2001 coming in at only £22 and from Savoie, with the lovely Mondeuse Vieilles Vignes 2002 from the Quénards at £29. Among the Loire reds, Pierre-Jacques Druet's top *cuvée*, the Bourgueil Vaumoreau 1995 (great vintage), stands out at £59.

There follows several pages of top Bordeaux reds, culminating in Château Mouton Rothschild 1945 at £10,000. There are several vintages of all the first growths at mainly 4-figure prices, but Château d'Armailhac 2000 at £49 looks reasonable enough here. German whites follow next and a pretty big selection of them, too, making choice difficult. On the basis that we have hardly found any Trocken wines to go well with food, we would stick to the Graacher Domprobst Riesling Spätlese 2000 from Reichsgraf von Kesselstatt at £29. Austrian whites are top quality with **Grüner Veltliner Kammerner Lamm 2003** from Schloss Gobelsburg at £36 being the best value. Italian whites don't match up to the quality of the reds, but Cusumano's 2001 Cubia from Sicily, is a good bet at £42. The selection of Italian reds is impressive with superb choices, particularly from Piemonte and Toscana. La Spinetta's Pin blend 1999 at £75 is good value as one of the least expensive offerings; you could also go all the way up to the legendary 1985 vintage of Sassicaia at £1,400, if you so desire. Spanish reds, too, are more interesting than the Spanish whites, ranging from the entry-level Les Terrasses 2002 from Alvaro Palacios at £44, to Pingus 1997 at £560. There is an interesting section on Greek wines, including a Viognier 2003 from Domaine Gerovassiliou in Macedonia at £32.50 and a Xinomavro 1999 from Kir-Yanni in the same area at £28.

Apart from Australia and the USA, New World wines are fairly scant, but of course high quality. **Vergelegen Shiraz 2001** at £38 would seem to be the best of the South Africans and Achavál Ferrer 2000 at £79 the best from Argentina. In Chile, Orzada Carmenère 2002 from Odfjell, is solid 3-star value at £33, whilst in New Zealand, old favourite Ata Rangi Pinot Noir 2001 at £72 looks best, although there are many places in the UK where you could find this for less than £50. There is a good page of Australian wines, with the ubiquitous Penfold's Grange coming in at £445 for the 1998 vintage, but Craiglee Shiraz 2001 seems good value at £50 and Giaconda Roussanne Aeolia 2001 intriguing at £96. North American wines are substantially represented with most wines being of extremely high quality. You would be paying for scarcity value with Colgin's Herb Lamb Vineyard Napa Valley 1997 at £900 – Caymus Cabernet Sauvignon Special Selection Napa Valley 1997 at £300 is a better bet. Customers with less stratospheric budgets would do well with Duck Pond Cellars' aromatic Pinot Gris 2003 from Oregon at £28, or **Cline Cellars Contra Costa County Ancient Vines Mourvèdre 2002** at £36, both being a wonderful change from Chardonnay and Cabernet.

There are 2 full pages of sweet wines with 6 vintages of Château d'Yquem in halves and 5 in bottles, plus the 1995 in an imperial (8 bottles) at £3,500. Or you could go for a bottle of the 1878 at £7,000. Sauternes generally seem to be excessively expensive so it may be better to go for I Capitelli Recioto di Soave 1997 from Roberto Anselmi at £85, or if you really miss Sauternes, the de Bortoli Noble One Botrytis Semillon 2000 at £48 the half-bottle. Finally, there are 3 pages of half-bottles and 2 pages of magnums with the Grüner Veltliner Kamerner Lamm 2003 from Schloss Gobelsburg Austria at £18 and Clos Puy Arnaud 2000 Côtes de Castillon at £22 being the best value white and red halves (magnums of the same are £85 and £90 respectively).

This is a fascinating list with many wines of the highest quality. If only the management could be persuaded to lower their prices by 20% or so, this would be the clear overall winner.

Neville's Best Buy: **Cline Cellars** Contra Costa County Ancient Vines Mourvèdre 2002 at £36

Score: *Quality* 140.30   *Value* 0.67   *Impression* 21.00   *Total* **161.97**

Ranking: *Quality* 1   *Value* 100   *Impression* 28 =   *Overall* **5th**

Recommendations:
NB: 1997 **Jean-Louis Chave** Hermitage at £195
DM: 2001 **Vergelegen** Shiraz at £38
PW: 2003 **Schloss Gobelsburg** Grüner Veltliner Kammerner Lamm at £36

Find out more about wine and wine producers at *www.winebehindthelabel.com*

27th

GREAT EASTERN HOTEL-AURORA

Liverpool Street EC2M 7QN
020 7618 7000

Part of the Conran Group of restaurants, this establishment boasts a wine list of very high quality, but alas, also of very high prices. Our criteria of 3 stars or more is reached by around 70% of this 636-strong selection, but only 22 of these wines meet our value criteria. Nevertheless, if you are feeling flush enough there are some wonderful choices to be made and hopefully this little appraisal will point you in the direction of some of the better value drinking.

The list kicks off with Champagne, where there are a number of really first class wines. Jacquesson Avize Grand Cru Blanc de Blancs 1995 at £70 is as good value as you can get from this list, but there is also the super 5-star Taittinger Comtes de Champagne Blanc de Blancs 1995 at £135. White Burgundies bristle with great names but the prices are very steep. As in many places, the best value is to be found in Chablis with the 2002 1er Cru Vaillons from Louis Michel at £50. Elsewhere the 1992 Musigny Grand Cru from Comte Georges de Vogüé is a rare and interesting treat at £350. White Rhônes are better value all round and Jean-Louis Chave's super 5-star Hermitage Blanc in the good (but not great) 1997 vintage at £95 would seem worth drinking. The white Languedoc-Roussillon section has two 3-star wines under £30 – Château de la Negly's La Brise Marine 2003 at £27 and **Château Mourgues du Grès Terre d'Argence 2003** at £26, whilst the white Loire section has a similar price/quality ratio with Didier Champalou's Vouvray Sec 2001 at £25. Alsace has Marc Kreydenweiss's Riesling Andlau 2000 at £39 and if you want to go up a step, there is the Riesling Vorbourg Grand Cru Clos St-Landelin 2001 from René Muré at £55. In the German section, **Riesling Auslese Goldkapsel Wehlener Sonnenuhr 1995** from Joh. Jos. Prüm is super 5-star quality at £70, but there is a more down-to-earth choice in the Austrian section with the Riesling Smaragd Loibner Loibenberg 1999 from Freie Weingärtner Wachau at £35. There are no bargains, nor is there anything overly exciting in the whites from Switzerland, Italy, Luxembourg or Greece, but in the Spanish section Palacio de Bornos Verdejo 2003 is 3-star quality at only £20. California turns up some good whites, notably some pretty steeply priced bottles from Kistler with Les Noisetières Chardonnay 2000 at £115 and Durell Vineyard Chardonnay 1998 at £149.50. A better bet is probably the Caymus Conundrum 2000 (guess the varietals) at £65, but that's no bargain either. In South Africa, Glen Carlou's Reserve Chardonnay 2002 is passably priced at £38, but there is better value in Australia with Shaw and Smith's M3 Vineyard Chardonnay 2002 at £43 and Tyrrell's Vat 1 Semillon 1997 at £50, which are 4-star wines. Felton Road Block 1 Riesling 2002 from Central Otago at £32 is the best value of the New Zealand whites.

There is a plethora of good clarets in drinkable vintages, but there's not a lot for under £100 a bottle, although Domaine de Chevalier 1996 is in at £75, which is relatively good value. There are some great names in Burgundy, too, but again, little of real merit

under £100. The 2000 Chambolle-Musigny from Alain Hudelot-Noëllat at £59 is probably worth a look. At the other end of the spectrum, there is a good little range of wines from the Domaine de la Romanée-Conti, culminating with Romanée-Saint-Vivant 1990 at £900 a bottle. Somewhere in the middle, Roumier's Bonnes-Mares 1988 at £250, is super 5-star quality. There's much better value in the Rhône, although Guigal's Côte-Rôtie La Turque 1997 will set you back £305 a bottle. However, there is a quartet of good value wines from the south – Côtes de Ventoux Fayard 2003 from Domaine de Fondrèche at £25, Costières de Nîmes Les Galets Rouge 2002 from Château Mourgues at £26, **VdP Côteaux de Peyriac Château Massamier la Mignarde 2003** at a mere £20 and Côtes du Rhône Saint Cosme 2003 from Barruol at £27. The 5-star Mas de Daumas Gassac 2001 is value at £46, if a little young to drink – if you want a bit of maturity here, the 1996 is available at £80. In the South-West, the 1999 Cahors from the Michel Rolland-influenced Château Lagrezette is value at £42. It seems that this little corner of France is the place to be on this list. Italian reds shine with a number of wines from top producers in Piedmont and Tuscany, but the best value would seem to be the 2000 Fatagione blend of Nero Mascalese and Nero d'Avola from Cottanera in Sicily at £39. In Spain Vega Sicilia Unico 1962 at £470 and Les Terrasses 2001 from Alvario Palacios at £48 are the best of a poor value lot. There is 4-star quality from Portugal, however, with the 2000 Chryseia from Prats and Symington at £55. Plenty of big names at big prices turn up in the Californian section (Harlan Estate 1999 at £450, Cask 23 1994 at £250), but the one to go for here must be the 5-star Ridge Geyserville Zinfandel 1998 at £68. South Africa has a good value red with the Double Barrel Tinta Barocca/Cabernet Sauvignon Blend 2001 from The Foundry at £38. There is a long list of Australian reds including 4 vintages of Penfold's Grange at prices from £295 to £440 a bottle, but there is 4-star value in the **Cape Mentelle Cabernet Sauvignon 1999**, which just meets our price criteria at £50. In New Zealand the Ata Rangi Célèbre Cabernet blend at £38 is worth a look.

In the list of French sweet wines the 1997 Bonnezeaux La Montagne from Domaine du Petit Val is the best value at £42 the bottle and in the rest of the world's stickies, the Auslese Riesling 'R' Wachenheimer Gerümpel 1990 from Dr. Bürklin-Wolf is worth drinking at £28.75 the half-bottle. There is a good selection of vintages ports but it's all 3-figure prices for the decent ones. The list finishes off with the selections in half-bottles and in magnums, most of which are of high quality. As is apparent throughout, prices are not cheap, although it's probably worth having a look at a half-bottle of Ridge Lytton Springs Zinfandel 1999 at £29. You could, of course, go for broke and have a double magnum of Luciano Sandrone's Barolo Cannubi Boschis at £500 if you are in the mood!

Neville's Best Buy: **Château Massamier la Mignarde VdP** Côteaux de Peyriac 2003 at a mere £20

Score: *Quality* 103.36   *Value* 5.65   *Impression* 17.00   *Total* **126.01**

Ranking: *Quality* 8   *Value* 92   *Impression* 64 =   *Overall* **27th**

Recommendations:
NB: 1995 **J. J. Prüm** Wehlener Sonnenuhr Riesling Auslese Goldkapsel at £70
DM: 2003 **Château Mourgues du Grès** Terre d'Argence at £26
PW: 1999 **Cape Mentelle** Cabernet Sauvignon at £50

67th

KENSINGTON PLACE

201-209 Kensington Church Street W8 7LX

020 7727 3184

From one of London's trendiest restaurants of the early 90s, this has always had a very upbeat wine list with plenty of half-bottles and wines by the glass to suit the sylph-like darlings who frequent it. The current list has almost 200 wines, of which some 40% reach our quality criteria of 3-stars or higher, and of these, just under a quarter reach our value criteria, too. Prices generally are very reasonable for trendy London. There are 25 wines available by the glass, three of which are of 3-star quality or greater, but a number of 2-star wines figure among them, too. Out of 14 half-bottles listed 4 are of 3-star quality or more. The wine list is divided mainly by style, although Italy, Spain and Portugal seem to defy style, but it's not difficult to get the hang of what the list is trying to communicate, despite the absence of any tasting notes.

There is good value in the Champagne section with **Larmandier-Bernier 1er Cru Blanc de Blancs NV** at £38.50, whilst at the top end a Jeroboam of the super 5-star Pol Roger Cuvée Sir Winston Churchill 1988 at £500 works out at only £125 a bottle, which is as cheap as you will find this wine in London. In the 'Riesling and other aromatics' section Grosset's Clare Valley Polish Hill Riesling 2003 is 4-star quality at £37.50. In the 'Sauvignon Blanc, Sémillon and Chenin Blanc' section (aren't they aromatic, too?) Life from Stone Sauvignon Blanc 2004 from Springfield Estate in South Africa is value at £27.50. A number of top quality wines make the value grade in the Chardonnay and Similar section, with the 4-star Shaw and Smith M3 Vineyard Chardonnay 2003 at £36, **Petaluma's Piccadilly Valley Chardonnay 2001** at £40 and Grosset's Piccadilly Chardonnay 2001 at £45, all from South Australia. There is not so much quality and value in 'Rhône and similar', nor in the Italian and Spanish whites, so it's best to look elsewhere.

In reds 'Cabernet Sauvignon, Merlot and other claret styles' has the 3-star High Trellis Cabernet Sauvignon 2002 from d'Arenberg in South Australia at £29.50, but better value is the 4-star **El Principal 1999** from Chile at £35. If you are into mature classed growth clarets, there are no real bargains here but Château Ducru-Beaucaillou 1989 at £110 might be worth a look. The list of 'Rhône, South of France and similar' is certainly far more interesting (and longer) than its white counterpart, with the 4-star Côte Rôtie 2001 from Clusel-Roch and Charlie Melton's Nine Popes 2000 from the Barossa Valley just on the button at £50, and for those who must drink nothing but the best, the super 5-star **Jean-Louis Chave Hermitage 1997** is worth drinking even at £120. In 'Italy and similar' (although we failed to find any 'similars' listed) value is not very apparent, but at a pinch you could stretch a point and go for the 5-star Amarone della Valpolicella Classico 2000 from Allegrini at £65. 'Spain and Portugal' has Dehesa la Granja 2000 from Alejandro Fernandez at £25, but 'Beaujolais, Loire, Burgundy and Pinot Noir' has little at all to offer as value. There is a nice selection of half-bottles with the 4-star Sally's Paddock Bordeaux blend 1999 at £25 from Redbank in Victoria, Australia and the equally rated Cornas Vieilles Vignes 2001 from Alain Voge at £27.50

Neville's Best Buy: 1999 **El Principal** from Chile at £35

Score: *Quality* 57.81   *Value* 20.83   *Impression* 16.00   *Total* **94.64**

Ranking: *Quality* 51   *Value* 49   *Impression* 67 =   *Overall* **67th**

Recommendations:
NB: 1997 **Jean-Louis Chave** Hermitage at £120
DM: **Larmandier-Bernier** 1er Cru Blanc de Blancs NV at £38.50
PW: 2001 **Petaluma** Chardonnay Piccadilly Valley at £40

14th

LA TROMPETTE

5-7 Devonshire Road Chiswick W4 2EU
020 8747 1836

A super London suburban restaurant wine list from the Nigel Platts-Martin stable. Wine has been important in all his restaurants and this one, sister restaurant to the Glasshouse in Kew (qv), is no exception. There over 500 bins here, of which over 60% are of 3-star quality or above. Prices are of course the issue, although they are not overtly excessive for London.

The wine list is topped and tailed by a Champagne and sparkling wine section at the beginning and pages of half-bottles, magnums, sweet wines and sherry, port and Madeira at the end. Dry wines are divided into colour sections and then conventionally arranged by country and region, so you may have to rely heavily on advice from the sommelier team in making your choices. A page of wines by the glass precedes everything with 3 Champagnes and a French cider offered in 150ml glasses and 15 other dry wines offered in either 175ml or 250ml glasses.

In Champagnes and sparkling wines few of the usual suspects appear. Instead, there is a grand selection of small growers' wines, with Larmandier-Bernier's Né d'Une Terre de Vertus Non Dosé at £45 being the pick of the non-vintage wines and 1997 Egly-Ouriet Ambonnay Grand Cru Brut, disgorged November 2003, the vintage choice at £70. The 1996 Nyetimber Classic Cuvée Brut at £37 is also a good buy. Loire whites are of a consistently high standard, with the 1999 Savennières Clos du Papillon from Domaine du Closel well priced at £29.50. There are good choices in Alsace, too, with Trimbach's Riesling Cuvée Frédéric Emile 1997 at £45 being the best on account of its age and vintage. Burgundy whites are divided into minor appellations (mostly Mâconnais and generic wines from the Côte d'Or), Chablis, Meursault, Chassagne-Montrachet, Puligny-Montrachet and *grands crus*. It's really hard to make choices here – William Fèvre's 5-star Chablis Grand Cru Valmur at £50 is certainly worth having a look at, as is Comte Lafon's super 5-star Meursault 1er Cru Perrières 1998, although you will have to pay £120 for that, but you could well look at the Saint-Véran Les Rochats 2001 from Domaine de la Croix Senaillet at £27.50 if you are on more of a budget. There is an excellent selection of white Rhônes, with André Perret's Condrieu, Côteaux de Chéry 2002 looking good at £51.50. French regional whites are a bit of a mixed bag, but the **Jurançon Sec Cuvée des Casterrasses 2000** from Domaine Bru-Baché at £24 looks interesting. There is nothing of outstanding quality in the Italian whites section, but the Verdicchio di Castelli di Jesi Superiore Podium 2001 from Garofoli, is well priced at £24.50. Spanish whites are not quite of the same high standard as other sections of the list, but in Portugal, we have Dirk Niepoort's **Redoma Branco 2003** at £32. There is a good array of 3-star German whites with Armand Diel's Dorsheimer Pittermänschen Riesling Spätlese 1998 at £33 probably being the best choice because of the quality of the vintage. There are some fine Grüner Veltliners and Rieslings from Austria, with the 5-star Riesling Smaragd Dürnsteiner Kellerberg 1999 from F-X Pichler at £59.50 providing top quality. From the nice page of Australian whites the rich Brokenwood Aged Reserve ILR Sémillon 1998 from the Hunter Valley at £29.50 would provide very acceptable drinking for the price. The top New Zealand white by far on the list is the 2002 Dry River Craighall Riesling at £42.50 whilst South Africa produces the Boekenhoutskloof Semillon 2003, a little pricey at £37, but good. There is a top quality range of Californian Chardonnays – the best value being the 2000 vintage of Brewer-Clifton's Sweeney Canyon Chardonnay at £55.

The single page of clarets fits in nicely with the rest of the list. Famous Bordeaux wines are usually in drinkable vintages with Château Palmer 1986 at £120 fairly priced as well as Château Lynch Bages 1970 at £165. Even Château Pétrus 1983 at £500 is very fair. There is a good selection of red Burgundies with Monthelie Clos les Champs Fuillot 1er Cru 1988 from Bouchard Père et Fils looking good value at £35 and 1992 Romanée Saint-Vivant from Robert Arnoux providing super 5-star quality at £185. There are a lot of good bottles in the red Rhône section, with Hermitage la Chapelle 1996 at £72 looking reasonable value in the north and Gigondas Prestige des Hautes Garrigues 1999 from Domaine Santa Duc taking the honours in the south at £36. Among Loire reds the 2003 Touraine Gamay Vinifera from Henri Marionnet at £26 should be interesting, and mentioning Gamay, there are three good Beaujolais on the list, with Brouilly Réserve du Château 2003 from Château de Pierreux at £31 looking best. There is a plethora of wines from the French regions, many of real quality. Try the Côtes de Roussillon-Villages Tautavel Vieilles Vignes 2001 from Domaine Gardiés at £31.50.

Italy delivers a lot of fine quality reds, particularly from Piedmont and Tuscany, with Roberto Voerzio's 1997 Vignaserra blend of Nebbiolo and Barbera at £45 and Poliziano's Vino Nobile di Montepulciano Asinone 1999 at £48.50. There are a couple of good 3-star red wines from Greece – Nemea Barrel Agiorgitiko 2001 from Domaine Vassiliou at £20 and Naoussa Xinomavro 2000 from Kir-Yianni at £25. Spanish reds get a good look in with 5-star quality wines such as René Barbier's Clos Mogador 2002 at £55 and of course Vega Sicilia Unico 1987 at £137.50, whilst Portugal has the 4-star Quinta do Vale Doña Maria 2000 at £32.50. South America is not without quality, but Nicolas Catena's Zapata 1999 from Argentina is not exactly value for money at £95. The **2001 Achaval Ferrer Quimera** blend of Malbec, Cabernet Sauvignon and Merlot at less than half the price (£45) is a better bet. The Estate Reserve Welgemeend 1998 at £27.50 looks good value in the South African section and the 2002 Massaya Selection from the Tanaï Property in the Bekaa Valley in Lebanon at the same price looks interesting, too. There is a fine selection of New Zealand Pinot Noirs, with Ata Rangi 2001 at £49.50 and Mount Edward 2002 at £43 heading the list. Australian reds outnumber the clarets and a very interesting mix they make. Dean Hewitson's **Old Garden Mourvèdre 2001**, from vines planted in 1853, will knock your socks off at £35.50, whilst Quintet 1999 (Cabernet Sauvignon, Merlot, Cabernet Franc, Malbec and Petit Verdot) from the Mount Mary Estate in Victoria will lull you into a sense of sublimity, even if a bottle will set you back £93. North America brandishes some huge guns at huge prices, but there is variety too: go for either the Harrison Hill Bordeaux blend 1999 from De Lille Cellars in Washington State at £65 if you are into finesse or John Alban's Lorraine Syrah 1998 at £51 if you are into power.

The selections of halves and magnums contain some good quality bottles – in halves, best value seems to be Chablis Grand Cru Bougros 1998 from William Fèvre at £28.50, while in magnums it's Ridge Lytton Springs Zinfandel 1998 at £110. An incredible array of 34 sweet wines from around the globe follows, which includes only one Sauternes. Obviously the emphasis is elsewhere – 4 Tokajis from Hungary with 1983 Essencia from Oremus at £60 for 25cl (probably – it's not specified) being the most interesting, but you could easily go for Alois Kracher's No. 7 Chardonnay TBA 1999 at £53 for a half-bottle, 1998 Ihringer Winklerberg Riesling TBA from Dr Heger in Baden at £79.50 the half, or a whole bottle of Robert Plageoles' Gaillac Vin d'Autan 1999 at £65. There aren't many places in Britain that can boast a wine list better than this and the residents of Chiswick are lucky to find such a gem on their doorstep.

Neville's Best Buy: **Hewitson** Old Garden Mourvèdre 2001, from vines planted in 1853, at £35.50

Score: *Quality* 102.03   *Value* 23.49   *Impression* 19.00   *Total* **144.52**

Ranking: *Quality* 9   *Value* 42   *Impression* 43 =   *Overall* **14th**

Recommendations:
NB: 2001 **Achaval Ferrer** Quimera at £45
DM: 2000 **Domaine Bru-Baché** Jurançon Sec Cuvée des Casterrasses at £24
PW: 2003 **Niepoort** Douro Redoma Branco at £32

62nd

LE CAFÉ DU JARDIN

28 Wellington Street WC2E 7BD
020 7836 8769

This Covent Garden haunt is handy for when you tumble out of the Opera House (as is its sister restaurant – Le Deuxième; qv), and it is also a pleasure to find a fairly compact wine list with some good quality wines – and above all, reasonable prices. The 128-bin wine list is simply written out on two closely typed pages – no tasting notes, but with availability by either the half-bottle or by the glass indicated in additional price columns. Over 20% of the wines listed meet our quality criteria and of these, nearly 40% meet our value criteria, which is pretty unusual for London. There are 14 half-bottles listed and 15 wines by the glass, and whilst only one of them meets out quality criteria, there is, nevertheless, great scope for experimentation. We noticed that at the end of the list there was a statement saying 'please ask your waiter if you want to see our fine wine list' – they did not send this to us, but who knows, if they had done so, this list might have finished up with a higher rating

The list is arranged conventionally by country and region and starts off with Champagnes where there is nothing that meets our price/quality ratio. Nor is there anything in any of the other regions until we get to the Loire where Henri Bourgeois's La Vigne Blanche Sancerre 2004 at £27 (£14 the half) scores. In white Burgundies, Jean-Claude Bessin's Chablis Grand Cru Valmur 2001 at £50 is right on the value limit for a 4-star wine. **Au Bon Climat Wild Boy Chardonnay 2001** from Santa Barbara in California is well priced at £30, whilst Australia has the Coldstream Hills Reserve Chardonnay 1998 at £28 and Plantagenet Mount Barker Chardonnay 2003 at £30 as 3-star value wines and the 4-star Grosset Piccadilly Chardonnay 2001 at £45.

There is more value in the reds with the **Costières de Nîmes Galets 2003** from Château Mourgues de Grès coming in at only £18 and the **Domaine de la Suffrène Bandol 2001** at £26. Also in this section is the 5-star Mas de Daumas Gassac 2002, terrific value at £35 the bottle and £18.50 the half, although it may be a little too young to drink. Burgundy and Bordeaux have quality wines but none that are any great bargain, but in Italy, **Piaggia Carmignano Riserva 2000** is well priced at £40. Australia has its fair share of quality wines, with the Seville Estate Pinot Noir 2002 at £30 and Grosset's Gaia Cabernet Sauvignon 1999 at £48 looking the best bets.

Neville's Best Buy: 2003 **Ch. Mourgues de Grès** Costières de Nîmes Galets at £18

Score: *Quality* 24.80   *Value* 57.05   *Impression* 15.00   *Total* **96.85**

Ranking: *Quality* 93   *Value* 11   *Impression* 75 =   *Overall* **62nd**

Recommendations:
NB: 2001 **Au Bon Climat** Chardonnay "Wild Boy" at £30
DM: 2001 **Domaine de la Suffrène** Bandol at £26
PW: 2000 **Piaggia** Carmignano Riserva at £40

Find out more about wine and wine producers at *www.winebehindthelabel.com*

81st

LE DEUXIÈME

65A Long Acre WC2E 9JH
020 7379 0033

This is the second restaurant owned by Robert Siegler and Tony Howarth and, like it's sister restaurant Le Café du Jardin (qv), it is an excellent watering hole for visitors to Covent Garden. Of nearly 180 wines listed just over 25% are of 3-star quality or higher, and of these, some 30% meet our price/quality ratio. There are 25 half-bottles of dry wines listed and 15 wines by the glass, which is useful, although few of them meet the ratio we are seeking. The wine list is set out without tasting notes on 4 closely typed pages in a conventional manner by country and region, white wines and then reds. We couldn't find any good value quality white wines in any of the lesser French regions, but in the white Burgundy section, Jean-Claude Bessin's 4-star Chablis Grand Cru Valmur 2001 hits the button at £50. Bonneau du Martray's super 5-star Corton-Charlemagne 1998 is good value at £90. In Alsace, the Riesling Engelgarten 1999 from Marcel Deiss comes in at £30. The USA has the 3-star Qupé Bien Nacido Viognier/Chardonnay 2003 at £30 and the 4-star Beringer Private Reserve Chardonnay 2000 at £50. There's value, too, in Australia with Cullen's Chardonnay 2000 at £40 and Grosset's Piccadilly Chardonnay 2001 at £45.

In the reds, there is good value in Provence with the 3-star Bandol 2001 from the Domaine La Suffrène at £26 (£14 the half bottle) and the 5-star **Vin du Pays des Bouches du Rhône 1998** from Domaine de Trévallon at £50. The Languedoc scores, too, with the Costières de Nîmes Galets 2003 from Château Mourgues du Grès at only £18 and the ubiquitous Mas de Daumas Gassac Rouge 2002 at £35 (£18.50 the half bottle). The Northern Rhône section has the super-5 star Hermitage La Chapelle 1996 well priced at £55, even if this was from a pretty moderate vintage. Clarets and red Burgundies don't make the cut, although there is 5-star value with the Volnay Santenots de Milieu 2001 from the Domaine des Comtes Lafon at £60 in the Burgundies and **Château Le Tertre Rôteboeuf Grand Cru Saint-Émilion 1986** at £85 in the clarets. Italy has the 4-star Carmignano Riserva 2000 from Piaggia at £40, whilst Spain has the 3-star Urbina Seleccion Rioja 1997 at £30. There is value, too, in Argentina with the French-owned **Clos de los Siete** blend of Merlot, Cabernet Sauvignon, Syrah and Malbec 2003 at £28, whilst in California there is the 5-star Ridge Geyserville Zinfandel 2000 at £45. Australia has its share of quality wines as well, with Seville Estate Pinot Noir 2002 from the Yarra Valley at £30 and the **Jasper Hill Georgia's Paddock Shiraz 2001** from Heathcote at £50. There is nothing of interest in the Champagne, Rosé, or House selections, but there is a fine wine list (available on request) which was not sent to us, so we presume that had it been done so, the list might have found itself a bit higher in the rankings. The big plus point for this list is that some of the prices are very reasonable for central London – let's hope they stay that way.

Neville's Best Buy: 1998 Vin du Pays des Bouches du Rhône from **Domaine de Trévallon** at £50

Score: *Quality* 30.80   *Value* 31.57   *Impression* 18.00   *Total* **80.37**

Ranking: *Quality* 89   *Value* 30   *Impression* 53 =   *Overall* **81st**

Recommendations:
NB: 1986 **Château Le Tertre Rôteboeuf** Saint-Emilion Grand Cru at £85
DM: 2003 **Clos de los Siete** Mendoza at £28
PW: 2001 **Jasper Hill** Georgia's Paddock Shiraz at £50

Find out more about wine and wine producers at *www.winebehindthelabel.com*

18th

LOCANDA LOCATELLI

8 Seymour Street W1H 7JZ
020 7935 9088

This list has one of the greatest percentages of 4- and 5-star wines (over 50% of the list) with a further 25% of 3-star quality. With the exception of a few Champagnes and fortified wines, all the wines come from Italy, and over 300 of them on are offer. Head sommelier Max Salli has put together one of the most exciting Italian lists in the UK and it's mostly the prices that prevent this list from obtaining an even higher score. A small selection of dry wines by the glass and the near absence of half-bottles has further reduced the score. A complete absence of tasting notes doesn't help either.

'Spumante and Champagne' is the first heading on the list, and whilst there are a number of top quality Champagnes (dominated by Taittinger), you would do far better to go for the brilliant Franciacorta Cuvée Satén NV from Bellavista at £45. In white wines, the top Piedmont choice is the 2002 Chardonnay Gaja & Rey, but at £129 it's a bit of a stiff price to pay for just 4-star quality. In Alto Adige, Cantine Terlano's Pinot Bianco Riserva Vorberg 2002 is well priced 3-star quality at £27.50. The unoaked Piere Sauvignon Blanc 2002 from Vie di Romans in Fruili-Venezia Giulia at £39.50 shows intense varietal flavours and is well worth drinking. Inevitably, under this section, you will find Silvio Jermann's famous 'Dreams' Chardonnay 2002 but you will have to pay £77 for the privilege. From the Marche, Verdicchio dei Castelli di Jesi Classico Riserva 2000 from Villa Bucci at £33 is a large cut above most other Verdicchios. Antinori's Chardonnay-based Cervaro della Sala 2001 from Umbria is good 4-star drinking at £53. An interesting find on the list is the Vermentino di Gallura Vendemmia Tardiva 2001 from Capichera in Sardinia, at £61. It is *barrique* aged, late harvest but dry, and the hefty price tag is not entirely due to the mark up in the restaurant.

There are a lot of top quality wines amongst the reds, but prices are generally high. Lombardia has a couple of 4-star wines – Nino Negri Sfursat 5 Stelle 2002 at £65 made from semi-dried grapes in the Valtellina and Ca' del Bosco's Bordeaux blend Maurizio Zanella from a mature 1990 vintage at £110. Good value prevails, however, with Elisabetta Foradori's Teroldego Rotaliano 2002 at £26 from Trentino and even possibly with the **Moschioni Pignolo Colli Orientali 2001** at £75. In the Veneto, the 5-star La Poja 1999 from Allegrini at £75 is a good buy considering the prices generally, and Allegrini's 5-star Amarone della Valpolicella Classico 1997 at £120 might be preferred to Romano Dal Forno's from the same vintage at £475, but Dal Forno's Amarones are legendary and you may well think it's worth paying that much for undoubted super 5-star quality. From Umbria, Poggio Bertaio's intensely tangy Sangiovese Cimbolo 2001 at £37, contrasts nicely with the rich and opulent super 5-star Montefalco Sagrantino 25 Anni from Arnaldo Caprai at £115. In Lazio, Falesco's Montiano Merlot 2000, is reasonably priced for a 5-star wine at £60. The 5 entries on the list from Campania are all of at least 4-star quality, with the 5-star **Serpico 1999** (Irpinia Aglianico) from Feudi di San Gregorio at £65 being the best value. More value is apparent from the south of

Italy and the islands, with Torcicoda Primitivo del Salento 2003 form Tormaresca in Puglia at £28.00, Aglianico del Vulture Il Viola 2001 from Tenuta Le Querce in Basilicata at £29, Tancredi Contessa Entellina 2002 from Donnafugata in Sicily at £33 and Rocca Rubia Carignano del Sulcis Superiore 2002 from Cantine Santadi in Sardinia at £27.

But it is in Piedmont and Tuscany that the selection reaches dizzy heights of both quality and price, culminating in the fabled 1985 Sassicaia at an extraordinary £1,385. In fairness, that's streets ahead of most other prices, with wines from mature vintages commanding the highest. For instance, Barolo Vigna del Gris from Conterno Fantino, is £395 for the 1985 vintage, but only £78 for the 2000. Whether the difference is worth it, is something you will probably have to ask the sommelier. In Piedmont, Dolcetto di Dogliani Vigna Tecc 2001 from Luigi Einaudi at £30 is a worthy entry-level wine, whilst moving up a notch, Oberto's Barbera d'Alba Giada 1998 at £45 should be drinking well now, as should Matteo Corregia's Roero Rocche d'Ampsej 1999 at £75. Big guns include Barbarescos from Bruno Rocca, La Spinetta, Bruno Giacosa, and, of course Gaja – all at 3-figure prices and many of them a bit on the young side. Barolos are similarly placed, with top quality wines from Conterno Fantino, Armando Parusso, Aldo Conterno, Roberto Voerzio, Domenico Clerico, Paolo Scavino, and, again, Gaja. In Tuscany, the entry-level blend of Cabernet and Sangiovese Belcore 2000 from I Giusti & Zanza at £28 should be well worth exploring, as should the **Rocca di Montegrossi Chianti Classico 2001** at £31. Most of the blended wines are a bit young again, as are the Chianti Classicos, the Brunellos and the Vino Nobile di Montepulcianos, but should all drink reasonably well. If you want to go back to more smooth and mature vintages then there is a choice (at a price) with wines from Ornellaia, Sanmarco, L'Apparita, Massetto, Solaia and, of course, Sassicaia.

On a page of first class magnums the Terre Brune Carignano del Sulcis 1998 from Santadi in Sardinia at £110 looks good value for the list and the outstanding super 5-star **Barbera Riserva Pozzo dell'Annunziata** from Roberto Voerzio is offered in 3 vintages (1998, 1999 and 2000) at prices between £385 and £455. There is a small selection of half-bottles, none of them cheap, with Tignanello 2000 at £43 looking to be the best value. The list finishes up with a good selection of sweet wines (although some of them are not so sweet, such as Vin Santo and Recioto della Valpolicella), with a bottle of I Capitelli 2003 from Anselmi at £48 producing enough richness and finesse to satisfy the sweetest of desserts. Despite the prices, this is a model list, containing much of the best of Italy and much to be commended.

Neville's Best Buy: the 5-star 1999 **Feudi di San Gregorio** Serpico at £65

Score: *Quality* 117.72   *Value* 5.11   *Impression* 15.00   *Total* **137.83**

Ranking: *Quality* 4   *Value* 93   *Impression* 74 =   *Overall* **91st**

Recommendations:
NB: 1998 **Roberto Voerzio** Barbera Riserva Pozzo dell'Annunziata (magnum) at £385
DM: 2001 **Rocca di Montegrossi** Chianti Classico at £31
PW: 2001 **Moschioni** Colli Orientali del Friuli Pignolo at £75

Find out more about wine and wine producers at *www.winebehindthelabel.com*

76th

McCLEMENTS

2 Whitton Road Twickenham TW1 1BJ
020 8744 9610

This is a pretty high-falutin' wine list for a local suburban restaurant in south-west London – maybe they are out to catch the punters after they fall out of their hospitality boxes at Twickenham, or drive back from the races at Ascot. There are nearly 400 wines on the list of which just over a third are of 3-star quality or more, but of these only a handful meet our value criteria. A fair number of half-bottles are available, many of which are of high quality (and price) and there are also 14 wines by the glass, of which two reach our quality standard. Quality, therefore is undoubted, but it's the prices that hurt, and it's not helped by a list that is difficult to read with a number of context errors.

The list starts off with a fair number of good quality Champagnes at fairly stiff prices, so it's probably best to stick with the basic Roederer Brut NV, 3-star quality at £54. White wines are conventionally arranged by country and region. In Alsace there is nothing under £30 and the best wine here is probably Trimbach's 4-star Cuvée Frédéric-Emile Riesling 1999 at a whopping £95. In white Burgundies, the 4-star Meursault-Charmes 1er Cru 2000 from Henri Germain at £85 is as good as you will get here. In 'Rhône Vallée and the Midi whites', the white **Mas de Daumas Gassac 2001** is 5-star value at £42, if they have any left by the time you read this; otherwise you will have to pay £55 for the 2004. The Loire has Didier Dagueneau's super 5-star Pouilly-Fumé Silex 2002 at a fairly reasonable £70 for the quality, although it may be a bit on the young side. There's not much else to consider in the 'European whites' but there is value in the Greek section, with the Santorini 2003 from Domaine Sigalas at £28 and the Malagousia 2003 from Domaine Gerovassiliou at £30. From Australia, there is 4-star quality in the Piccadilly Valley Chardonnay 1999 from Petaluma at £45 and in the USA section there is Jade Mountain's Paras Vineyard Viognier 1999, but you will have to pay £59 for that.

Reds start off with Burgundies and here, it might be well worth considering the super 5-star Chambertin Clos de Bèze from Louis Jadot at only £115, but the catch is that it is from the 1976 vintage – a vintage with a good reputation, but it's probably best to enquire of its provenance from the sommelier. At the other end of the scale, the Beaujolais section has the **Chénas Domaine des Vieilles Caves 2003** from Fernand Charvet at £30. In the northern Rhône, **Jean-Louis Chave Saint-Joseph 2002**, doesn't look a bad shot at £32, but you could also go for his super 5-star Hermitage 1995 at £350. There is better value in the southern Rhône section with the Côtes du Rhône-Villages 2003 from Domaine Chapoton at £26 and the **Vacqueyras 2000 Domaine La Garrigue** at £30. The Madiran 2001 from Domaine Berthoumieu is also good value at £25. Clarets come next, with Château La Dauphine 1999 from Canon-Fronsac looking good value at £25 and it may be well worth trying the Château Beauséjour Saint-Émilion 2000 at £56, even if it may be a bit on the young side. There is really nothing else in the reds that we could recommend as having a good price/quality ratio, although Ktima Pavlidis 2002 from Greece is just off the cusp at £32. Many of the long list of half-bottles are of good quality, but finding value is another matter. Still, Henri Pellé's Ménétou-Salon 1994 is in at £17 in the whites, (although it may be a bit past it), and Domaine du Chapoton's Côtes du Rhône 2003 is in at £18 in the reds. In the dessert wine list, there is a section headed 'South west Rhône', which is a bit confusing, especially when it includes Côteaux du Layon, Rancio Grande Reserve Rivesaltes, Muscat Beaumes de Venise, Banyuls Reserva and 'Condrieux' – all from unspecified producers, so it is impossible to give any assessment on these wines. There are a couple of good Sauternes there but they are rather pricey, so it may be best to enquire of further and better particulars from those others mentioned above.

Neville's Best Buy: **Mas de Daumas Gassac** Blanc 2001, 5-star value at £42

Score: *Quality* 68.58   *Value* 6.21   *Impression* 9.00   *Total* **83.79**

Ranking: *Quality* 41   *Value* 89   *Impression* 97 =   *Overall* **76th**

Recommendations:
NB: 2002 **Jean-Louis Chave** Saint-Joseph at £32
DM: 2000 **Domaine La Garrigue** Vacqueyras at £30
PW: 2003 **Fernand Charvet/Domaine des Vieilles Caves** Chénas at £30

Find out more about wine and wine producers at *www.winebehindthelabel.com*

37th

OXO TOWER

Oxo Tower Wharf Barge House Street SE1 9PH
020 7803 3888

This is the sister restaurant to the Harvey Nichols Fifth Floor (qv) and is similar in style but with some differences in the contents. Prices for the best known names (and there are plenty of those) are pretty steep, even for London, but there are some bargains to be had amongst the host of quality wines on the list. Over 65% of the wines listed meet out quality criteria, but only just over 10% of those meet our value criteria. There are only 18 dry halves listed out of nearly 500 wines, but a fair proportion of them meet the quality standard, and 20 wines by the glass, with 5 meeting the quality standard. So, as you can see, this is a very good list if you can afford the prices. It is conventionally arranged by country or region. There are no tasting notes, but we are sure the sommelier team would be up to providing the necessary information

Nothing in the Champagne section meets the price/quality ratio, but out of several super 5-star Champagnes, Veuve Clicquot la Grande Dame 1996 seems the best value at £165. The next page lists magnums, most of which are of impeccable pedigree, at a price. The best value here would appear to be the 5-star Alion Reserva 1998 from the Vega Sicilia stable in Spain at £135. Bordeaux wines follow but again with little to excite those seeking a good price/quality ratio. There is a good spread of first growth clarets from the outstanding 1982 vintage – Margaux is £1,000, Mouton-Rothschild £1,100, Latour £1,200, Cheval Blanc £1,350 and Pétrus £4,200, but for us the best value for the vintage is undoubtedly the Pichon Lalande at £630, a marvellous wine with so much still to give. For those with shallower pockets, Léoville Barton 1999 at £85 is fair value for this list, if a little too young to drink. In the Burgundy reds, the Chambolle-Musigny 1996 from Confuron-Cotétidot at £48.50 looks reasonable value with enough bottle age to soften this normally very sturdy wine. There is the usual clutch of *grands crus* at pretty big prices, but none from the DRC, although there is a Richebourg 1990 from Mme Leroy at £1,450. The Côte de Beaune is rather scantily represented compared with the Côte de Nuits. White Burgundies has the 4-star Chablis 1er Cru Vaillons 2002 from Billaud-Simon, a relative bargain at £35 and the 3-star Viré-Clessé Mont Châtelaine 2000 from Domaine Rijckaert at £22.50, but if you insist on a Côte d'Or wine, then the Meursault Le Meix Sous le Châteaux 2002 from Jean-Philippe Fichet at £65 looks best. Of course, you could go for Domaine Leflaive's Bâtard-Montrachet 2000, super 5 stars at £315, but you might prefer to go for Richard Fontaine-Gagnard's 5-star **Criots-Bâtard-Montrachet 2001** at a mere £150. There is nothing exciting in the Loire section, but the Rhône has Crozes-Hermitage 2002 from Domaine Gilles Robin at £33. The 'French country' section offers better value with Arbois en Paradis Vieilles Vignes 2000 from Domaine Rijckaert coming in at £23.50, Jurançon Sec 2002 from Camin Larredya at £26.50 and Roussette de Savoie 2003 from A & M Quenard at £27.50. In the reds, the 3-star **Château Mas Neuf Costières de Nîmes 2002** is remarkable value at £18.50. There is some good value from Alsace, too, with Pinot Blanc Barriques 2002 from Ostertag at £22 and Pinot Blanc Mise du Printemps 2003 from Josmeyer at £24.50, both 3-star wines. Josmeyer's Riesling Grand Cru Hengst is 4-star quality for £43 for a 50cl bottle in the 1993 vintage and £50 for a full 75cl bottle in the 1997 vintage.

Turning away from France, in Italy, Massolino's Barolo Vigna Rionda 2000 looks good value at £50, if a little on the young side, as does Selvapiana's Chianti Rufina Riserva Bucerchiale 2000 at £42. Surprisingly, there are no really great Barolo or Barbaresco wines on the list. In Spain, **Casa Castillo Monastrell 2002** from Jumilla is worth drinking at £22 and among Vega Sicilia wines the Reserva Especial at £245 is as good as you will get. Australia provides good value as usual – Tahbilk's Marsanne 2002 from the Goulburn Valley in Victoria is only £18, whilst Plantagenet Riesling from Mount Barker in Western Australia is £20. Better value still is **Grosset Watervale Riesling 2003**, 4-star quality at £32.50. Petaluma Piccadilly Valley Chardonnay 2001 is also good value at £38.50. There is less value overall in the reds, but Plantagenet Mount Barker Shiraz 2001 is 4-star quality at £44. Two wines from New Zealand sport a good price/quality ratio – Kumeu River Chardonnay 2002 at £42.50 and Unison's estate red 1999 from Hawkes Bay at £35 – nice to see the bottle age on this one, too. Chile has Casa Lapostelle's Chardonnay Cuvée Alexandre 2002 at £28 and Valdivieso's Reserve Cabernet Franc 2001 at £26.50 as good value 3-star wines, while South Africa offers Spice Route Pinotage 2003 at £27.50. Wines from the USA are not normally noted for their value, but there are exceptions, and on this list they are provided by wines from Ridge, with their York Creek Petite Sirah 1999 at £45 and their Geyserville Zinfandel 2000 at £50, both being of 4-star quality. The 'Stickies' page is neatly divided into Bottle, Half Litre and Half-Bottle sections. Alois Kracher's super 5-star Chardonnay No. 3 TBA 2001 at £53.50 the 50cl bottle (£12 the glass) lends some Austrian finesse, whilst a half-bottle of Yalumba's Museum Muscat from Rutherglen, at £25, provides some Australian power.

The half-bottle list provides a good selection of Champagnes at a price, but the best value here is to be found in the Chablis 1er Cru Vaillons 2003 from Billaud-Simon, 4-star quality at £19, and the Vino Nobile di Montepulciano 2001 from Avignonesi, 3-star quality at £16.50. A reasonable selection of dry wines by the glass takes in the Avignonesi Vino Nobile as above, at £8 a glass, and a Chablis 1er Cru Beauroy 2002 from Alain Geoffroy at £8.10 a glass. Fortified wines by the glass include Dow's 20-year-old Tawny at £11.50 a glass and three *muy viejo* sherries, Noé Pedro Ximénez, Matusalem Oloroso and Apóstoles Palo Cortado from González Byass at £7. These three are also available by the half-bottle at £27.50. There is a large selection of vintage ports at all prices, with Warre's 1985 and Dow's 1983 being the cheapest at £90, but it might be better to go for a little more ageing with Warre's 1977 at £107.

Neville's Best Buy: **Château Mas Neuf** Costières de Nîmes 2002 at £18.50

Score: *Quality* 85.34   *Value* 12.96   *Impression* 19.00   *Total* **117.30**

Ranking: *Quality* 20   *Value* 72   *Impression* 43 =   *Overall* **37th**

Recommendations:
NB: 2001 **Richard Fontaine-Gagnard** Criots-Bâtard-Montrachet at £150
DM: 2002 **Casa Castillo** Jumilla Monastrell at £22
PW: 2003 **Grosset** Watervale Riesling at £32.50

Find out more about wine and wine producers at *www.winebehindthelabel.com*

London restaurants

6th

RANSOME'S DOCK

35-37 Parkgate Road SW11 4NP
020 7223 1611

Why is it that so many wine merchants are seen eating at Ransome's Dock? Is it because that they know that there there they will find one of the most exciting wine lists in London (in the whole country, even), or is it because they hope that Martin Lam's ever expanding cellar will accommodate even more of their wines?! Whatever it is, this is a list that is in the vanguard of modernity:it has pzazz, buzz, beat – a pot pourri of all that's new in the wine world – and this is probably why this has taken over from the Tate Gallery as the wine merchant's favourite watering hole. Martin was one of the first in the country to list his wines by style rather than by region and his innovative approach still continues to this day. Well over half the wines on the 300-plus list qualify on our quality criteria, but of those, less that a quarter qualify on our price criteria, so prices are not *that* cheap, but for London, they are pretty fair. There is a better quality/price ratio on the halves and it is very refreshing to see such an outstanding proportion of dry wines by the glass of real quality.

The 'Ransome's Dock selection', an ever changing *mélange* of modern tastes, opens proceedings – no boring old clarets here. On the list we saw, we liked the look of Grüner Veltliner Kies 2003 from Kurt Angerer in Austria at £15.50 and the **Pondalowie Vineyards Shiraz/Viognier 2002** from Victoria in Australia at £22.50. Wines by the glass include Larmandier Bernier Champagne 1er Cru Brut Vertus at £6.75 and Kevin Mitchell's Prodigal Grenache 2000 at £6.95 from Clare Valley, South Australia. A page of half-bottles follows with Bandol 2001 from Domaine la Suffrène looking the best value at £12.75. Champagnes are by no means cheap, but there is better value at the top end, with Dom Pérignon 1993 looking good at £135. The sparkling whites are interesting with the Roederer Estate Quartet Brut NV at £32 a good alternative to Champagne. The list swings on with some Sauvignon Blancs and some Semillons, with Rockford Local Growers Sémillon 1999 from the Barossa Valley at £24 catching the eye. A full page of Rieslings follows, from the keenly-priced Clare Valley Riesling 2004 from Tim Adams at £17, to the sumptuous, super 5-star Clos Ste-Hune 1996 from Trimbach at £100 (£50 the half). Aromatic and dry white wines include Joël Gigou's **Jasnières Cuvée Saint-Jacques 1999** from the Loire at £27.50 and the equally aromatic (but in a different way) **Condrieu Côteaux du Chéry 1999** from the talented André Perret in the Rhône Valley at £50. The whites are completed by a page containing some very high class Chardonnays, with Jeffrey Grosset's 4-star Piccadilly Chardonnay 1999 from Clare Valley at £35 in for value and Domaine Billaud-Simon's Chablis Grand Cru Vaudésir 2000 at £70 for 5-star quality.

The first page of reds is devoted to Pinot Noir, with Au Bon Climat's Bien Nacido and Le Bon Climat Vineyards 2000 vintage at £37 providing good value and Domaine Ponsot's Clos de la Roche Vieilles Vignes 1997 at £190 providing super-5 star quality in a vintage which should just about be ready to drink. There is an interesting lighter, fruity 2003 red from Planeta in Sicily made from Nero d'Avola and Frappato called

Cerasuolo di Vittoria at £22.50, whilst the collection of big Zinfandels has Cline Cellars Ancient Vines 2002 at the value end at £26 and Ravenswood Wood Road-Belloni vineyard at £70 at the top. 'Bigger reds' follows (can you get any bigger than a Ravenswood Zinfandel?). There's not a lot of high quality stuff at the cheaper end of this section, but Jaboulet's Hermitage La Chapelle 1996 at £80 is reasonably enough priced, although it's not the greatest of vintages. 'Cabernets; Sauvignon and Franc' kicks off with a finely valued Franc from Yannick Amirault in Bourgeuil in the Loire Valley – his Les Quartiers 2002 at £22.50. The 5-star Boekenhoutskloof Cabernet Sauvignon 2000 from South Africa at £50 is at a good price/quality ratio and the cult Harlan Estate Napa Valley 1995 is not overpriced at £230. The short list of pure Merlots and Malbecs has Craggy Range Merlot 2002 from New Zealand reasonably priced at £29, but there are more interesting offerings in the Bordeaux-style blends with the **Joseph 'Moda Amarone' Cabernet Sauvignon/Merlot 1998** from South Australia coming in at £30 and the 5-star 1999 Cullen Cabernet Sauvignon/Merlot coming in at £50. The last page dedicated to red wine in bottles is entitled 'Very big reds'. Well, how big can you get? We suppose that Penfold's Grange 1990 would fit the bill, as would Beaucastel's Hommage à Jacques Perrin 1994 – they are both just about ready to drink, but at £310 and £250 a bottle respectively, you may have to hold your breath.

The next section of the list is for 'Bigger and very big bottles', both red and white. There's not a lot of value in the selection of whites – Verget's Puligny-Montrachet Les Ensegnières 1999 at £95 a magnum is only 3-star quality, but seems to be the best value, but in the reds you can go from the 4-star Nine Popes 1998 Châteauneuf-du-Pape look alike from Charlie Melton in the Barossa Valley at £100 right up to the super 5-star Chambertin Clos de Bèze 1996 from Armand Rousseau at £290. In the *really* big bottles there's an unconventional 500cl of another Châteauneuf-du-Pape look alike, Le Cigare Volant 1996 from Randall Grahm's Bonny Doon Vineyard in California at £270, or you could play safe with an Imperial (600cl – 8 bottles) of Ch. Pichon-Longueville-Lalande 1997 at £600.

The list of dessert wines is conveniently divided into sizes, from a glass to whole bottles. A half of Domaine Cauhapé's Jurançon Ballet d'Octobre 1999 at £14.50 is good entry-level value, whilst the only Sauternes on the list, Ch. Coutet 1998, is not bad value at £34 the half in a reasonable vintage. Quite interesting, too, is a whole bottle of Domaine Soumade's Rasteau Vin Doux Naturel 1999, made from red Grenache, at £31. Finally, there is a page of very fine sherries available either by the glass or half-bottle from Emilio Lustau at £19.50 the half or £5.50 the glass. There is a feel-good factor about this list, although it is not as cheap as you might hope, but if you pick your way through it carefully enough, there are some good value wines to be had.

Neville's Best Buy: Joseph 'Moda Amarone' Cabernet Sauvignon/Merlot 1998 from **Primo Estate** at £30

Score: *Quality* 109.05 *Value* 23.37 *Impression* 24.00 *Total* **156.42**

Ranking: *Quality* 6 *Value* 40 *Impression* 15 = *Overall* **6th**

Recommendations:
NB: 1999 **André Perret** Condrieu 'Côteaux du Chéry' at £50
DM: 1999 **Joël Gigou** Jasnières Cuvée Saint-Jacques at £27.50
PW: 2002 **Pondalowie** Shiraz/Viognier at £22.50

 Find out more about wine and wine producers at *www.winebehindthelabel.com*

3rd

RSJ

33 Coin Street SE1 9NR
020 7928 4554

This restaurant is a long-time specialist in wines from the Loire Valley and whilst there is a tiny selection from elsewhere, you will have to content yourself in mainly furthering your knowledge of the wines from this remarkably diverse region of France. There is a detailed explanation at the beginning of the list about grape varieties, vintages and peculiarities of each part of the region, so that you will be fully familiar with what the Loire Valley has to offer. Vintage information is particularly important, since there are enormous variations in quality between one year and the next and even between one part of the region and another, so you should read this section carefully. And even if Loire wines don't exactly turn you on, you do have the certain knowledge that by and large, these wines offer exceptional value for money.

The list starts off with House wines and new arrivals, but you will also find these wines in the main body of the list. The first section deals with the dry whites from Anjou and Saumur and quality wines start at £15.75 with a 2003 Anjou Blanc from Domaine Ogereau although there are plenty of others under £30. At the top of the pile is the super 5-star **Savennières Clos de la Coulée de Serrant 1985** at £85 – a great wine from a great vintage. Dry whites from Touraine lists Vouvrays and Touraine Sauvignons with a little run of wines from Huët to add some real class to the section with the 1995 Le Haut Lieu at £29.95 looking good value. The *demi-secs* follow, mainly from Huët, culminating with the 1959 Le Haut Lieu at £125, but you won't go wrong with Vouvray Demi-Sec Cuvée des Fondraux 2002 from Didier Champalou at £19.95. The wines from the Nivernais (Sancerre, Pouilly-Fumé, etc.) have some top class producers, none better than Didier Dagueneau, whose 5-star Pouilly-Fumé Pur Sang 2003 is very reasonably priced at £45.

On to the reds, this time working our way back towards the mouth of the Loire. So we start off with red Nivernais, in which Alphonse Mellot's Sancerre Rouge les Demoiselles 2003 stands out at £45. In Anjou-Saumur, Thierry Germain's Saumur-Champigny Terres Chaudes 2002 at £23.50 is good drinking value, but J P Chevalier's Le Grand Clos, made only in good years, is available in both the 1995 and 1996 vintages at £39.95. In Chinon, there is a choice of *cuvées* from Philippe Alliet, one of the top producers in the appellation, with the 2002 Vieilles Vignes looking the best value although probably not yet ready to drink. In Saint-Nicolas-de-Bourgueil and Bourgueil, Frédéric Mabileau's Les Rouillères 2003 is light and fruity at a comfortable £18.95, whilst Yannick Amirault's Bourgueil Le Grand Clos 1999 at £27.95 will have more structure.

This list really comes into its own in the sweet wine department. A superb selection of Côteaux du Layon wines from various producers includes renowned 'sugar hunters' such as Patrick Baudouin and Jo Pithon, culminating in Baudouin's rare and extraordinary **Aprés Minuit 1997**, an outstanding sweet wine vintage, at £69.95 for

50cl. It's truly amazing to find this on ANY list, it is so rare and the price is very reasonable for the quality. In older top-quality vintages, there is Bonnezeaux, Château de Fesles 1985 at £85 a full bottle and an extraordinary quartet of **Vouvray Moelleux** from Huët in the first class 1990, 1989, 1971 and 1959 vintages at prices from £87.50 to £150.

There are 18 wines on the list that do not come from the Loire Valley, including five Champagnes, of which Bollinger 1996 is very well priced at £49.95. The rest is a mixed bag of wines from Burgundy, Beaujolais, Bordeaux, Languedoc and Italy, of which there is little of outstanding merit, although the **Côte de Brouilly 2003** from Nicole Chanrion at £21.50, and also available in halves at £11.95, is very good. There are a few Loire halves, both red and white, with the best value being Champalou's 2002 Vouvray Sec at £10.25 and Ogereau's Anjou Villages 2000 at £10.95. All in all, this is an intriguing wine list from which you can make many new discoveries at prices that won't break the bank.

Neville's Best Buy: **Patrick Baudouin's** Côteaux du Layon Aprés Minuit 1997 at £69.95 for 50cl

Score: *Quality* 67.30 *Value* 84.05 *Impression* 20.00 *Total* **171.35**

Ranking: *Quality* 43 *Value* 4 *Impression* 34 = *Overall* **3rd**

Recommendations:
NB: 1985 **Clos de la Coulée de Serrant** Savennières Coulée de Serrant at £85
DM: 1971 **Huët** Vouvray Moelleux
PW: 2003 **Nicole Chanrion** Côte de Brouilly at £21.50

Find out more about wine and wine producers at *www.winebehindthelabel.com*

London restaurants

THE TATE RESTAURANT

Millbank SW1P 4RG

020 7887 8825

3 0-odd years ago, you might have been surprised, as you slipped into the restaurant at the Tate Gallery to take a break from viewing all those Turners, to find the place absolutely heaving with members of the wine trade guzzling down smart clarets at extraordinarily cheap prices to accompany the pretty *ordinaire* food on offer. Sadly, all that wine has gone and whilst it is still the policy of the Tate to cellar their wines for many years, prices have inevitably crept up, but then so has the quality of the food! Nevertheless, this is one of the finest lists that you will come across – it has moved away from the traditional Tate stronghold of fine clarets and Burgundies, with much more exciting offerings elsewhere, particularly from Australia and the USA. You will be hard pressed to find better drinking value in the centre of London, the only drawback being that the restaurant is only open for lunch.

The list kicks off with a couple of pages of Sommelier's Recommendations – generally of less expensive wines and mostly available by the glass. It's then followed by a list of some 58 wines available in half or 50cl bottles, of which some three-quarters rate 3, 4 or 5 stars. For us, maybe a half-bottle of Meursault Les Tillets Cuvée Speciale 1999 from Patrick Javillier at £22, followed by a half bottle of Ornellaia 1996 at £32 and then a half of the Tokaji Noble Late Harvest 2000 from Oremus at £13.50 would make a great alternative to drinking a single bottle with the meal.

The Champagnes are dominated by Billecart-Salmon and the chance to try the rare **Cuvée Elisabeth Salmon Rosé** shouldn't be missed, even if it is at £87. White Burgundies are impressive with perhaps the Bâtard-Montrachet from the great 1996 vintage from Gagnard-Delagrange at £85 topping the bill in terms of quality and value. Also consider

a magnum of straight Puligny-Montrachet 1998 from Domaine Leflaive at only £90. The White Rhône selections are not prolific, but Clusel-Roch's 2002 Condrieu stands out at £42, whilst the Loire section lets you drool over the choice of either Huët's Vouvray Moelleux Clos du Bourg 1971 at £79, or Le Haut-Lieu Demi-Sec 1949 at a mere £63.50. Decisions, decisions! In Alsace, 5 out of 8 selections rate 4 stars or more, led by the super 5-star Riesling Clos Sainte-Hune 1985 from Trimbach at £98. But if you think that's a bit too much to pay for a Riesling, then why not try the Bernkastler Badstübe Spätlese from the superb 1990 vintage by Joh Jos Prüm, for a mere £35. Australian whites put up a good showing with Giaconda 1999 Chardonnay at £75 leading the quality stakes and Keith Tulloch's 2003 Hunter Valley Semillon offering extraordinary value at £21. New Zealand weighs in with **Kumeu River Chardonnay 2002**, a snip at £28, as well as the same producer's Maté's Vineyard Chardonnay 2002 *en magnum* at £70. The 2 Californian Chardonnays on offer from Au Bon Climat are both 5-star wines – the Sanford & Benedict Reserve 1996 at £42 and the Nuits Blanches au Bouge 1996 at £47. There's a good selection of sweet wines ranging from the Oremus Tokaji Noble Late Harvest 2000 at £13.50 (half-bottle) to a bottle of Yquem 1986 (great vintage) at £240.

The longish list of clarets (perhaps not as long as it used to be) features a number of goodies without anything of particular merit standing out. The list of Burgundies, too, is a roll call of the good and the great with the Volnay 1996 from the Marquis d'Angerville at £46 looking to be good value. In the Rhône, Clape's 1997 Cornas at £40 looks good value, whilst the 2000 Châteauneuf-du-Pape from Domaine Marcoux at £29 looks even better. Trévallon 1997 from Provence at £34 is worth trying, too. In Italy, whilst the selection from Piedmont lacks some of the best names (with the exception of Gaja, which is basically overpriced anyway), the Amarone 1999 from Allegrini in the Veneto at £48 is a 5-star wine at a reasonable price. In Tuscany, Ornellaia 1996 at £61 (£32 for a half) is a very fair price for the quality offered. There are some interesting ports, but you may well be tempted to try the Barbeito 20-year-old Malvasia Lote 4122 Madeira at £58 as an alternative. The Spanish red selection is 100% class with Vega Sicilia Unico 1989 at £135, but try the 100% Monastrell Pie Franco 1998 from Casa Castillo in Jumilla at £28.50 for a good wine at a good price. The outstanding price/quality wine from Australia is undoubtedly Torbreck's The Steading 2000 at £27, a Grenache, Shiraz and Mourvèdre blend with lovely fruit and a supple and long finish. There is a fine selection of USA reds with **Ridge Geyserville Zinfandel 1999** at £37 and **Brewer-Clifton Julia's Pinot Noir 2000** at £47 being the pick of the bunch.

Neville's Best Buy: **Ridge** Geyserville Zinfandel 1999 at £37 (with half a dozen others close behind).

Score: *Quality* 121.05   *Value* 34.31   *Impression* 22.00   *Total* **177.36**

Ranking: *Quality* 3   *Value* 29   *Impression* 21 = *Overall* **2nd**

Recommendations:
NB: **Billecart-Salmon** Cuvée Elizabeth Salmon Rosé at £87
DM: 2000 **Brewer-Clifton** Pinot Noir Julia's at £47
PW: 2002 **Kumeu River** Chardonnay at £28

Find out more about wine and wine producers at *www.winebehindthelabel.com*

57th

LE CHAMPIGNON SAUVAGE

24-26 Suffolk Road Cheltenham Gloucestershire GL50 2AQ
01242 573449

This long-standing bastion of good cuisine in the Cheltenham area is not let down by its wine list. Not that it panders in any way to the expense account mob, but rather to sensible drinkers who like to get value for their money. There are around 150 wines on the list, of which about one third are of 3-star quality or more, and of these about two fifths meet our price criteria. A goodly number of half-bottles show some of real quality, too. Wines by the glass, however, do not pander to the quality-conscious, so it's best to stick to the halves if you want to do a bit of experimenting. Apart from the House selections, the list is conventionally arranged by country and region.

First come the Champagnes and sparkling wines. No bargains here (there rarely are with Champagne) but Roederer's super 5-star Cristal 1990 at £155 is very fairly priced. The still white wines are kicked off by the House wines. A commendable entry here is the **Hamilton Russell Chardonnay 2003**, 3-star quality on the value limit at £30. In Loire Valley whites, Henry Pellé's Ménétou-Salon Clos de Blanchais 2002 is good value at £24, and there are some wines at exceptional prices from Albert Mann in the Alsace section. The Pinot Blanc/Auxerrois blend 2001 is in at only £14 (£8 for a half bottle), the 1997 Riesling is at £16 and the Gewürztraminer 2001 is at £19 (£10 for a half bottle). These are all 3-star quality wines, but there is also the 4-star **Gewürztraminer Grand Cru Steingrubler 2000** at only £25 (£13 for a half bottle). It's worth coming here just for the Alsace! In the Côte Chalonnaise, Jacqueson's **Rully Blanc 1er Cru La Pucelle 2002** is

good value at £25, whilst in the Côte d'Or the 4-star Meursault 1er Cru Bouchères 1999 from Domaine Latour-Giraud at £39 has by far the best price/quality ratio in the section. The Californian section has Saintsbury's Carneros Chardonnay 2002, 3-star quality at £29, and similarly, Australia has Mountadam Eden Valley Chardonnay 1998 at £30 (£18 for a half bottle), but they are both beaten hands down for value by the 4-star 2002 Chardonnay from Kumeu River in New Zealand at £37 – one of the best Chardonnay producers in that country. The dessert wine section ends the list of whites with Château Filhot 1997 looking good value at £38, as does a half-bottle of the 4-star Château Coutet 1er Cru Sauternes at £39, and there's Château d'Yquem 1985 at £375.

In red wines nothing really excites in the House selection, Beaujolais or the Loire Valley, but in the Côte Chalonnaise, the Mercurey 1er Cru Les Naugues 2000 from Domaine Raquillet looks pretty good value for a red Burgundy at £28. We can't find the same value in the Côte de Nuits section, but if you want to have a splash, **Clos de la Roche Grand Cru 1999** is 5-star quality from Armand Rousseau, but you will have to pay £125 for the privilege. There is good value in the Rhône, however, with the Gigondas 2001 from Domaine Saint Gayan at £23 (£12 for a half bottle) and the Saint-Joseph 1999 from the Courbis brothers at £24, but these are overtaken by the 4-star Côte Rôtie 1996 from Jasmin at £45 and the 5-star Cornas 1998 from Clape at £50. Clarets follow but nothing offers outstanding quality and value. Château Grand-Ponter Saint-Émilion Grand Cru 1995 should be worth a punt at £37 and Château Léoville-Barton 1989 at £115 is from a good vintage but the price is a little steep. For a real treat, though, Latour 1988 should be drinking really nicely now, but at £235? Well, why not? New Zealand reds don't thrill, but in Australia, Wynn's Coonawarra Cabernet Sauvignon 2000 at £21 is excellent value for a 3-star wine. The Californian reds disappoint.

This is a good list, but in our view many improvements could be made which would be entirely in keeping with the philosophy of the establishment.

Neville's Best Buy: 2000 **Albert Mann** Gewürztraminer Grand Cru Steingrubler at £25 (£13 for a half bottle)

Score: *Quality* 45.35   *Value* 39.91   *Impression* 18.00   *Total* **103.26**

Ranking: *Quality* 66   *Value* 23   *Impression* 53 =   *Overall* **57th**

Recommendations:
NB: 1999 **Armand Rousseau** Clos de la Roche Grand Cru at £125
DM: 2003 **Hamilton Russell** Chardonnay at £30
PW: 2002 **Henri et Paul Jacqueson** Rully 1er Cru La Pucelle at £25

87th

CHARLTON HOUSE

Charlton House Charlton Road Shepton Mallet Somerset BA4 4PR
01749 342008

oger Saul's Mulberry Restaurant in his baronial hall just outside Shepton Mallet has a wine list born of passion. The list has been put together by style, thus obviating a lot of head scratching as to which wine would go best with the food. However, it starts off with a little collection of current discoveries which Roger thinks he ought to bring to your attention. So wines like the Justin Vineyard Syrah 2002 from Paso Robles in California appear with a matching reference to one of the dishes on the menu. Mind you, at £49 it's not cheap, but then Roger has a lot of

The South West

expenses to keep the place in apple pie order for the well-heeled customer he is keen to attract. The 13 wines by the glass are not exactly designed to attract the big spenders, but **Krug 1988** (not offered by the glass, of course) at £150 probably will, especially as it's not a bad price for what it is and only £20 more expensive than the NV. 'Unoaked white and rosé wines' feature **Didier Champalou's Vouvray Cuvée Fondraux 2003** at £23, which is good value and the 'Aromatic dry white' section has Plantagenet Riesling 2004 at £26, which is quite good value too

'Oak aged white wines' has Beringer Napa Valley Private Reserve Chardonnay 1999 at £54.50 and in 'Classic white wine' Domaine Bonneford's Condrieu Côte Chatillon 2002 at £43 looks to be the best balance of price and quality. 'Light red wines' has Nepenthe Pinot Noir 2002, a very good example of Aussie Pinot, but at £34 a bit pricey. **Glaetzer The Wallace 2002** (a blend of Shiraz, Cabernet and Grenache) at £31 in the 'Medium weight red' section is also interesting if no bargain. In the 'Full bodied red wines' section, the **Prats & Symington Chryseia 2001**, a dry wine from the Douro at £54, shows boldness of choice, and in the 'New World, Old World classic red wine' section, Ridge Lytton Springs Zinfandel 1999 at £58.50 stand out for best drinking value, even though these are really London prices.

Getting slightly confused with the headings, the list then moves on to the 'Classic red wines' section, with Château Cissac 1990 probably drinking extremely well now, but at £81.50 a bottle, it's a bit of a steep price to pay. Maybe better to choose Château Margaux 1994 from 'Roger's own cellar' at £150 – not a great vintage, but Margaux is Margaux and you shouldn't go wrong here. The 5 dry half-bottles have nothing of outstanding quality, but the 2001 Saumur-Champigny, Château du Hureau at £14.50 is certainly worth a stab. There is a choice of 7 dessert wines (and all available by the glass) with the **Maury Cuvée Spéciale 10 years** from Mas Amiel at £34 (£8 a glass) being of special interest.

Neville's Best Buy: **Krug** 1988 Champagne at £150!! For a more affordable alternative go for: **Didier Champalou** Vouvray Cuvée Fondraux 2003 at £23

Score: *Quality* 41.10   *Value* 15.09   *Impression* 19.00   *Total* **75.19**

Ranking: *Quality* 73   *Value* 65   *Impression* 43 =   *Overall* **87th**

Recommendations:
NB: 2001 **Prats & Symington** Douro Chryseia at £54
DM: **Mas Amiel** Maury Cuvée Spéciale 10 Ans at £34
PW: 2002 **Glaetzer** The Wallace at £31

83rd

COMBE HOUSE

Gittisham Honiton near Exeter Devon EX14 3AD
01404 540400

W e agree wholeheartedly with Combe House's stated 'philosophy' of deprecating the ease of putting together a long list of wines which reflect more of a desire to impress rather than to please and of eschewing pomposity and snobbery. Of these 237 wines, around 40% meet our quality criteria, and of those, just around one eighth meet the value criteria, too. There is also a big selection of half-bottles for those who like to experiment a bit, a few of which are of 3-star quality or better, but in the short list of wines by the glass, there is nothing of real interest. The list is laid out conventionally by country and region, with France, and particularly Chablis, dominating.

The list opens with Champagne and sparkling wines, but with nothing of exceptional interest until you get to the vintage and prestige Champagnes where 5 vintages of Dom Pérignon are listed from the 1996 at £105 back to the 1959 at £470. There follows a good selection of clarets with the entry-level **Château Cap de Faugères Côtes de Castillon 1998** good value at £26.50. Much further up the scale, there are some impressive mature clarets with **Château Léoville Barton** from the superb 1982 vintage looking good at £95, or if you save up enough, you could get Château Pétrus from the same vintage at a mere £1,800! There's not much to write home about in the Côte d'Or section of the Burgundies, but a passion for Chablis brings up a few good value choices, notably the Premier Crus from William Fèvre, with the 1999 Vaillons looking best at £35.30. In the Grands Crus, the pick of the bunch is William Fèvre's super 5-star **Chablis Grand Cru Les Clos 1999** at £55 with Les Preuses 1999 not far behind at the same price. Due to adverse growing conditions, the 1998s should generally be avoided. Rhône reds has the 3-star Vacqueyras Cuvée Floureto 2001 from Domaine le Sang des Cailloux at £30 and the super 5-star Hermitage La Chapelle 1996 (not a great vintage, though) at £85, whilst in the Loire reds there is great value in the **Château de Villeneuve Saumur-Champigny 2003** at £19 and for white, the super 5-star Clos de la Coulée de Serrant Savennières 1999 from Nicolas Joly at £75.

Away from France, there is value in the Australian section with Petaluma Clare Valley Riesling 2003 at £23.80 and the Cabernet/Merlot 2001 from Vasse Felix in Margaret River at £22.40. New Zealand has Hunter's Marlborough Sauvignon Blanc 2004 at £24, whilst the Americas have the 4-star Ridge Lytton Springs Zinfandel 1999 at £50.80 in an otherwise poor selection. Sweet wines include the Muscat de Beaumes de Venise 2001 from Domaine de Durban at £28.50 and Château d'Yquem 1988 at £250.

Having thought that we had come to the end of the list, we then discovered a page called 'Personal selection of Australian gems' which included a range of 4 vintages of the **Parker Coonawarra Estate Terra Rossa First Growth**. Go for the 1998, a great vintage and the cheapest at £39. The pages of magnums and half-bottles follow, with

a magnum of Bodega Muga's Rioja Reserva Especial 1994 looking good at £68.90. Halves include the 4-star Puligny-Montrachet 1er Cru Les Folatières 2001 from Gérard Chavy at £32 and the 5-star Ridge Geyserville Zinfandel 2000 at £32.50 and in dessert halves there is the 5-star Château Lafaurie-Peyraguey 1996 at £41.40 – all good wines, but none of them reaching our price/quality criteria.

Neville's Best Buy: 1982 **Château Léoville Barton** at £95!! For a more affordable alternative go for: **Château Cap de Faugères** Côtes de Castillon 1998 at £26.50

Score: *Quality* 43.32   *Value* 13.81   *Impression* 21.00   *Total* **78.13**

Ranking: *Quality* 69   *Value* 71   *Impression* 29 =   *Overall* **83rd**

Recommendations:
NB: 1999 **William Fèvre** Chablis Grand Cru Les Clos at £55
DM: 2003 **Château de Villeneuve** Saumur-Champigny at £19
PW: 1998 **Parker Coonawarra Estate** Terra Rossa First Growth at £39

55th

CORSE LAWN

Corse Lawn Gloucestershire GL19 4LZ

01452 780771

This establishment has been in the hands of the Hine family for many years and there is a certain maturity in the list. Nevertheless, it has moved with the times to include some of the young Turks who are setting the world of wine alight. There are over 400 wines on the list of which around one third are of 3-star quality or higher and of these, over a quarter reach our price/quality ratio. There is a really lengthy list of half-bottles, many of which are of high quality, but wines by the glass are a little scant. The list is arranged conventionally by country and region with any sweet wines being incorporated into their particular regions.

There are comprehensive tasting notes for House wines and wines available by the glass but not for the rest of the list. But from these a glass of Pol Roger White Foil Champagne NV at £8 is just about all that we would consider before turning to the next page. Here there are some fine half-bottles of Lustau sherries which are also available by the glass. There follows a list of half-bottles from around the world (but mainly French) with some good value ranging from Vieux Château Gaubert 2001 from the Graves at £15.50 to the 4-star Le Cigare Volant 1995, Randall Grahm's Châteauneuf-du-Pape clone from Paso Robles in California, at £24.50. In Sauternes, a half-bottle of Château Rabaud-Promis 1996 at £17.80 looks promising, too.

Clarets come next, where you can find all qualities at all prices. At the value end, Vieux Château Gaubert 1999 at £24.80 looks a steal for claret lovers and the Chasse Spleen 1982 at £66.50 should be good value if it hasn't dried out. Other clarets worth considering are the magnum of the 4-star Château Haut-Marbuzet 1995 at £110, or Clos l'Eglise 1983 at £58.75, which is a wine that ought to have stood the test of time. Dry white Bordeaux takes in 2 expertly crafted wines from Denis Dubourdieu – Château Reynon Vieilles Vignes 2003 at £22 and Clos Floridène 2001 at £31.30. A couple of decent Beaujolais are listed in the shape of the Morgon Côtes du Py 2001 from Potel-Aviron at £23 and a Fleurie 2002 from André Colonge et Fils at £25.40, but as usual, it is difficult to find real value in the wines from the Côte d'Or. However, Jean-Marc Morey's red Chassagne-Montrachet 1999 looks good at £27.40, as does Clos Vougeot 1999 from Domaine René Engel – 5-star quality at £90 but almost certainly too young to drink. In the white Burgundy section, the Saint-Véran Terroirs de Davayé 2001 from Verget should be a good buy at £25.80 as should the 4-star Chablis Grand Cru Vaudésir 2000 from Louis Michel at £52. The wines from the Rhône Valley are lumped together with wines from the rest of the south of France, but the best value here comes from far to the west, near the border with Spain, with Domaine La Soula's 4-star white and 5-star red, both in the 2001 vintage and both at £34.80. The **4-star Bandol La Migoua 1999 Domaine Tempier** in Provence is also listed in this section at £32.80 and Domaine de Trévallon 1997 is well priced at £48.75. In the Loire Valley, **Domaine Baumard Savennières Clos du Papillon 1999** is 4-star quality at a superb £26.30, while there is 3-star value at under £30 from Huët (Vouvray) and Vacheron (Sancerre). There is value in the Alsace wines listed with Paul Blanck's Gewürztraminer Altenbourg 2000 at £26.40 looking best, but the real thrill here is the listings of 2 late harvest wines from 2 superb early vintages – the **1983 Riesling Bergheim Burg Vendanges Tardives** from Marcel Deiss at £44 and the 1976 Gewürztraminer SGN from Hugel at £95. Champagne comes next with a real treat in the super 5-star Bollinger RD 1988 at £125. If you think that's too much, you could always have a magnum of Pol Roger White Foil NV at £75.

The rest of the world kicks off with some wines from Spain, with the Mas Collet Negra 2000 from Tarragona at £16.70 and the junior wine from Alejandro Fernández, Condado de Haza Crianza 2001, at £23.20. There are no really big hitters from Italy, but **Valpolicella Superiore Marion 1998** from Campedelli family at £26.20 and Carignano del Sulcis Riserva Rocca Rubia 2000 from Santadi in Sardinia at £26.80 represent good value here. From Austria, there is 4-star quality in F-X Pichler's Riesling Steinertal Smaragd 2002 at £46.70, but it may still be a little too tight to drink. California Reds are unexciting, unless you want to fork out £400 on the Harlan Estate 1994 (it's probably worth it) and in the whites, the only wine worth drinking for value would be the Au Bon Climat Chardonnay 1997 at £33.60. There are some value Australian reds, of course, with the Cabernet/Merlot 2001 from Vasse Felix in Western Australia looking best at £21.85. Burge family The Renoux Shiraz/Merlot/Cabernet Sauvignon 2001 from the Barossa at £30 is just on the value limit, whilst in the whites, Cullen's Margaret River Reserve Semillon/Sauvignon 2002 at £30.80 is just over it. Avoiding the relatively overpriced reds from New Zealand, (and some whites, too) the best option here is the 4-star Kumeu River Chardonnay 2002 at £39. The best Cabernet Franc in South Africa is listed here, from Warwick Estate, and the 1997 is £26.50; Bouchard Finlayson's Walker Bay Chardonnay 2003 is also good value at £24. Vintage ports are also relatively inexpensive with Quinta do Noval 1966 at £105 looking best.

Neville's Best Buy: 1983 **Marcel Deiss** Riesling Bergheim Burg Vendanges Tardives at £44

Score: *Quality* 50.74   *Value* 27.16   *Impression* 27.00   *Total* **104.90**

Ranking: *Quality* 59   *Value* 35   *Impression* 8 =   *Overall* **55th**

Recommendations:
NB: 1999 **Domaine Baumard** Savennières Clos du Papillon at£26.30
DM: 1999 **Domaine Tempier** Bandol La Migoua at £32.80
PW: 1998 **Marion** Valpolicella Superiore at £26.20

COTSWOLD HOUSE

Cotswold House The Square Chipping Camden Gloucestershire GL55 6AN
01386 840330

Juliana's Restaurant has a very interesting high quality list, but it is let down a lot by some very stiff prices. There are over 160 wines on the list, of which around half meet our quality criteria, but of those we could only find 6 wines that met the price criteria as well. Many other wines are in at astonishingly high prices. There are very few half-bottles, but 16 wines by the glass (although 6 of them are Champagnes) do have some quality offerings among them, so it may be better to stick to one or two of these to keep your costs down a bit. A glass of Bollinger NV, followed by a glass of Kumeu River Chardonnay 2002, followed by a glass of Chianti Vigna del Sorbo from Fontodi, and finishing with a glass of the Off the Rack Chenin Blanc Passito 2003 from Plantagenet in Western Australia, will set you back £48.50, but at least they are all wines of 3-star quality or higher and this still works out cheaper than a bottle of Cloudy Bay Sauvignon Blanc 2004, which will set you back £60. A big saving grace for this wine list is the inclusion of very comprehensive tasting notes for each wine. The list is arranged conventionally by country and region.

Red and white sections entitled 'From the private cellars of Cotswold House' list some of the more expensive wines (and some of the most interesting) – of which practically all are of 3-star quality or better and of which none meet our price criteria – before the list proper goes on by country and region. In the white private cellar you could

The South West

have Bollinger RD 1990 at £170, or Joseph Phelps Napa Valley Viognier 2000 at £85. In the Australian section of the white wine list proper, Shaw and Smith's Sauvignon Blanc 2003 from the Adelaide Hills is in at £30, whilst the **2002 Kumeu River Chardonnay** from New Zealand is 4-star value at £45.

From the red private cellar, there is a host of goodies, particularly from the USA. It would be hard to choose between the **Arietta Variation One 2002** at £140, the Arietta Variation H Block 2002 at £150 and the Herb Lamb Cabernet Sauvignon 2001 at £160, let alone the Hundred Acre Cabernet Sauvignon Kayli Morgan Vineyard 2001 at £400, but they all may be a bit on the young side to drink. On the other hand, if you have £400 to spend on a bottle of wine, you might feel more comfortable with the 1988 Château Mouton-Rothschild, or the 1989 for £40 less. In the red list proper, the 4-star **Brokenwood Rayner Vineyard Shiraz 2001** from New South Wales is well worth buying at £39, whilst in Spain, the Viña Izadi Crianza Rioja 2001 is on the value cusp at £30. Italy has the super 5-star **Aldo Conterno Barolo Cicala 1998**, a vintage that is beginning to drink well, at a surprisingly modest £65. Value wines are completed by the Ata Rangi Pinot Noir 2001 from New Zealand at £48. Finally, there are choices to be made in the vintage ports – is it to be Dow's 1997 at £250 or Warre's 1977 at £300? Maybe we'll plump for just a glass of the Dow's at £25 and then go for the whole bottle of Warre's 1945 at £400, if we haven't already spent it on the Mouton 1988!

Neville's Best Buy: 2001 **Brokenwood** Shiraz Rayner Vineyard Hunter Valley at £39

Score: *Quality* 61.75   *Value* 8.20   *Impression* 22.00   *Total* **91.95**

Ranking: *Quality* 46   *Value* 86   *Impression* 21 =   *Overall* **71st**

Recommendations:
NB: 2002 **Kumeu River** Chardonnay at £45
DM: 2002 **Arietta** Variation One at £140
PW: 1998 **Aldo Conterno** Barolo Cicala at £65

59th

LES MIRABELLES

Forest Edge Road Nomansland Nr Salisbury Wiltshire SP5 2BN
01794 390205

It's difficult to imagine that a tiny restaurant deep in the heart of the New Forest could boast such a tremendous wine list. Nearly 1,000 wines are listed of which around three-quarters are of 3-star quality or above, although only just over 10% of those meet our value criteria. There are a number of half-bottles available, but generally not many of them reach the quality mark – and as for wines by the glass, these seem to be geared to those who can't be bothered to read the wine list. But for those who can, there is a veritable treasure trove of goodies to discover. A number of great wines are available in several vintages, with some of the younger wines having no price but only the word 'cellar' – in other words the establishment has the foresight to lay down wines and only make them available when the proprietor thinks that they are ready to drink.

The list starts off with a House selection– 37 wines, among which there are several good quality bottles, particularly from the French regions, with the Faugères 1997 from Domaine Léon Barral at £21.80 looking to be the pick of the bunch. The list continues conventionally by country and region, starting off with wines from Alsace, where there is some good value to be found, the best being the 4-star **Tokay-Pinot Gris Grand Cru Steinert 1999** from Domaine Riéflé at £25.30. In the Loire Valley section the 3-star Pouilly-Fumé 2000 from Château de Tracy at £26.90 looks good, but looking better is the Chinon La Cure 2000 from Charles Joguet at only £19. Spanish wines come next, but here the value is not so apparent, so it may be better to go for one of the 8 vintages of the 5-star Clos Mogador, with prices ranging from £53 to £94. Probably the best drinking vintage at the moment would be the 1996 at £56. In Italy the white section has the 4-star Vintage Tunina white blend 2000 from Jermann at £48.50 (better value than 'Dreams'), whilst the best value in the Italian red section is the Chianti Classico 2000 from Castello di Fonterutoli at £23.50 (but only if it is the premium version with Castello di Fonterutoli, and not simply Fonterutoli, on the label). Of course, there are some top quality names, particularly from some of the Antinori estates in Tuscany, but these are all at 3-figure prices with the exception of the Guado al Tasso 1998 at £81.

There is good value, however, among the South American wines – standing out are the Odfjell Vineyards Merlot 2001 from Chile at £16.20 and the Anubis Bonarda/Merlot 2000 from Argentina at £20.20. South Africa has two good value Chardonnays in the shape of the Glen Carlou Reserve 1999 at £26.60 and the Thelema Mountain Chardonnay 1999 at £29, whilst in the reds, Thelema Mountain Merlot 1999 is the best value, although there are better, older, vintages of this wine available at a higher cost. In the better 1997 vintage, there is the Meinert Estate Cabernet Sauvignon at £29.90. The 4-star Hamilton Russell Pinot Noir is available in five different vintages from 1997 to 2001 at prices from £39.50 to £52. There is some exceptional value in the Australian white section, with 4-star entries from Moss Wood, Dalwhinnie, Cullen and Grosset – all coming in under £50 – but the pick of the bunch must be the **Grosset Piccadilly Chardonnay 1998** at £27.10. Leeuwin Estate Art Series Chardonnay 1998 is 5-star quality at £49. There is not, perhaps, quite the same value for money in the Australian reds, with the 4-star Leeuwin Estate Art Series Cabernet Sauvignon 1998 looking best at £39.50. A number of verticals from top estates come with prices to match, especially in the older vintages. Penfolds Grange 1981 is £690. Isabel Estate Sauvignon Blanc is far and away the best value in the New Zealand whites and the 2002 vintage is available at £23.40. The reds don't match the whites for value.

There is an orgy of fine wines from the USA – again, many in multiple vintages. As you can imagine, these are not cheap, but in the whites, there is 3-star value in Cline Cellars Marsanne 1998 at £24.60 and 4-star value (just) in Steele Wines Durrell Vineyard Chardonnay 1998 at £52 (Kistler's is £160), whilst in the reds, Foppiano's Petite Sirah 2000 takes the 3-star honours at £25 and Ridge Lytton Springs Zinfandel 1995 is the best value 4-star wine at £37. But there are also many top wines to drool over in this section. Three pages of white Burgundies follow with Chablis proving better value than wines from the Côte d'Or. The 1er Cru Vaillons 2001 from Domaine Defaix is reasonably priced at £26.50, while the 5-star Grand Cru Les Preuses 1998 from Dauvissat comes in at £53. But if you are feeling bold enough (or flush enough) you could well try the rare white Clos de Vougeot 1999 from Domaine de la Vougeraie – not overpriced for what it is at £95, and to put it in perspective DRC Montrachet 2000 is £1,560. There is not a lot in the value for money stakes in the red Burgundies, either, so maybe it's best to go for the top – Armand Rousseau's Gevrey-Chambertin Clos Saint-Jacques 1996 is a super 5-star wine and at £88.60 it's a far better bet than most other top names featured. In the Beaujolais and Rhône section Paul Janin's Moulin-à-Vent 2001 looks good value at £21.10, as does the Gigondas 2000 from Domaine de Font-Sane at £21.50 – there is 5-star quality in the **Vieux-Télégraphe Châteauneuf-du-Pape 1998** at £41 which looks better value than that from the poor 1996 vintage at £34. In the Northern Rhône, there's Côte Rôtie 1996 from Domaine Bonnefond at £49, and value in the super 5-star **Jaboulet Hermitage La Chapelle** in the underrated 1994 vintage at £74.80. There is an enormous choice of clarets at all prices and in the case of the classed growths, it's really a question of what you fancy and what you can afford, but if you are looking for value here we could suggest Vieux Château Gaubert Graves 1996 at £26, or for 4-star quality, Château Haut-Marbuzet Saint-Estèphe 1996 at £64. There are no great bargains either in the Champagne list, although Deutz Blanc de Blancs 1990 at £52 should be well worth a try. There is an interesting selection of pudding wines, some of which are from very old vintages – Château Coutet 1916 is £999.99 and Domaine de Theuley Monbazillac 1911 is £450, but for the less adventurous, the Gewürztraminer Vendanges Tardives in the superb 1983 vintage from the Caves de Turckheim co-operative at £56.80 should be at least equally satisfactory. Finally, there is a good little list of half-bottles with Gérard Chavy's Puligny-Montrachet 1er Cru Les Folatières 2002 at £28.40 looking to be the best value.

Neville's Best Buy: 1999 **Domaine Rieflé** Tokay Pinot Gris Grand Cru Steinert at £25.30

Score: *Quality* 73.45   *Value* 11.57   *Impression* 16.00   *Total* **101.02**

Ranking: *Quality* 31   *Value* 75   *Impression* 67 =   *Overall* **59th**

Recommendations:
NB: 1994 **Paul Jaboulet Aîné** Hermitage La Chapelle at £74.80
DM: 1998 **Domaine du Vieux-Télégraphe** Châteauneuf-du-Pape at £41
PW: 1998 **Grosset** Piccadilly Chardonnay at £27.10

Find out more about wine and wine producers at *www.winebehindthelabel.com*

The South West

73rd

LEWTRENCHARD MANOR

Lewdown Devon EX20 4PN

01566 783222

For an upmarket country house hotel (it belongs to the same group as Sharrow Bay; qv), the wine list looks pretty bare and also a bit downmarket, but there are some hidden quality gems to be found at good prices, although there seems to be some inconsistency in pricing. Of over 260 wines listed here, just under a third reach our quality criteria and of these, just over a third are in the value frame, too. A reasonable amount of half-bottles include some of high quality, but the wines by the glass are totally geared to the bottom end of the market. The wine list is conventionally arranged by country and region and there are no tasting notes. A few wines have been inadequately identified, so you will have to ask the staff further about those.

There are some well priced Champagnes and all the NV bottles listed can be drunk with confidence. Of the vintage Champagnes, the 5-star Bollinger Brut Grande Année 1996 is worth drinking at £89, but you might try the Cloudy Bay Pelorus 1998 at £29 as an alternative. Value is hard to find on the list of 23 clarets, so you might as well just go all out for quality with the 1989 Château Léoville-Barton at £119 – it should be delicious. Under the umbrella of Burgundy, in the Beaujolais section, the Fleurie 2003 from Domaine Métrat is value at £25, but the wines of the Côte d'Or suffer from the same problem as the clarets as far as value for money is concerned, with the Corton Perrières Grand Cru 1998 from Domaine Belland getting nearest to the mark at £53. There is better value in the Rhône, with the 4-star Côte-Rôtie 2001 from Robert Niero coming in at £43, but Château de Beaucastel 2000 seems a bit overpriced at £85 for such a young wine. In the Loire, the Ménétou-Salon Morogues 2002 from Henry Pellé is excellent value at only £18; Jacques Sallé's Silices de Quincy 1998 is made of sterner stuff and is still good value at £29. The 4-star **Trimbach Riesling Cuvée Frédéric-Emile 1995** at £49 is the one to go for in the Alsace section.

Away from France, there is 4-star quality in Spain with the Tinto Pesquera Reserva 1997 at £41 from Alejandro Fernández in Ribera del Duero. Italy serves up 3-star value in the Chardonnay 2001 from Planeta in Sicily at £29 and in the 1996 **Carignano del Sulcis Riserva Rocca Rubia** at £23 from Santadi in Sardinia. There is good value, too, from Austria in the shape of Dr Unger's Grüner Veltliner Reserve Trocken Ried Gottschelle 2001 at £19 and his **Riesling Reserve Trocken Silberbügel 1999** at £22. The Californian section has 3-star value in Frog's Leap's Sauvignon Blanc 2000 at £29 (£16 for the 2001 half) and 4-star value in Bonny Doon's Le Cigare Volant 2000 at £41 (£22 the half). The 3-star Alpha Domus Chardonnay 1999 from New Zealand comes in at only £23, while from Chile, there is also 3-star value with the 2000 Cabernet Sauvignon Cuvée Alexandre from Casa Lapostolle, at £27. There are good choices from Australia, too, with Tyrrell's 4-star Vat 1 Semillon 1993 in at £39 (we can vouch for the current quality of the 94 but ask whether the 93 has also stood the test of time), while the Print Shiraz 1995 from Mitchelton at £49 should have had no trouble with ageing at all. Highlights from quite a long list of South African wines are the Thelema Chardonnay 2000 at £29 in the whites and the Saxenberg Private Collection Pinotage 1999 at £21 in the reds. There are two good 4-star wines in the dessert section, both in half-bottles – **Château Rabaud-Promis 1er Cru Sauternes 1996** at £16 the half (£8.00 the glass) and Yalumba Museum Release Muscat NV from Australia at £17.50 the half-bottle and £6.50 the glass. (Odd pricing for these glasses.) A nice little selection of vintage ports has Warre's 1970 looking good value at £95.

Neville's Best Buy: **Château Rabaud-Promis** 1er Cru Sauternes 1996 at £16 the half (£8.00 the glass)

Score: *Quality* 38.61   *Value* 38.31   *Impression* 13.00   *Total* **89.92**

Ranking: *Quality* 81   *Value* 26   *Impression* 87 =   *Overall* **73rd**

Recommendations:
NB: 1996 **Santadi** Carignano del Sulcis Riserva Rocca Rubia at £23
DM: 1995 **Trimbach** Riesling Cuvée Frédéric-Emile at £49
PW: 1999 **Dr Unger** Riesling Reserve Silberbügel at £22

52nd

LITTLE BARWICK HOUSE

Barwick Somerset BA22 9TD
01935 423902

his is an interesting list, principally arranged by style rather than by country or region, which is a great deal of help to the reader, even if there are no tasting notes for any of the individual wines. There is an extensive list of half-bottles, many of good quality, but dry wines by the glass are pretty scant. Of almost 250 bins on the list, around 40% reach 3-star quality or more and of these around 20% have the added bonus of reaching our price criteria as well.

There is nothing to commend at the entry level of the Champagne section, but £84 for the 5-star Bollinger Grande Année 1990 and £98 for Krug NV is as little as you will pay almost anywhere. Best value in 'Zesty, crisp and refreshing whites' is Jane Hunter's 2003 Sauvignon Blanc at £23.95, while the **Vouvray Cuvée des Fondraux 2002** from Didier Champalou at £16.50 is even better value in the 'Aromatic, medium and fruity white wine' section. Also in this section is the 4-star Muenchberg Grand Cru Riesling 1997 from Ostertag at a very reasonable £32.50. 'Fuller, non oaked dryish whites' has for choice the stylish **Lugana Brolettino 2002** from Ca' dei Frati at £23.50, or the Chablis 1er Cru Mont de Milieu 2002 from Domaine Pinson at £29.50. There's less obvious value in the 'Oak aged dryish whites' section, but the Châteauneuf-du-Pape Blanc 2003 from Domaine de la Roquette looks good value at £32.50.

Red wines kick off with 'Light and fruity reds yet with plenty of character' and Paul Janin's Moulin-à-Vent 2002 at £22.75 fits the bill here. There is a long list of wines in the 'Soft, mellow and fuller reds', but good 3-star value rests with the Vacqueyras Cuvée Floureto 2001 from Domaine Le Sang des Cailloux at £25.95, while one of the rare cult wines from California, **Sine Qua Non No. 6 Oregon Pinot Noir 2001**, is excellent value (for this wine) at £87.50. 'Lightly oaked, more structured reds' includes a whole host of Bordeaux and Bordeaux-type wines, so there is not a lot of scope for real value here. The 1998 Château Cap de Faugères Côtes de Castillon (wrongly described here as a Saint-Émilion) is very good, even if a little overpriced at £40.50. 'Heavier, full bodied and rich reds' has the well-priced Directors Cut Shiraz 2000 from Heartland in South Australia at £20.50 (although the 2002 and 2003 vintages are much superior) and the fashionable Shiraz/Viognier blend 2002 from Homtini in South Africa at £28.50, but the best value is probably the 4-star Bandol Cuvée Migoua 1999 from Domaine Tempier in Provence at £36.95, even if it is not yet ready to drink. Other 4-star value wines in this section are Charlie Melton's Nine Popes 1998 from the Barossa Valley at £43.75 and Underhill Shiraz 1998 from Yarra Yering in Victoria, just on the value cusp at £50.75. There is plenty of 4-star Australian Shiraz to play with in this section (the proprietor must have a propensity for muscle), but there's a lot better value with two super 5-star wines from California which have both muscle and finesse – Mondavi Napa Valley Cabernet Sauvignon Reserve 1992 at

£89.50 and Ridge Monte Bello Cabernet Sauvignon in the same vintage at £110 – both should be drinking superbly now. For the more conventionally minded, Château Léoville-las-Cases 1982 shouldn't be a bad drop, even if it is at £235, and probably better value than the Château Margaux of the same vintage at £420.

There are lots of half-bottles and the Chablis 1er Cru Mont de Milieu 2001 from Domaine Pinson looks good value at £13.25 in the whites, with Gèrard Chavy's Puligny-Montrachet 1er Cru Folatières 2001 not far behind at £26.75. In the reds, Qupé Winery's Syrah 2000 is value at £13.50 as is the **Crozes-Hermitage Cuvée Albéric Bouvet 2001** from Gilles Robin at £13.95. There are some pretty old halves of claret at 3-figure prices which must pose some questions, but you should be safe with a half of Château Haut-Bailly 1982 at £45. There is a fair choice of dessert wines with Campbell's Rutherglen Muscat NV seeming the best value at £16.50 for a half (£4.50 the 65ml glass). Otherwise a half-bottle of Château Lafaurie-Peyraguey 1997 at £38.50 may do the trick, which you can also have by the glass at £5.95. In vintage ports, Dow's 1983 at £77 may take precedence over Fonseca 1985 at £71.50, but at least you can have the latter at £6.75 the 65ml glass.

Neville's Best Buy: Vouvray Cuvée des Fondraux 2002 from **Didier Champalou** at £16.50

Score: *Quality* 71.07 *Value* 19.16 *Impression* 18.00 *Total* **108.23**

Ranking: *Quality* 36 *Value* 518 *Impression* 53 = *Overall* **52nd**

Recommendations:
NB: 2001 **Sine Qua Non** Pinot Noir No.6 Oregon at £87.50
DM: 2001 **Gilles Robin** Crozes-Hermitage Albéric Bouvet (half-bottle) at £13.95
PW: 2002 **Ca' dei Frati** Lugana Brolettino at £23.50

79th

LONGUEVILLE MANOR

St Saviour Jersey JE2 7WF
01534 725501

One of the grandest hotels in the Channel Islands sports this very grand wine list of nearly 370 bins, of which some 40% are of 3-star quality or more. Unfortunately, only a mere handful qualify for our value criteria and prices generally are very fierce. The saving grace here is the range of 33 dry wines available by the glass, of which 6 are of 3-star quality or higher, and the 46 half-bottles of dry wines of which 16 are of 3-star quality or higher. The list is conventionally arranged by country and region without tasting notes.

It starts off with a substantial array of clarets, some in more than one vintage. None, of course, meets our price/quality criteria so it really boils down to choosing something mature and expensive or something young and more reasonably priced. For the former, Château Ducru-Beaucaillou 1982 should be smashing if you have £250 to fork out on a bottle, and for the latter, the Clos du Marquis 1997 (the second wine of

Château Léoville-las-Cases) at £48.50 should be exciting enough. In white Bordeaux, there are 4 vintages of Château d'Yquem, with a bottle of the 1934 setting you back £2,500. In white Burgundies, the 4-star **Chassagne-Montrachet 1er Cru Morgeot 2001** from Domaine Ramonet is as good as you will get from this list at £59. In red Burgundies there is a similar situation with Vincent Girardin's Nuits-Saint-Georges 1er Cru Les Damodes 2001 at £57. For a real treat, though, the super 5-star Clos de Tart 1996 will set you back £162. There is nothing that excites us in the Rhône (at least not at these prices) but there is value, however, in the Loire wines, with the 4-star **Savennières Clos de Saint-Yves 1999** from Domaine Baumard at £25 and the super 5-star **Pouilly-Fumé Silex 2001** from Didier Dagueneau at £70. Chinon Les Grézeaux 1999 from Bernard Baudry is 3-star value in the Loire reds at £29. There is nothing of value in the Italian section – Sassicaia 1999 is £247.50 a bottle (compare this with £130 for the 2000 vintage at Firenze; qv) – but in Portugal, the white Heradade do Esporão Reserva 2001 at £28 and the red **Quinta da Terrugem Alentejo 2000** from Caves Aliança at £29 are both 3-star value wines.

From the New World, Australia delivers value with Cape Mentelle Semillon/ Sauvignon 2003 at £25 and Plantagenet's Omrah Mount Barker Shiraz 2001 at £26. The New Zealand choices are not so inspiring, and while there is more quality in the Californian choices, they are poor value for money. South America doesn't shine either and top wines such as Almaviva, which are already overpriced to buy, look really bad value for money. The list then moves on to the Champagnes, where Laurent-Perrier Rosé is not badly priced at £55 (£117.50 a magnum). Ruinart 1995 is 5-star quality and at £55 must be a star buy. The super 5-star Taittinger Comtes de Champagne 1994 looks to be good value at £95. On an extensive half-bottle list the Sancerre Blanc 2001 from Lucien Crochet looks best at £17 the half. Dessert wines are pretty expensive too, with Château d'Yquem 1996 at £205 for a half-bottle and £42.50 a glass.

Neville's Best Buy: 1999 **Domaine Baumard** Savennières Clos de Saint-Yves at £25

Score: *Quality* 57.50   *Value* 4.32   *Impression* 20.00   *Total* **81.82**

Ranking: *Quality* 52   *Value* 96   *Impression* 34 = *Overall* **79th**

Recommendations:
NB: 2001 **Domaine Ramonet** Chassagne-Montrachet 1er Cru Morgeot at £59
DM: 2001 **Didier Dagueneau** Pouilly-Fumé Silex at £70
PW: 2000 **Caves Aliança** Alentejo Quinta da Terrugem at £29

Find out more about wine and wine producers at *www.winebehindthelabel.com*

LUMIÈRE

Clarence Parade Cheltenham Gloucestershire GL50 3PA
01242 222200

This is a very modern and forward-looking list for genteel Cheltenham, with lots of interesting wines from the New World and the Med. There are just under 100 wines on the list of which almost half are of-3 star quality or above and on the whole the pricing is very fair. There are a reasonable amount half-bottles on the list, some of which are of excellent quality, but little in the way of decent wines by the glass. The main body of the list is arranged roughly in order of weight, from light to heavy and there are often guest wines, which the front-of-house staff are willing to describe.

Among the lighter white wines a Verdejo from Palacios Bornos in Rueda, Spain at £19 is excellent value for the quality as is the slightly fatter Sancerre PMG 2003 from Gérard Morin at £28, also available in halves at £15.75. The **Cuvée Jacques Charvet Pouilly-Fuissé 2002** from Jean-Michel Drouin at Domaine des Gerbeaux is also good value at £34. There is also a good little selection of Californian whites with Luna Pinot Grigio 2002 and Alban Viognier 2000 both representing value at £33.

In red wines, quality claret at a reasonable price comes in the shape of Château Cap les Faugères Côtes de Castillon 1997 at £25, while from the appellation of Faugères,

The South West

Léon Barral's gamey 2001 at £30 is also good value on the main list. Other guest wines which pleased were Roberto Voerzio's Vignaserra Nebbiolo/Barbera blend 2000 at £30, **Domaine Tempier Bandol 2000** at £33 and La Spinetta's new Sangiovese offering from Tuscany, **Sezzana 2001**, at £52. The best 4-star quality, however, come from a brace of wines each from Cline and Ridge in California: **Cline Small Berry Vineyard Mourvèdre 1999** at £39 and their Big Break Vineyard Zinfandel at £45, as well as Ridge's Petite Sirah 1999 at £42 and their Lytton Springs Zinfandel 2000 at £48. As well as the Faugères, the main list has Foppiano Petite Sirah 1999 at £30 and Domaine Richeaume Cuvée Tradition 2002 from the Côtes de Provence at £30. There are some good dessert wines, but nothing particularly cheap – a bottle of Cyprès de Climens 1998 at £45 looks the value for the quality on the list, but a half of 1996 Tokay-Pinot Gris SGN from Domaine Rieflé at £35 is also well worth looking at. This is a good little list, carefully put together.

Neville's Best Buy: 1999 **Cline** Small Berry Vineyard Mourvèdre at £39

Score: *Quality* 58.39   *Value* 49.00   *Impression* 17.00   *Total* **124.39**

Ranking: *Quality* 50   *Value* 14   *Impression* 61   =   *Overall* **30th**

Recommendations:
NB: 2002 **Dom. des Gerbeaux** Pouilly Fuissé Cuvée Jacques Charvet at £34
DM: 2000 **Domaine Tempier** Bandol at £33
PW: 2001 **Casanova della Spinetta** Sezzana at £52

97th

THE MANSION HOUSE

Thames Street Poole Dorset BH15 1JN
01202 685666

This is a neat list comprising 165 bins of mainly inexpensive wines. The list is divided into 3 sections: 'Recommended wines of the house', 'Good value wines of the world under £35' and 'Classic wines'. There are also 16 sparkling wines (including Champagnes) and 22 half-bottles listed. The scores would have been higher had there not been the slightly irritating habit of listing alternative vintages which were not of the same quality for some of the wines.

Standing out for quality and value on the House section is the Errazuriz Cabernet Sauvignon Reserva Don Maximo Estate at £22.50, whilst the under-£35 section can claim 3-star wines such as Hunter's Sauvignon Blanc from New Zealand at £26.50, **Wynns Coonawarra Estate Cabernet Sauvignon 2000** at £26.50 and Kanonkop Estate Pinotage (vintage not shown, but it's a consistent wine) at £34.50.

However, it is in the fine wine section that this list scores with clarets such as Cos d'Estournel 1996 at £92.50, Pontet-Canet 1995 at £69.50, Ducru-Beaucaillou 1996 at £92.50 and Cheval Blanc 1979 at £295. Burgundies score, too, with a magnum of **Chablis Mont du Milieu 1998** from Pinson at only £65 and a bottle of **Vosne-Romanée Les Suchots 2001** from Louis Jadot at £57.50. Vasse Felix Heytesbury Cabernet/Shiraz 1997 and Ridge Cabernet Sauvignon 1995 at £68.75 weigh in for the New World. There is a good choice of Champagnes, especially Vintage Champagnes, with Pol Roger Cuvée Sir Winston Churchill 1995 at £138 looking good. Of the half-bottles **Domaine La Roquette Châteauneuf-du-Pape 2001** at £15.95 comes out best for the price/quality ratio.

Neville's Best Buy: A magnum of 1998 **Pinson** Chablis 1er Cru Mont du Milieu at £65

Score: *Quality* 23.09   *Value* 15.71   *Impression* 20.00   *Total* **58.80**

Ranking: *Quality* 96   *Value* 63   *Impression* 21 =   *Overall* **97th**

Recommendations:
NB: 2001 **Louis Jadot** Vosne-Romanée 1er Cru Les Suchots at £57.50
DM: 2001 **Dom. La Roquette** Châteauneuf-du-Pape (half-bottle) at £15.95
PW: 2000 **Wynns Coonawarra Estate** Cabernet Sauvignon at £26.50

Find out more about wine and wine producers at *www.winebehindthelabel.com*

The South West

85th

THE WINDMILL

Salisbury Road Marten Wiltshire SN8 3SH
01264 731372

Ex-wine merchant Chris Ellis admits that he had a lot of difficulty in putting together this wine list, mainly because of having to decide what to leave out! He's still managed to get together nearly 400 wines, of which almost half are 3-star quality or above. However, he seems to have abandoned his wine merchant margins for that of a London restaurateur since only 10% of these meet our value criteria. There are a reasonable amount of half bottles and 22 wines by the glass, but these are not geared towards the quality end of the list. The list is divided into two parts – the regular list, which is arranged by style, and the 'Fine and rare' list, which is arranged more conventionally by country and region.

Conventionally, too, the list starts off with the Champagne section, but there are certainly no bargains here. 'Light dry white wines (Europe)' offers inexpensive wines, but no wine of real quality. It is not until you reach 'Medium bodied, aromatic, dry whites (New World)' that you begin to get somewhere. Springfield Estate Life from Stone Sauvignon Blanc 2004 from South Africa is good 3-star value at £24.50, as is the Matakana Estate Pinot Gris 2003 from New Zealand at £27.50. 'Full bodied, richly flavoured whites (Europe and New World)' has some well priced big hitters, with the 4-star **Petaluma Chardonnay 1999** from Coonawarra at £35 and Jean-Marc Brocard's Chablis Grand Cru Les Clos 2002 at £44.50. The 5-star **Savennières Coulée de Serrant 2000** from Nicolas Joly's Clos de Coulée de Serrant is also good value at £49. 'Fruity, medium bodied reds (Europe)' comes next and delivers 3-star value with the Fleurie Domaine de la Madone 2002 at £26.95. 'Structured, characterful and full bodied reds (Europe and New World)' has 4 wines under £30 worth considering, the least expensive being the Domaine Clavel Les Garrigues Vin du Pays d'Oc 2002 at £26.50. The other three are Australian. Australia scores in the 4-star department, too, with the Petaluma Coonawarra Cabernet/Merlot blend 1999 coming in at £45.

The fine and rare section offers little value in white Burgundy, but in the Loire there is the 4-star Savennières Clos du Papillon 1997 from Domaine Baumard at £47.50. Vouvray Clos du Bourg Moelleux from Huët in the great 1971 vintage should be superb if you have £145 to spend. There is good value in Alsace with the Gewürztraminer Grand Cru Eichberg 2001 from Bruno Sorg at £45, and for pure quality, a couple of SGNs from the superb 1989 vintage, Gewürztraminer from Hugel at £175 and Riesling from Trimbach at £125. A good selection of mature clarets runs back to the 1929 Ducru-Beaucaillou at £600, but it's probably less of a risk to plump for the 1996 Lynch Bages at £99.50. In the red Burgundy section, the 5-star Volnay Clos des Ducs 1993 from Marquis d'Angerville is worth a look at £110, while in Rhône reds, **Château de Beaucastel 1995** is a 5-star Châteauneuf-du-Pape at £90. There is quality in both Italy and Spain, with the best value probably being the super

5-star Pesquera Gran Reserva 1995 at £95. No bargains from the USA either, but the 5-star Ridge Geyserville Zinfandel 1997 comes in at £69.50. There is 4-star value in the Moss Wood Glenmore Vineyard Cabernet Sauvignon 1999 from Western Australia at £45 and in the 1992 vintage you have a choice of Penfolds Grange at £235, or Henschke Hill of Grace at £285. In South Africa, the Hamilton Russell Pinot Noir 2002 is 4-star value at £49.90. There is a good choice of dessert wines with **Seppelt's Cask DP63 Show Muscat NV** from Victoria, Australia, best value at £24.50 for a half-bottle. There is always a half-bottle of Château d'Yquem 1994 at £145 if you have to turn your nose up at the Aussie stickies, but the vintage was lousy. Finally, Warre's 1983 port is served at £15 a glass, but is apparently not available in bottle, which seems a little strange. There are good sherries from Hidalgo by the glass, too.

Neville's Best Buy: 1999 **Petaluma** Chardonnay at £35

Score: *Quality* 47.01   *Value* 9.78   *Impression* 20.00   *Total* **76.79**

Ranking: *Quality* 64   *Value* 82   *Impression* 34 =   *Overall* **85th**

Recommendations:
NB: 2000 **Clos de Coulée de Serrant** Savennières Coulée de Serrant at £49
DM: 1995 **Château de Beaucastel** Châteauneuf-du-Pape at £90
PW: NV **Seppelt** Show Reserve Cask DP 63 (half-bottle) at £24.50

Find out more about wine and wine producers at *www.winebehindthelabel.com*

11th

CHERWELL BOATHOUSE

50 Bardwell Road Oxford OX2 6ST
01865 552746

The wine list at Tony Verdin's (literally) converted boathouse in donnish Oxford has impressed under- and postgraduates for many years, for both quality and value. No doubt his partnership with Jasper Morris, MW, in forming one of the best wine merchant's in the country has more than something to do with it. Although the list is dominated by Morris & Verdin (now part of Fields, Morris & Verdin) wines, there is a lot of good kit bought elsewhere to enhance the quality.

The list is not a very long one – just a tad shy of 200 bins – but with nearly 40% of the wines listed of 4- or 5-star quality, and a further 20% of 3-star quality. It's a percentage that has been beaten by only a handful of other restaurants. Prices are, on the whole, very fair. For example, the ubiquitous Isabel Estate Sauvignon Blanc 2004 is listed at only £20, some £10 or more cheaper than in many London restaurants – but then, it is a Morris & Verdin wine, so we suppose the Cherwell Boathouse qualifies for a special discount. Champagnes, on the other hand, are priced pretty well up to standard, with Krug Vintage 1989 at £150. Maybe a magnum of Bollinger 1990 for the same £150 is a better bet.

The list is firmly divided into white wines and red wines, so you are initially confronted with the 'House Selection' of whites followed by a small selection of white halves. The quality of wines served by the glass is very good – the above-mentioned 4-star Isabel Estate Sauvignon Blanc 2004 is one of them at £5 and there is also Wild Boy Chardonnay 2001 from Au Bon Climat in Santa Barbara, California – 3 stars at the same price. A half-bottle of Puligny-Montrachet Charmes 2002 from Gérard Chavy at £18 looks well priced. The 4 Alsace wines are all from Ostertag, with the 1999 Gewürztraminer Fromholz at £26 the 4-star choice. Menetou-Salon Clos de Blanchais from Henri Pellé is the most expensive Loire white at £21, but then it probably deserves to be. The Rhône Valley whites include Qupé Marsanne 2003 from California at £23, but Robert Niero's excellent Condrieu 2002 is more conventionally listed at £34. Under the general heading of 'White Burgundy and other Chardonnay', there are 4 sections – Australia and California (one Australian and four Californians – Au Bon Climat 2001 Chardonnay at £25 looks best), generic Burgundy, Mâconnais and Chalonnais (leaving aside the Aligoté, Olivier Merlin's **Mâcon-La Roche Vineuse Vieilles Vignes 2002** at £20 stands out for value), Chablis (go for Denis Race's Montmains Vieilles Vignes 2002 at £24) and a huge selection of top whites from the Côte d'Or. If we had to make a stab at one, we would probably choose Comte Lafon's 1992 Meursault Genevrières at £150, but it would be a hard choice over the other 7 Lafon Meursaults, not to mention the two vintages of Le Montrachet – 1986 at £220 and 1987 at £250. There are some more down to earth choices such as Puligny-Montrachet Les Charmes 2002 from Gérard Chavy at £34 and even 1988 Bonneau du Martray Corton Charlemagne at £85. The white section finishes off with 'The

Riesling page'. This lists several from Germany – the best being the Maximin Grünhauser Herrenberg 153 Auslese from von Schubert at £58, but it's pretty sweet. There's one from Alsace (Ostertag's Muenchberg Grand Cru 2001 at £32 – not mentioned on the Alsace page) and one from Austria (Riesling Achleiten Smaragd 2001 from Prager at £36), but surprisingly, none from the New World.

'House Selection' reds include a proper House wine – Morris & Verdin's **Beaune Les Pertuisots 2001** at £7.50 the glass, £25 the bottle – surely something to swig down with impunity. It's 3-star rated and a bargain for a bottle of single-vineyard Burgundy. The small selection of red halves include Ridge Lytton Springs Zinfandel 2000 at £19 and their Montebello Cabernet Sauvignon 1996 at £60 (not cheap). A long list of Bordeaux wines follows, most of which are at a good drinking age. Top choices – Palmer 1983 at £160 (they made a better 83 than 82), Lynch-Bages 1982 at £140, or Latour 1985 at £200. For the more budget-conscious, 1993 Grand-Puy-Lacoste at £32 is less exciting but with a good price/quality ratio. There's not a lot of rewarding stuff in the 'Cabernet & Merlot blends from the New World' section except Ridge Montebello 1995 at £120. There is some Cabernet Franc from Charles Joguet – Chinon Clos de la Cure 2002 at £20, which looks good value. In red Burgundies, Volnay 1er cru Santenots de Milieu 1991 from Comte Lafon at £50 should still be drinking well, as should the 1988 Clos de Vougeot Grand Cru from Domaine Rion at £78. New World Pinot Noir has Au Bon Climat's Rosemary Vineyard 1993 at £36, which should also still be drinking well. As one would expect from the Morris & Verdin connection, the list is strong in the 'Rhône Valley and Rhône Rangers' section. In the Rhône Valley itself, André Perret's Saint-Joseph 2002 at £20 looks a snip and from the New World, Qupé 2003 Syrah is particularly well priced at £19. There is very little of interest outside of France and California, with the possible exception of Spain, where Bodegas Alion 1999 is well priced at £35 and **Vega Sicilia Unico 1970** reasonably priced at £200.

Finally, there is a big stab at pudding wines – all from the Old World – ranging from a half-bottle of **Domaine Cauhapé Vendanges de Novembre 2001** at £15 (£5 a glass), through Oremus Tokay Essencia 1995 at £95 for 25cl and on to Château d'Yquem 1983 at £280 the full bottle. All in all, this is a good list, full of high quality offerings with many at exceptionally low prices. The layout of the list is a bit confusing and although there are some tasting notes, we could probably have done with clearer information all round. Nevertheless, it's certainly worth a punt into this Boathouse at any time!

Neville's Best Buy: 2001 **Morris & Verdin** Beaune Les Pertuisots 2001 at £7.50 the glass, £25 the bottle

Score: *Quality* 95.33   *Value* 43.34   *Impression* 13.00   *Total* **151.67**

Ranking: *Quality* 12   *Value* 18   *Impression* 87 =   *Overall* **11th**

Recommendations:
NB: 1970 **Vega Sicilia** Unico at £200
DM: 2001 **Domain Cauhapé** Jurançon Vendanges de Novembre (half-bottle) at £15
PW: 2002 **Olivier Merlin** Mâcon-La Roche Vineuse Vieilles Vignes at £20

Find out more about wine and wine producers at *www.winebehindthelabel.com*

10th

THE CROOKED BILLET

2 Westbrook End Newton Longville Buckinghamshire MK17 0DF
01908 373936

John Gilchrist has used all his experience as a head sommelier in some of the top hotels in the country to produce this masterpiece in his own gastro-pub and this is one of the most remarkably impressive wine lists we have seen. Not because of its size (at 342 bins, it's middle-ranking in length), nor for its overall quality (there are other lists with a greater percentage of quality wines), but for the remarkable fact that 97% of the wines listed are available by the glass. What a fantastic way of exploring your way through the list! The only downside, however, is that the prices are pretty stiff, both for wines by the glass as well as full bottles. You could start the meal with a glass of Dom Pérignon 1996 at £35, go on to a glass of Le Montrachet 1998 from Etiènne Sauzet at £150 with your fish course, continue with a glass of Château Pétrus 1999 at £550 with the meat course and finish up with a glass of Château Suduiraut 1996 at £38 to finish off with the puds. Of course, you could drink for a lot less, but there is little of real quality at under £9 a glass.

Another plus point for the list, is that it is not only listed conventionally by country and region, but also by flavour, which is a most useful aid when considering what wine to choose with your food. The listing by flavour is very well compartmentalised and described and is a very useful adjunct to the list by country. A minus point, however, is that the pricing of glass versus bottle has, on occasions, brought up some strange anomalies and inconsistencies. For example, Vouvray Haut-Lieu 1989 from Huët is listed at £32 a 100ml glass and £120 a 70cl bottle in the dessert wine section, which means, if you have 7 glasses, it will cost you £224, but the wine is also listed in the Loire white wine section, where the glasses are of 175ml size, at the same price, which means that your four glasses to the bottle will only cost you £128 – a much better bet!

The list is headed by a page of 'The Most Popular Wines' – 37 of them ranging from the white Le Midour VDP de Gers 2003 at £14.50 a bottle (£3.75 a glass), to Penfold's Grange 1994 at £240 a bottle (£62 a glass). The wine list proper kicks off (by country and region) with Champagne and Sparkling wines, with some good vintage Champagnes including Drappier Millésime Exceptionnelle 1999 at £35 (£9 the 175ml glass). In Loire whites, the above-mentioned Vouvray is 5-star quality, but you could get the 4-star Demi-Sec 2000 Le Clos de Bourg, from the same producer for £38 (£9.75 the glass). The Alsace section is dominated by Zind-Humbrecht, with **Gewürztraminer Wintzenheim 2000** at £43 (£9 the glass) being the best value. Rhône whites has Guigal's Condrieu 2001 at £75 (£19 the glass), whilst the white Burgundies has 5-star **Bouchard Père et Fils Chevalier-Montrachet 1995** at the comparatively easy price of £160 (£40 the glass). There's little in the way of top quality whites from Italy, Spain, Germany and Austria, but Australia boasts Petaluma's excellent 1999 Chardonnay at a hefty £50 (£11.50 the glass). New Zealand whites are surprisingly uninspiring and the only wine of note in the South African whites is the **Bouchard-Finlayson Kaaimansgat Chardonnay 1999** at £28

(£7.25 the glass). The USA whites has Saintsbury's 3-star Carneros Chardonnay 1999 at £52 (£14 a glass), not exactly great value, but there's little else to choose from.

The reds, in general, score more heavily on quality than the whites, with Regional France weighing in well with the Bandol 2000 from Château de Pibarnon at £63 (£16 the glass). The list is very strong on Bordeaux, with good selections all round and some good mature wines on the left bank, although the right bank selections are generally a bit on the young side. Saying that, if we had to pick out a best buy claret, we would probably go for the super 5-star Château Ausone 1998 at £220 (£56 the glass), just about approachable now, especially if you have it by the glass. There's a clutch of 5-star red Burgundies with Domaine Trapet's Latricières-Chambertin from the very drinkable 1997 vintage at £150 (£40 the glass) seemingly the one to go for. In the Northern Rhône, it's worth paying the extra £20 a bottle (£5 a glass) for Guigal's super 5-star **1997 Côte Rôtie La Turque** over his Château Ampuis at £180 (£50 the glass) – should just be beginning to drink well now. At the other end of the spectrum, there's good 3-star value in the Southern Rhône section with Château Val Joanis Les Griottes 1996 at £36 (£9.25 the glass). Italian reds do make a mark, with **Fontodi Chianti Classico** from the excellent 1999 vintage at £48 (£12.25 the glass) scoring over some more highly regarded (and more expensive) offerings. Australian reds has 4 successive vintages of Penfold's Grange, 1993 to 1996, at prices varying from £240 to £280 (£62 to £72 the glass), but if you want value, then try the 1998 Cabernet Sauvignon from Edwards & Chaffey at £27 (£7 the glass). South Africa has Bouchard-Finlayson's Galpin Creek Pinot Noir 2000 at a fairly stiff £47 (£12 the glass), whilst USA includes Dominus 1984 and 1995 and Opus One 1991 at heftier prices still.

Sweet wines include the confusingly priced wines from Huët and some classy Sauternes from Château Suduiraut – 1995 vintage at £115 (£30 the glass) and £145 (£38 the glass) for the 1996 vintage – but probably the best value would be the 2001 Muscat de Rivesaltes from Domaine de Cazes at £36 (£9.50 the glass). All the dessert wines prices by the glass would have to be carefully calculated as there appear to be even more anomalies. The few half-bottles on the list (not really needed since there are so many wines by the glass) include Alain Graillot's Crozes-Hermitage 2000 at £17.

All in all, John Gilchrist has put together a very user-friendly list – it's a pity that the wastage that must occur by serving so many wines by the glass results in inevitably very high prices – a 10% or 15% reduction might have made him the overall winner.

Neville's Best Buy: 1997 **Guigal** Côte-Rôtie La Turque at £180 (£50 the glass)!! For a more affordable alternative go for: **Bouchard-Finlayson** Kaaimansgat Chardonnay 1999 at £28 (£7.25 the glass)

Score: *Quality* 67.85   *Value* 3.84   *Impression* 81.00   *Total* **152.69**

Ranking: *Quality* 42   *Value* 98   *Impression* 1   =   *Overall* **10th**

Recommendations:
NB: 1995 **Bouchard Père et Fils** Chevalier-Montrachet at £160
DM: 2000 **Zind-Humbrecht** Gewürztraminer Wintzenheim at £43
PW: 1999 **Fontodi** Chianti Classico at £48

Find out more about wine and wine producers at *www.winebehindthelabel.com*

63rd

GRAVETYE MANOR

Vowels Lane East Grinstead West Sussex RH19 4LJ

01342 810567

One of the first modern country house hotels established in the UK, Gravetye Manor is now seen as one of the more conservative outlets for fine wining and dining and this is reflected in no small degree in its wine list. The wines from France dominate, but there is a fair lick of wines from the New World, particularly Australia. It's a sizeable list – over 500 bins – with just under half meeting our quality criteria, but alas, of these, there are only 14 wines in total that make our value criteria. However, there are 72 dry halves, many of which are quality wines, and 9 wines by the glass, which are not. The list is arranged by country and region, with each section having its own sub-list of magnums, bottles and half-bottles – and no separate list of halves.

The tone is set in the Champagne section where there are some pretty swingeing prices – and some oddities, too. It's difficult to understand, for instance, why the 3-star Bollinger NV should be listed at £72 (ouch), when the 4-star 1997 Grande Année is in at £80, only £8 more – even more inconsistent when you look at the price of the super 5-star **Bollinger RD 1985**, which is only £75. No prizes for guessing which one of those we would go for. In the Alsace section that follows, there is outstanding value in the 4-star **Domaine Paul Blanck Riesling Grand Cru Schlossberg** from the superb 1983 vintage at £29.50. The Loire offers Henri Bourgeois' Pouilly-Fumé 2001 at £30 (£17 the half), but there is better value in Huët's Vouvray Le Haut Lieu 1995 at £35. It is listed under the 'Sweet wine' section of the Loire wines, but does not indicate as to whether this is the Demi-Sec or the Moelleux – the former is a 4-star wine and the latter rates 5 stars. There are no bargains in the white Burgundy section – a magnum of Corton-Charlemagne 1997 from Bonneau du Martray seems particularly excessive at £450, so maybe it's best to stick to the Saint-Véran Terres Noires 2001 from Verget at £36, although that isn't exactly cheap, either. Sweet Bordeaux turns up some real quality, with the super 5-star Château Climens 1986 at £87 having the best price/quality ratio in the section. In dry white Bordeaux there is value in the Vieux Château Gaubert Graves 2002 at £30 (£16 the half) and Château Reynon Vieilles Vignes Premières Côtes de Bordeaux 2003 at £29 (£15 the half).

The white wines from Australia and New Zealand are lumped together and good value comes in the shape of 3-star Cape Mentelle Semillon/Sauvignon 2003 from Western Australia at £25 and the 4-star Grosset Polish Hill Riesling 2001 from South Australia at £50. New Zealand's Cloudy Bay Chardonnay 2002 is not as overpriced as one might expect here at £35, nor is the Sauvignon Blanc at £34. In the red wine section there is 4-star value in the Cape Mentelle Cabernet Sauvignon/Merlot 2001 at £33 and **Felton Road Block 3 Pinot Noir 2002** from sexy Central Otago in New Zealand, also at £33. There is nothing of real value in South African whites, but in the reds, there is the Stellenzicht Golden Triangle Shiraz 2002 at £28. Californian offers

quality but cannot match other regions for value, whilst in South America, there are low prices, but not the quality. Several pages of clarets follow, listed in vintage order, most of which are at pretty stiff prices. **Château Ducru-Beaucaillou 1981** at £85 could be interesting, whilst a half-bottle of Mouton-Rothschild 1979 at £245 is decidedly not, but you might well consider a magnum of Château Pavie-Macquin 1995 at £180, which should be quite jolly as long as you have someone to share it with. Red Burgundies, too, lack value options – you could lash out a grand on the 1982 La Tâche from the Domaine de la Romanée-Conti, but it isn't even from a good vintage (although that shouldn't really matter from that estate). It's the same story in the Rhône – Hermitage La Chapelle 1985 is £350 (it's £115 at Tyddyn Llan; qv) and if you want a bottle from the cult 1990 vintage you will need to fork out £600. The Italian section disappoints, too, and whilst there are some good 3-star selections (at a price), there are only two 4-star wines and they are both over £100. Spain doesn't fare much better, either, with the 1970 Castello Ygay Gran Reserva Especial from Marqués de Murrieta at £250, although it's probably not too bad a price considering the age of the wine. Best value here is the entry-level Condado de Haza 2001 from Alejandro Fernández in Ribera del Duero, at £30.

Neville's Best Buy: 1985 **Bollinger** RD at £75

Score: *Quality* 66.29   *Value* 5.08   *Impression* 25.00   *Total* **96.37**

Ranking: *Quality* 45   *Value* 94   *Impression* 13 =   *Overall* **63rd**

Recommendations:
NB: 1981 **Château Ducru-Beaucaillou** at £85
DM: 1983 **Domaine Paul Blanck** Riesling Grand Cru Schlossberg at £29.50
PW: 2002 **Felton Road** Pinot Noir Block 3 at £33

Find out more about wine and wine producers at *www.winebehindthelabel.com*

The South East

88th

THE GREYHOUND INN

31 High Street Stockbridge Hampshire SO20 6EY
01264 810833

This list has around 200 wines of which some 35% are of 3-star quality or higher. Of these, around a quarter meet our value criteria, which is pretty good going for a gastro-pub seeking to attract well-heeled fishermen on the Test. There are 11 dry wines available by the glass, but none of them reach our quality criteria, but some in the 23-strong dry wine half-bottles list do. Apart from the 'Greyhound Inn selection' of cheaper wines at the beginning, the list is arranged conventionally by country and region.

A short selection of Champagnes and sparkling wines is dominated by the wines from Joseph Perrier, the most expensive of which is Cuvée Josephine 1990 at £69. In the white wine section, André Perret's Saint-Joseph Blanc 2001 is value at £29, whilst at the other end of the scale, the Corton-Charlemagne 1998 from Bonneau du Martray is reasonably priced at £95. In the Loire whites, Didier Dagueneau's Pouilly-Fumé Pur Sang 2002, is 5-star quality at £69, whilst his super 5-star Silex 2001 comes in at £79. Spain has the 3-star Albariño 2002 from Pazo de Señoráns at £29, but there is nothing of great interest from Italy. From Australia, Jasper Hill's Georgia's Paddock Riesling 2003 is in at £35, while in the USA whites, the 5-star **Kistler Les Noisetières Chardonnay 2002** is reasonably priced for what it is at £75.

In the red wine section, regional France offers plenty of value, with the Madiran Chapelle l'Enclos 1996 from Patrick Ducournau at £22 and the Côteaux du Languedoc La Côte 2002 from Château de la Négly at £19. The Rhône Valley, too, has value with the **Séguret Côtes du Rhône-Villages** from Domaine du Mourchon – the 1998 at £22 and the 2000 at £20. In red Burgundies, the 3-star Santenay 1er Cru Commes 2002, is just off the value cusp at £32. A fairly lengthy list of clarets turns up value in the 4-star Château Grand-Puy-Lacoste Pauillac 2001 at £46. The excellent 1995 is also available but you will have to pay £95 for this. Italian reds include the Benuara Nero d'Avola/Syrah blend 2001 from Cusumano in Sicily at £26 and, at the other end of the spectrum, the Monferrato Rosso Pin 2000 from La Spinetta comes in at £69 and the **Barolo Le Vigne 1998** from Luciano Sandrone at £99. There is value in Spain with the Cal Pla Tinto 2002 from Mas d'en Compte in Priorat at £20 and the Monastrell 2001 from Casa Castillo in Jumilla at £26. Australia has a couple of value wines in Lake Breeze's Cabernet Sauvignon 2000 from Langhorne Creek in South Australia at £28 and their **Bernoota Cabernet/Shiraz 2001** at £26. There is no value in the USA section, but in South Africa, the Warwick Estate Three Cape Ladies 2001 (Cabernet Sauvignon, Merlot and Pinotage) at £29 is 3-star value. For those with a sweet tooth, the Banyuls Cuvée Reserva NV from Domaine la Tour Vieille at £22 is good value, too. From a good choice of half-bottles, Vieux Château Gaubert Graves 1999 at £18 and Castello di Ama Chianti Classico 1999 at £19 look the best value.

Neville's Best Buy: 2002 **Kistler** Chardonnay Les Noisetières at £75

Score: *Quality* 39.91   *Value* 18.47   *Impression* 18.00   *Total* **76.38**

Ranking: *Quality* 78   *Value* 46   *Impression* 81   =   *Overall* **88th**

Recommendations:
NB: 1998 **Luciano Sandrone** Barolo Le Vigne at £99
DM: 2000 **Domaine du Mourchon** Côtes du Rhône-Villages Séguret at £20
PW: 2001 **Lake Breeze** Cabernet/Shiraz Bernoota at £26

Find out more about wine and wine producers at *www.winebehindthelabel.com*

The South East

89th

THE GRIFFIN INN

Fletching East Sussex TN22 3SS
01825 722890

The Griffin Inn is the personal fiefdom of Ebury Wine director Nigel Pullen and this shortish, but neat wine list shows some pretty astute choices. Whilst there are plenty of bottles under £20, the wines of real merit tend to reflect stockbroker-belt prices, so you may need to choose between very good or very cheap.

The Champagne and sparkling wine page has Taittinger Comtes de Champagne Blanc de Blancs 1995 at £120, but you might care to experiment with the Breaky Bottom Cuvée Rémy Alexandre 1999 fizz from nearby Lewes at £27.50. Nigel says in his notes that it is 'at least the equal and in many cases superior to well-known Champagne' – he's probably right, and it's cheaper, too.

Red and white wines are divided into 'Wines from Europe' and 'New World Wines', with the New World Wines further sub-divided by grape varietals and blends put into the 'Other grape varieties' sub-sections, which makes it all a bit confusing, but there are useful tasting notes on all the wines to guide you through. White wines from Europe include wines from England, France, Spain and Italy, with François Mikulski's 2001 Meursault at £49.50 being the pick of the bunch. The Thelema Mountain Vineyards Chardonnay 2001 (£28.50) from South Africa tops the choice of New World whites.

There is greater choice in the reds with **Château de Capitoul Les Rocailles 2002** from the Languedoc showing an excellent price/quality ratio at £21.50 and top Chianti Classico Castello di Brolio 1998 (£45) taking the European honours. The European connection is also present in our top choice New World red, that being the **Clos de los Siete 2002** from Argentina (£29.80), which has the involvement of top consultant, Michel Rolland. The 'Connoisseur's list' of 6 wines has 4 bottles worthy of 4 stars or more, with the top spot going to **La Brancaia Il Blu 2000**, a Super-Tuscan blend of Sangiovese, Cabernet and Merlot at £65. Dessert wines include a 25cl bottle of Royal Tokaji Blue Label 5 puttonyos at £19.50 or a half-bottle of Pantelleria **Morsi di Luce 2001** from Cantine Florio (£16.50 or £5.20 a glass).

The 14 dry wines available by the glass are firmly geared to the lower end of the spectrum and, if you are reading this book, are probably not what you are looking for. Nigel advises us that the list is ever changing, so perhaps in the future we might see a greater number of 3- and 4-star wines by the glass, which would certainly up his score no end. Choosing a Best Buy from this list was extremely difficult, owing to the clear distinction between quality and price. In the end, quality prevailed.

Neville's Best Buy: 1982 **Château Léoville-las-Cases** Saint-Julien at £250!! For a more affordable alternative go for: **Château de Capitoul** Les Rocailles 2002 from the Languedoc showing an excellent price/quality ratio at £21.50

Score: *Quality* 30.44   *Value* 23.53   *Impression* 21.00   *Total* **74.97**

Ranking: *Quality* 90   *Value* 41   *Impression* 29 =   *Overall* **89th**

Recommendations:
NB: 2000 **La Brancaia** Il Blu at £65
DM: 2002 **Clos de los Siete** Mendoza at £29.80
PW: 2001 **Cantine Florio** Morsi di Luce (half-bottle) at £16.50

74th

HOTEL DU VIN, BRIGHTON

2-6 Ship Street Brighton East Sussex BN1 1AD

01273 718588

Hotel du Vin group wine lists are all similar but the emphasis varies, so people won't be bored by repetition from one establishment to the next. This one concentrates a bit more on value than some of the others, although quality is not forgotten. The list has over 450 entries, of which just under 40% are of 3-star quality or more, and of these, about one sixth meet our price criteria. With the list sent to us, there were 27 wines served by the glass, but they had mainly an Italian theme, so we assume that the selection changes from time to time and it is difficult to assess the overall quality. Two of the 27 wines were of 3-star quality or more, but there were a few 2-star wines as well, so we can assume that most of these would follow a similar pattern. The 35 dry wines sold by the half-bottle had around a quarter that met out quality criteria. The wine list is laid out conventionally by country and region, without tasting notes.

There are no bargains to be found in the Champagne section that opens the list, nor even among sparkling wines, where the Nyetimber NV is a hefty £49. If you must drink fizz, it's probably best to stick to the Chapel Down Brut from Kent at £26. White Burgundy, too, doesn't lend itself naturally to value for money and the Chablis Grand Cru Bougros 1999 from William Fèvre at £59.50 is about as close as you will get. There's better value in the South of France with the Costières de Nîmes Vieilles Vignes 2002 from Château de la Tuilerie at £28 and the 4-star Vin de Pays des Côteaux des Fenouilledes Le Soula 2001 from Gérard Gauby at £45. Gaillac Renaissence Sec 2001 from Domaine Rotier is also good value at £24. There is no value in the Loire whites nor in the Alsace section, but the Côtes du Jura 1999 from Domaine Rolet is 3-star quality at £29.50. Germany weighs in with the 4-star Eitelsbacher Karthäuserhofberg Riesling Auslese 1997 from Weingut Karthäuserhof at £45.50 and there is 3-star value from Austria with the Spitzer 1,000-Eimer-Berg Riesling Smaragd Trocken 1998 from Freie Weingärtner Wachau at £28.50. The whites from Luxembourg, Hungary and England don't score and neither do the whites from Switzerland, Thailand and even Italy, but Greece has the 3-star Biblia Chora Ovilos 2002 at £22.50. There's excellent value in the fruit-driven **Telmo Rodríguez Rueda Basa 2004** from Spain at £18, and there's even value in the Californian section with Cline Cellars Sonoma County Viognier 2002 at £26.50. The Terrunyo Sauvignon Blanc 2003 from Chile at £19.50 is also good value for money, but there is nothing in Uruguay or Argentina. In Australia, the Leeuwin Estate Art Series Riesling 2003 is well priced at £29, whilst in New Zealand Sauvignon Blancs (of which there are 9), the 4-star **Isabel Estate 2004** beats the rest hands down for value at £29.50.

Clarets head the red wine section and surprisingly there are very few classed growth wines. If we had to make a choice here, we would probably plump for Pavillon Rouge

1995, the second wine of Château Margaux, at £85. There's not a lot of value in Burgundy, either, so it's probably best to go for the top here with the 5-star Clos des Lambrays 1999, but it will set you back £110. There is an exciting array of red wines from the Rhône Valley, from Pierre Gaillard's Saint Joseph 2002 at £28 and the 4-star Châteauneuf-du-Pape 2002 from Domaine de Marcoux at £42, right through to 2 super 5-star cuvées from Chapoutier – Côte-Rôtie La Mordorée 1995 at £159 and Ermitage Le Pavilion 1996 at £179. Provence has the 4-star Bandol 2000 from Domaine du Gros Noré at £45, while in the Loire, the Anjou Rouge 2002 from Domaine Ogereau at £22.50 is good value, too. Savoie and Jura have good value wines in the Chignin Vieilles Vignes Mondeuse 2002 from André & Michel Quenard at £22.50 and the Arbois Trousseau 1999 from Domaine Rolet at £26.50. Greece's Domaine Biblia Chora scores again with the Vin du Pays de Pangee 2002 at £21. Italy has a number of reds, but surprisingly no Barolos or Barbarescos and also nothing to reach the price/quality ratio we are seeking. There are no other European reds that make it either except for Laurona's Montsant 2000 at £29.50. A very good selection of Californian reds has Harlan Estate 1996 available at £315, but we would probably stick with the Bien Nacido Reserve Syrah 1999 from Qupé Winery at £48. South Africa has the **Observatory Syrah 2000** at £50 and it would be interesting to compare this with the Qupé. There are some interesting red wines from Australia including the Petit Verdot 2002 from Heartland in South Australia at £29.50 and the Yarra Burn Shiraz/Viognier 2002 from Victoria at £29. Those wanting something more refined could go for the Quintet from Mount Mary Vineyard in the Yarra Valley, but you would have to pay £180 for the privilege. The best value sweet wine on the list is undoubtedly the **Rivesaltes Ambré NV Domaine Fontanel** at £30, but there are a host of different types of sweet wines in all sizes including the astonishing Côteaux du Layon Maria Juby SGN in the extraordinary 1997 vintage from Patrick Baudouin at £88 for 50cl. The list finishes up with the selection of half-bottles of dry wines, where the best value would appear to be the Crozes-Hermitage 2002 from Alain Graillot at £19.

Neville's Best Buy: 2004 **Telmo Rodríguez** Rueda Basa at £18

Score: *Quality* 38.61   *Value* 38.31   *Impression* 13.00   *Total* **89.92**

Ranking: *Quality* 60   *Value* 56   *Impression* 34 =   *Overall* **74th**

Recommendations:
NB: 2000 **The Observatory** Syrah at £50
DM: **Domaine Fontanel** Rivesaltes Ambré at £30
PW: 2004 **Isabel Estate** Marlborough Sauvignon Blanc at £29.50

77th

HOTEL DU VIN, TUNBRIDGE WELLS

Crescent Road Tunbridge Wells Kent TN1 2LY
01892 526455

This is one of the largest of the lists from the Hotel du Vin group – over 720 wines, with over 40% meeting our quality criteria, of which around one eighth meet the price criteria as well. There are 54 half-bottles listed, 19 of which are of 3-star quality or more, and 13 dry wines by the glass, which do not reach this status but do count some 2-star wines among them. The list is laid out conventionally by country and region, but there are no tasting notes.

The list starts off with Champagne, where there is nothing to excite at the lower end of the spectrum, but **Dom Pérignon 1996** is well priced at £79.50. (Compare this with £220 at McClements; qv). There is also a run of older vintages of Dom Pérignon, going back to 1959 at £600, which should keep somebody happy. White Burgundies follow and here you will see that there is some pretty heavyweight stuff (at a price) so maybe you might consider saving money by plumping for the Pouilly-Vinzelles Les Remparts 2002 from Bret Brothers at £36, although it still doesn't qualify as value in our book. In South-West France, there is value in the Gaillac Sec Renaissance 2001 from Domaine Rotier at £23.50, whilst in the Languedoc Côteaux du Languedoc La Brise Marine 2001 from Château de la Négly is indeed a breeze at £18.50. Savoie has the Roussette de Savoie 2003 from the Quenards at £25 and in the very impressive Alsace section, the best value comes from the Pinot Blanc Clos des Capucins 2002 from Domaine Weinbach at £28.50. There are a number of value wines to be found among the Loire whites – standing out are the Jasnières Cuvée Clos Saint-Jacques 1999 from Joël Gigou at £25 and the Ménétou-Salon Morogues 2003 from La Tour Saint-Martin at £23.50. There is good value in the Italian white section with the **2003 Friuli Grave Tocai Friulano Toh!** from Di Leonardo at £20, while Austria turns up 3-star value in the Wachau Spitzer Steinterrassen Riesling Federspiel 2001 from Franz Hirtzberger at £29. In Spain the Clos Nelin Priorat 2002 is also nicely priced at £29.50. America (North and South) doesn't do that well, but there is value in South Africa with the Mulderbosch Chardonnay 2002 at £26 and the Meerlust Chardonnay 2000 at £29. Australian whites has the 4-star Tyrrell's Vat 1 Semillon 1995 in at £49.50, while New Zealand scores 4 stars with the Kumeu River Chardonnay 2002 at £46.

The reds kick off with the wines from Burgundy, but there is no wine listed makes our price/quality criteria until the Beaujolais, where the Fleurie 2003 from Domaine de la Madone comes in at £25. If you still crave Pinot Noir, then you might consider the magnum of Jean-Marc Pavelot's Savigny-les-Beaune 2001 at £115, for there are no other 4- or 5-star quality wines under £100 a bottle. A full page of clarets follows, with a few stellar wines, but nothing to get too excited about. There is also a full page of wines from the South-West of France, where value really takes off. Vin du Pays Catalan Empreinte du Temps 2000 from Domaine Ferrer Ribière at £21, Saint-

Chinian 2000 from Domaine des Jougla at £19.50, and Faugères Vieilles Vignes 2002 from Château de la Liquière at £25 are but 3 of a number of good value wines from this region. There is lots of good value too in the Rhône reds, with the 4-star Cornas Cuvée des Côteaux 2000 from Robert Michel at £41.50 looking good and several 3-star wines at under £30. Provence has outstanding value in the 3-star Côteaux Varois Cuvée Le Trou de Infernet 1998 from Château Routas at £17. Loire reds are interesting, with the Saumur-Champigny 1999 from Château de Villeneuve at only £17 and the 4-star Bourgeuil Cuvée Prestige in the extraordinary 1989 vintage, from Domaine des Chesnaies, at £48.50. While there is terrific value to be found in the French regional reds, the same cannot be said for Italy, where the delicious 3-star **Dolcetto d'Alba Tiglineri 2001** from Enzo Boglietti at £29.80 and the 4-star Toscana IGT Torrione 2000 from Petrolo at £49 just scrape in under the wire in their respective value criteria. In Spain, however, there is outstanding 4-star value in the **Toro Viña San Román 2000** from Bodegas Maurodos at £27. There are some top quality wines from the USA, but nothing to meet our value criteria – if we had to go for something here it would be a toss-up between the Brewer-Clifton Santa Maria Valley Pinot Noir 2000 at £69.50 and the 5-star Andrew Will Ciel du Cheval Cabernet Sauvignon 1998 from Washington State at £77. In South Africa, the Meinert Synchronicity blend 2002 is value at £27. There is a good choice of Australian reds, some of which are pretty pricey, but the value prize here goes to the 4-star Trinders Cabernet/Merlot 2002 from Cape Mentelle at £26. There is quality, too, in the New Zealand reds, but only the Sileni Estates Merlot/Cabernets 2000 comes anywhere near our criteria at £31.

From a fair selection of vintage ports, Warre's 1983 looks best at £78 (£9.85 a glass). The range of sweet wines is excellent: pick of the bunch is the 4-star Côteaux du Layon-Chaume Les Onnis 1998 from Domaine des Forges at £30, although the vintage wasn't very good. Jo Pithon's Côteaux du Layon Clos des Ortinères in the superb 1997 vintage might be a better bet, but you would have to pay £60 for this. Another wine within the price/quality ratio is I Capitelli 2000 from Anselmi in the Veneto in Italy at £49.50.

Neville's Best Buy: 1996 **Moët et Chandon** Dom Pérignon at £79.50

Score: *Quality* 49.53   *Value* 14.73   *Impression* 18.79   *Total* **83.05**

Ranking: *Quality* 61   *Value* 67   *Impression* 52 =   *Overall* **77th**

Recommendations:
NB: 2003 **Di Leonardo** Friuli Grave Tocai Friulano Toh! at £20
DM: 2000 **Bodegas Maurodos** Toro Viña San Román at £27
PW: 2001 **Enzo Boglietti** Dolcetto d'Alba Tiglineri at £29.80

86th

THE JOLLY SPORTSMAN

Chapel Lane East Chiltington East Sussex BN7 3BA
01273 890400

There are over 200 wines on this country restaurant's list with around 30% of 3-star quality or more and, of these, around a fifth meet our value criteria. There is quite a large selection of half-bottles but just 8 dry wines available by the glass, all geared to the entry-level customer. The list is conventionally arranged by country and region without tasting notes, except for the wines by the glass.

In the Champagne and sparkling wine section, the 5-star Bollinger Grande Année 1996 is well priced at £69, but there is little to recommend at the entry level. Italian whites has the Lugana Brolettino 2002 from Ca' dei Frati at £28.75, whilst in Spain the Albariño Rias Baixas 2003 from Pazo de Senoráns is also good 3-star value at £27.50. In Australia, the Leeuwin Estate Art Series Riesling 2002, comes in at £27.50. There is good value, too, in Alsace, with Bruno Sorg's Tokay-Pinot Gris 2002 at £22.90. In white Burgundies, the super 5-star Chablis Grand Cru Les Clos 2001 from Domaine Dauvissat is good value for the quality at £62.50.

The reds kick off with an interesting selection from Italy, with the 4-star Brunello di Montalcino 1998 from Tenuta Argiano coming in at £49. If you want to see just how well this wine is capable of maturing, the 1990 is available at £89. In 'The Americas', there is 3-star value in **Seghesio's Sonoma County Zinfandel 2001** at £29.85 in an otherwise poor selection, but Australia offers better value with the 3-star Plantagenet Great Southern Pinot Noir 2001 at £28 and their 4-star Mount Barker Shiraz 2001 at £38. The new **Shaw and Smith Adelaide Hills** Shiraz is superb in the 2002 vintage and also good value at £34.75. In the Rhône selections, the Châteauneuf-du-Pape 2002 from Domaine du Vieux Lazaret is well priced at £29.65 and in Burgundy the Chambolle-Musigny 1er Cru Les Véroilles 1992 from Ghislaine Barthod is also well priced at £49, but 1992 was a pretty weak vintage, so you may need to ask how well it has stood the test of time. You may feel safer with the beefy Clos de la Roche 1995 from Dominique Laurent, but you will have to pay £93 for the privilege. Clarets come next and here you will find a few wines in the not-very-popular 1994 vintage at good prices. It wasn't a great year but it wasn't a bad year, either, and we wouldn't mind drinking Château Léoville-Barton or **Château Ducru-Beaucaillou** at £59. For those who mustn't drink anything so lowly as an 'off' vintage, there is always **Château Gruaud-Larose 1982** at a very reasonable £98.

Neville's Best Buy: 1994 **Château Ducru-Beaucaillou** Saint-Julien at £59

Score: *Quality* 39.91 *Value* 18.47 *Impression* 18.00 *Total* **76.38**

Ranking: *Quality* 77 *Value* 53 *Impression* 53 = *Overall* **86th**

Recommendations:
NB: 1982 **Château Gruaud-Larose** at £98
DM: 2001 **Seghesio** Zinfandel Sonoma County at £29.80
PW: 2002 **Shaw and Smith** Shiraz Adelaide Hills at £34.75

Find out more about wine and wine producers at *www.winebehindthelabel.com*

33rd

JSW

1 Heath Road Petersfield Hampshire GU31 4JE
01730 262030

his is a big list of around 550 entries with almost half being of 4- or 5-star quality and a further fifth of 3-star quality. There are a lot of big-ticket items with bottles from several vintages, generally not overpriced, but on the whole the list misses our criteria of finding 4- or 5-star wines at under £50 and 3-star wines at under £30. Had there been more of these, it would have achieved a considerably higher score. There is a very reasonable number of halves, many of which are of real quality, but there is a derisory list of wines by the glass, which would inhibit experimentation. The list is arranged conventionally by country and region with the usual pages for Champagnes and sparkling wines and dessert wines from around the globe at the beginning and end of the list respectively.

There are some big names in the Champagne list – mostly vintage Champagnes with Roederer Brut 1996 coming in at £85. Krug 1988 is £230, so you might consider going for the only non-Champagne sparkling wine on the list – Pelorus 2000 from New Zealand at £24. Red Bordeaux follows with a good selection of mainly drinkable vintages, culminating in a run of 4 mature vintages of Château Mouton-Rothschild, 3 vintages of Château Lafite-Rothschild and 2 vintages of Château Latour at prices varying between £275 and £580 the bottle. No Château Margaux, but then you can't have everything. There is Château Haut-Brion 1989 at £550, if you really must stick to first growths, but Château Haut-Bailly 1990 is another good Péssac-Léognan, which at £95 might be considered more approachable. There's a long list of red Burgundies, too. Here the prices are a bit more down-to-earth, with Comte Lafon's Volnay Santenots-de-Milieu in the now very drinkable 1997 vintage at £75 looking better value than other wines in more considered vintages, although Louis Jadot's Echezeaux 1996 is from a star vintage and tempting at only £65. Red Rhônes are another tour de force with a number of products from Chapoutier, 3 vintages of Château Rayas, 3 vintages of Hermitage from Chave, 4 vintages of Côte-Rôtie La Turque, 4 vintages of La Chapelle and 11 vintages of Château de Beaucastel and many others contributing to the quality of this section, but the value wine to go for is the 4-star **Châteauneuf-du-Pape Les Cailloux 2000** from André Brunel at £29. Italian reds have vintage choices for Sassicaia, Tignanello and Ornellaia and lots of quality wines from Piedmont and Tuscany, but again there is 4-star quality to be found at a reasonable price in the 1997 Chianti Classico Reserva from Castello di Fonterutoli at £39.50. Spain weighs in with a number of wines from Artadi, from the entry-level Rioja Viños de Gain 1999 at £29.50, to Viña El Pison 2001 at £110. René Barbier's Clos Mogador at £48.50 in both the 1998 and 1999 vintage is not badly priced either. Terrazas Alto Malbec 2003 at £17 is a quality entry-level wine in the Argentinian section. There is massive quality in the North American red wine section with Sine Qua Non's Flagrante and **Incognito 2000** at £140 and £160 respectively, but if you want to be more down-to-earth, then the Ridge Lytton Springs Zinfandel 2001 at £45 is your wine. New Zealand reds brim with Pinot Noirs, with Felton Road Block 3 2003 at £85 a rather

The South East

expensive purchase (contrast this with £33 for the 2002 at Gravetye Manor; qv). South African reds are well represented with Spice Route Syrah 2000 at £28 being a better bet than their Flagship Syrah 1999 at £45. The Vergelegen Red 2000 is one of the best reds coming out of South Africa and at £50 on the list represents good value. The Australian red section is full of big hitters from D'Arenberg, Torbreck, and Penfolds and it is apparent that subtlety is not the order of the day here. The Veritas Heysen Vineyard Shiraz 2000 is well priced at £29.50 and the 1997 super-5 star Henschke Hill of Grace should just about be starting to drink for your £125 investment.

White Burgundies score heavily with a plethora of famous names. Sauzet, Henri Boillot and Drouhin feature with lots of wines – and very good they are, too – but for super 5-star quality, Bonneau du Martray's 1995 Corton-Charlemagne at £120 looks good in the context of the list. Of course, the same rating applies to the 1999 Le Montrachet Marquis de Laguiche from Joseph Drouhin, but you will have to pay £225 for that. Alsace has lots of wines from Trimbach and Zind-Humbrecht with several vintages of some of their top wines. Zind-Humbrecht's Tokay-Pinot Gris Clos Windsbuhl 1996, 1998 and 1999, all at £49, is 5-star wine at an affordable price. Trimbach's super 5-star Riesling Clos Sainte-Hune 1989 should be drinking beautifully now and £120 is not over the top for this quality. There is a good German selection and the **Eitelsbacher Karthäuserhofberg Riesling Auslese** in both the 2001 vintage and the 1990 vintage are worth drinking at £33 and £45 respectively. Dry whites from Spain, Italy and the Rhône Valley do not live up to their red counterparts, although Beaucastel Blanc 2001, from the Perrin family, is 4-star quality at £55. Loire whites could be more exciting with the exception of Jean Baumard's Savennières Clos du Papillon 1996 at £39.50. For Australian and New Zealand whites there's value in Petaluma Clare Valley Riesling 2001 at £33 and Villa Maria's Taylor's Pass Sauvignon Blanc 1999 at £30, respectively. The best shot in South Africa is the Vergelegen Reserve Chardonnay 2000 at £34. Outstanding half-bottle selections include super 5-star **Zind-Humbrecht Riesling Brand Vendanges Tardives 1995** at £37, for white, and 4-star Ridge Lytton Springs Zinfandel 2002 at £28, for red.

There is a global list of dessert wines, including 5 vintages of Château Yquem in halves and one in full bottles, that being the 1945 at £750. More budget-conscious customers might consider a half-bottle of De Bortoli's 1999 Noble One from Australia at £20, or a bottle of Baumard's Quarts de Chaume 1990 at £62. There are some good bottles of vintage port available, too, with Fonseca's 1980 at £65 looking to be the best value. This is a fine list, full of big names, but inevitably at big prices.

Neville's Best Buy: 2000 **Les Cailloux** Châteauneuf-du-Pape at £29

Score: *Quality* 90.31   *Value* 10.20   *Impression* 20.27   *Total* **120.78**

Ranking: *Quality* 14   *Value* 80   *Impression* 34 =   *Overall* **33rd**

Recommendations:
NB: 2000 **Sine Qua Non** Incognito at £160
DM: 1995 **Zind-Humbrecht** Riesling Brand V T (half-bottle) at £37
PW: 2001 **Weingut Karthäuserhof** Eitelsbacher Karthäuserhofberg Riesling Auslese at £33

Find out more about wine and wine producers at *www.winebehindthelabel.com*

56th

NOVELLI AT AUBERGE DU LAC

Brocket Hall Lemsford Welwyn Garden City Hertfordshire AL8 7XG
01707 368888

This is a splendid high quality list with wines from some of the best producers in the world, but it makes it expensive to drink anything of quality with Jean-Christophe Novelli's excellent cuisine. From over 450 wines, around three-quarters are of 3-star quality or more – one of the highest proportions we have seen – but there is no concession to value on the list at all, which does make  it a difficult task to make any recommendations. Nevertheless, we have looked carefully and hopefully we can point you in the right direction, even if you have to sacrifice value for quality.

The list stars off with pages of 'Sommelier's suggestions' 'Jean-Christophe Novelli suggestions' and 'Wine club members' favourites', which presumably are there for people who are too lazy (sorry, we mean busy) to look through the whole list. A pity, really, because there are some very fine wines to be had – you just have to dig them out. We couldn't find any half-bottles listed for dry wines at all, but 22 wines are available by the glass, of which 8 are very commendably of 3-star quality. A glass of Gosset Grand Rosé at £15, followed by a glass of Gewürztraminer Harth Cuvée Caroline 2003 from Domaine Schoffit at £8 and then a glass of The Custodian McLaren Vale Grenache 2001 from D'Arenberg at £6.50 and a glass of pudding wine (which we shall come to later) to go with your meal is probably going to be a better bet than one of the fancy clarets or Burgundy in which the list abounds. In fact, we would say that this is one of the few places we have come across where drinking wines on offer by the glass is a pleasure. Keep up the quality, please!

The list is arranged conventionally by country and region and in the Champagne section the tone is immediately set by the page containing the five vintages of Dom Pérignon Oenothèque Champagnes at prices ranging from £270 for the 1988 to £1,200 for the 1962. Other Champagnes, of course, do get a look in and all are of impeccable provenance but wildly overpriced. Instead, try a bottle of Franciacorta 1997 from Ca' del Bosco at £59, as good a fizz you will get coming out of Italy. Alsace whites come next with the best value being the Tokay-Pinot Gris Grand Cru Pfingstberg 2000 from Lucien Albrecht at £44. No great value from Rhône Valley whites but some **Saint-Péray 1999** from one of the best producers of that wine, Alain Voge, at £39, has curiosity value. No value recommendations in the Loire and even paying £120 for Didier Dagueneau's Pouilly-Fumé Silex 2003, is still a bit excessive. There are certainly no bargains to be had in the white Burgundy section, but if money is no object we would plump for the super 5-star Bienvenues-Bâtard-Montrachet 1999 from Paul Pernot at £190, although it must be still a bit on the young side. There is nothing of great value nor of great quality in the rest of the whites until you come to the South African section and then Paul Cluver Elgin Chardonnay 2001 just gets its 3-star price/quality rating at £29.

There is no let-up in the red Burgundy section, but the best 4-star option is Chambolle-Musigny 1er Cru Les Charmes 1998 from Hudellot-Noëllat at £78 and the best 5-star Michel Gros' 2000 Vosne-Romanée 1er Cru 'aux Réas'(sic) – a top wine assuming this is the Clos des Réas, at £90. There is some value in the red Rhônes, with Domaine de Beaurenard's Châteauneuf-du-Pape 2002 at £45, a bit of a cry from Château de Beaucastel's Hommage à Jacques Perrin 1995 at £600. Still, it's nice to see both on the list. There is value, too, in the Languedoc, with **Domaine Léon Barral's Faugères 1999**, 3-star value at £27. There is a huge choice of clarets, and you may spend time making up your mind whether you should choose the Pétrus 1997 at £900 or Le Pin 1997 at £650. Probably best to ask the sommelier. If you have got a bit more to spend there is also a choice between the Mouton-Rothschild 1982 at £1,100 and Latour 1961 at £1,700, both excellent vintages. But for lesser mortals, you could do a lot worse than to go for the Clos du Marquis 1996 (the second wine of Château Léoville-las-Cases) at £69. Italy offers some of the top names in Piedmont and Tuscany, but the best value would appear to be the 4-star **Rosso del Conte 2000** (mostly Nero d'Avola) from Tasca d'Almerita in Sicily at £52. The best value Spanish red (if you can call it value) is the 4-star Priorat Indus 2001 from Vall Llach at £65, although it is doubtful whether it is ready to drink. Bodegas Alion 1999 is ludicrously priced at £80 and Vega Sicilia Unico 1985 is £380. There are better value wines from Australia with the 2001 Cabernet Sauvignon from Vasse Felix at £46 and **The Bishop Shiraz 1999** made by Ben Glaetzer at £47. D'Arenberg's The Custodian Grenache 2001 is a very respectable £26. There are also 8 vintages of Penfolds Grange to choose from at prices varying from £250 to £350.

Sweet wines follow, again at very high prices, but a bottle of 1989 Château Coutet at £90 is not bad for this list. Strangely, we could find no dessert wines listed by the glass, maybe they didn't send us the list, but this did rather put an end to the wine-by-the-glass programme that fired our enthusiasm at the beginning of this appraisal. A big selection of vintage ports has Warre's 1983 at £105. There are also a reasonable number of both red and white magnums, with the 4-star 'Dreams' 2001 from Silvio Jermann at £130 in the whites and Vino Nobile di Montepulciano Asinone 1999 from Poliziano in Tuscany at £120 in the reds looking to be the best value for money.

This is a very high quality list with some super choices – but oh, those prices! A little less mark up would send this list several places higher next year.

Neville's Best Buy: 1999 **Domaine Léon Barral** Faugères at £27

Score: *Quality* 85.79   *Value* 2.62   *Impression* 15.00   *Total* **103.41**

Ranking: *Quality* 18   *Value* 99   *Impression* 75   =   *Overall* **56th**

Recommendations:
NB: 1999 **Glaetzer** Shiraz The Bishop at £47
DM: 1999 **Alain Voge** Saint-Péray at £39
PW: 2000 **Tasca d'Almerita** Rosso del Conte at £52

 Find out more about wine and wine producers at *www.winebehindthelabel.com*

The South East

20th

THE SIR CHARLES NAPIER

Sprigg's Alley Chinnor Oxfordshire OX39 4BX
01494 483011

This long-running establishment has seen its wine list mature *and* move with the times. There are a lot of New World up and coming producers featured on the list, but alas, no tasting notes to guide the uninitiated. Still, there is a philosophy statement at the front of the list with some useful pointers and if you are not sure, we assume you can always ask any of the front of house team. About 50% of the list is of 3-star quality or above and there are a number which meet our quality/price criteria. There are a fair number of quality half-bottles of dry wines but not a lot by the glass. Nevertheless, this is a very fine list with reasonable prices for Home Counties fine dining.

The Champagnes and Sparkling wines are not overtly cheap, although Billecart-Salmon as the House Champagne at £35 is obviously better value than Pelorus from New Zealand at £38. Roederer Cristal 1996 at £140 is about par for the course. In Burgundy, premier cru Chablis under £30 is always worth a go and the 2002 Montmains from Jean-Claude Bessin at £29.50 just fits the bill. **Puligny-Montrachet 1er Cru Les Clavoillons 1999** from Gérard Chavy is good 4-star value at £49, whilst you could go for broke with the super-5 star Bâtard-Montrachet 1997 from Paul Pernot at £135. Loire whites include the super 5-star Savennières Clos de la Coulée de Serrant 1998 from Nicholas Joly at £75, which should just about be beginning to drink now, whilst in Alsace, Gewürztraminer d'Epfig 2003 from Ostertag is 3-star quality at £27.50. The best Rhône white on the list is the **Condrieu Les Ravines 2001** from Niero Pinchon at £38, which is pretty well priced for Condrieu. The short list of Italian whites has Manna Cru 2001 (a blend of Riesling, Chardonnay, Gewürztraminer and Sauvignon) from Franz Haas in the Alto Adige, 3-star quality at £26.50. There is good value in the Australian whites section, with Jeffrey Grosset's Sauvignon/Semillon Clare Valley 2001 at £19.50 and his Polish Hill Vineyard Riesling 2001 at £26.50. On the other hand, Leeuwin Estate 'Art Series' Chardonnay 1999 at £75 is not. Similarly, there is cracking value in the New Zealand section from Isabel Estate, the 1999 Dry Riesling coming in at £18.95 and the 4-star 2004 Sauvignon Blanc coming in at £24.50. The 3-star Cloudy Bay Sauvignon Blanc 2004 comes in at a whopping £48, but maybe that is often the way to fleece the *lumpenprolatariat* who can't be bothered to look for anything else. The 2003 Fairview Viognier from Paarl in South Africa at £24.50 is also an interesting listing.

In the reds there is a smallish selection of clarets, with not too many mature enough to drink yet. Of these, the Pichon Lalande 1989 at £160, or the Léoville-las-Cases 1985 at £180 are probably not out of line with current restaurant prices. Pichon Lalande's second wine, Réserve de la Comtesse 1997, is probably just beginning to drink now and at £36 is reasonably priced. Nearly every one's a winner in the short selection of red Burgundies, from a youthful **Gevrey-Chambertin Clos Prieur 2002**

from Frédéric Esmonin at £32.50, to the super 5-star Clos de Tart Grand Cru 1997 at £125. Similarly, in the Rhône the 1996 Cornas Champlerose from Domaine Courbis at £36 is good value for a 4-star wine, but you can also get super 5-star quality with Hermitage La Chapelle 1983 at £130, although you can buy the 1994 vintage for £66.50. Spanish reds include many of the usual suspects – Alion 1999 at £46 is not the cheapest we have seen it listed, but then, neither is it the most expensive.

The South East

There is not a lot of excitement in the Italian red section except for Antinori's Solaia 1990, but at £160 a throw one would hope that it would live up to its super 5-star rating. New World reds score heavily with Australia leading the way for price/quality ratio. Olmo's Reward 1998 (Merlot, Cabernet Franc and other Bordeaux varieties) from Frankland Estate in Western Australia is from a lesser vintage but well priced at £21.50, whilst Jeffrey Grosset's Gaia Cabernet Blend 1995 is 4-star quality at £48. The New Zealand selection is all Pinot Noir, with the Ata Rangi 2001 a little overpriced at £52 (especially given this is a weaker vintage), whilst in South Africa, the Boekenhoutskloof Cabernet Sauvignon 1998 is true 5-star quality at £48. California shines with impressive offerings from the amazingly low priced **Côtes du Soleil Mourvèdre/Syrah 1997** from Jade Mountain at £18.50, to the somewhat overpriced Shafer Hillside Select Cabernet Sauvignon 1998 at £250. In between, Ridge Geyserville Zinfandel 2000 is 5-star quality at only £35. South America has some big guns in the shape of the Rothschild/Concha y Toro Almaviva blend 1998 from Chile at £75 and from Argentina, Michel Rolland's Yacochuya blend 2000 at £68, but whilst they are both impressive, one can't help wondering if they are not falling short of their lofty price tags in the face of global opposition (not that that's the restaurant's fault!).

There is a nice page of dry halves with Gérard Chavy's Puligny-Montrachet 1998 at £21.50 and Au Bon Climat's Chardonnay 2001 from California coming in at £22.50 in the whites. In the reds, Vacheron's Sancerre Rouge 1999 is fairly priced at £11.50 and Ridge Lytton Springs Zinfandel 2000 is 4-star quality at £18.50. For a 5-star quality splash, you could do worse than a half of Gevrey-Chambertin 1er Cru Les Cazetières 1999 from Armand Rousseau at £42. Dessert wines have a good mix of bottles, halves and 50cl sizes from 5 different countries but regional France dominates. Jurançon VT Symphonie de Novembre 2001 from Domaine Cauhapé at £38.50 the bottle, £19.50 the half and £4.50 the glass stands out for value, whilst Banyuls 2000 from Domaine La Tour Vieille, seems only to be available by the glass (£4.75). From Australia there is a half of De Bortoli's Noble One 2000, but it's a bit pricey at £29.50 and from Hungary, the Tokay Furmint Noble Late Harvest 2000 from Oremus at £19.50 the half (£4.50 a glass), is probably better drinking value than the Tokaji Aszu 5 Puttonyos 1995 at £37.50 for 50cl. As the restaurant states on the introduction to the list, they are working hard on improving it – they have come a long way so far, and if it keeps going this way, it won't be long before it reaches the top 10 in the country.

Neville's Best Buy: 1997 **Jade Mountain** Côtes du Soleil at £18.50

Score: *Quality* 83.94   *Value* 30.65   *Impression* 19.00   *Total* **133.59**

Ranking: *Quality* 22   *Value* 32   *Impression* 43 =   *Overall* **20th**

Recommendations:
NB: 1999 **Gérard Chavy** Puligny-Montrachet 1er Cru Les Clavoillons at £49
DM: 2001 **Niero Pinchon** Condrieu Les Ravines at £38
PW: 2002 **Frédéric Esmonin** Gevrey-Chambertin Clos Prieur at £32.50

Find out more about wine and wine producers at *www.winebehindthelabel.com*

The South East

108

36th

36 ON THE QUAY

47 South Street Emsworth Hampshire PO10 7EG

01243 375592

This restaurant is a handy stop off before taking the ferry from Portsmouth over to Northern France, but the list is closer to something you would find in London or Paris, in terms of both range and price. There are over 200 wines on the list, with around 65% being of high quality. However, less than 10% of the quality wines listed met our price criteria – otherwise this list would have had a much higher rating – but there are still some goodies to be had at all prices. One of the saving graces of the list is the high proportion of quality wines offered in half-bottles, although the same cannot be said for wines by the glass. Nevertheless, this is an impressive list, despite the absence of any tasting notes except for the House wines, so we expect you will have to ask the front-of-house staff for advice.

At the front of the list is an End of Bin page. Don't expect any bargains here (a half-bottle of Les Forts de Latour 1995 was listed at £100), but you never know. The Recommended wines are 4 whites and 5 reds, most of which are available by the glass and some by the half-bottle, the only 3-star quality wine offered being the **Cape Mentelle Semillon/Sauvignon Blanc 2003** from Margaret River, Western Australia at £6.75 for 175ml or £26.75 the bottle. Strangely, for a restaurant of this quality, there appears to be no Champagne offered by the glass. The Champagne section itself follows with some pretty impressive names at pretty impressive prices – if you are going for broke, Taittinger Comtes de Champagne Blanc de Blancs 1995 is super-5 star quality at £145. A short list of Alsace whites follows, with Trimbach's Cuvée Frédéric-Emile 2000 looking best value at £45. There are some good quality clarets and certainly a half-bottle of Pavillon Rouge de Château Margaux 1995 at £56 (£110 the bottle) is infinitely better value than the bin-ended half of Les Forts de Latour of the same vintage mentioned above. In white Burgundies, Jean-Noël Gagnard's Chassagne-Montrachet 1er Cru Les Caillerets 1999 at £120 (£62.50 the half-bottle) is a 5-star wine and better value than the super-5 star Chevalier-Montrachet Les Demoiselles from Louis Jadot in the same vintage at £295. Red Burgundies has the 3-star Morgon 2003 from Jean Descombes in at £29.50 and better value than the wines from the Côte d'Or. There is better value drinking from the Rhône Valley as usual, with the super 5-star Hermitage La Chapelle 1996 from Paul Jaboulet Aîné coming in at £98. In Provence, **Château de Pibarnon 2000 Bandol** is good 4-star value at £38 and further afield Alain Brumont's **Château Bouscassé Vieilles Vignes 1993** is also good value at £35.

Away from France, the Italian section has Antinori's Castello della Sala Chardonnay 2002 from Umbria at £29.50 which is a good wine but shouldn't be mistaken for the premium Chardonnay-based Cervaro della Sala. There is little else of real value. Australian whites have Petaluma Chardonnay Piccadilly Valley 2000 as good 4-star value at £39, whilst Penfolds 4-star Yattarna Chardonnay 1998 is decidedly not at

£98. The North American section has as its best value wine the Newton Special Cuvée Unfiltered Chardonnay 2001 at £39, whilst Havens 1998 Carneros Syrah is also worth drinking at £39. There is a page of Rare American Finds, but only 2 out of the 12 wines are listed at under £100, although they are of undoubted quality. Australian reds are pretty upmarket, too, with three vintages of Penfold's Grange varying between £175 and £250 a bottle. Wynn's John Riddoch Reserve Cabernet Sauvignon 1994 is a 5-star quality wine at £65. There's not a lot of value in the Cloudy Bay-dominated listings in the New Zealand section, but South Africa has **Rustenberg Peter Barlow Cabernet Sauvignon Reserve 1999** at £49. Sweet wines from France are pretty stiffly priced and in the rest of the world section a half-bottle of Noble One 1997 from De Bortoli in Australia at £35 is about as good as one can get here.

Neville's Best Buy: 2000 **Château de Pibarnon** Bandol at £38

Score: *Quality* 93.90   *Value* 8.51   *Impression* 15.00   *Total* **117.41**

Ranking: *Quality* 13   *Value* 85   *Impression* 75 =   *Overall* **36th**

Recommendations:
NB: 1993 **Château Bouscassé** Madiran Vieilles Vignes at £35
DM: 1999 **Rustenberg** Peter Barlow Cabernet Sauvignon Reserve at £49
PW: 2003 **Cape Mentelle** Semillon/Sauvignon Blanc at £26.75

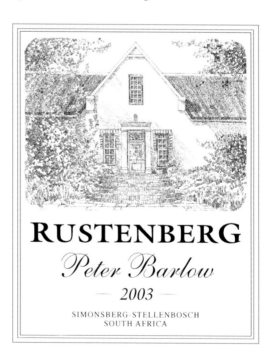

RUSTENBERG
Peter Barlow
— 2003 —
SIMONSBERG-STELLENBOSCH
SOUTH AFRICA

Find out more about wine and wine producers at *www.winebehindthelabel.com*

29th

THE GRANGE HOTEL, BRAMPTON

115 High Street Brampton Cambridgeshire PE28 4RA
01480 459516

ick Steiger's wine list for his Grange Hotel in deepest Cambridgeshire is rather short (113 bins) in comparison with other lists that we have been considering and maybe there's not quite the overall quality that we have seen elsewhere, but there are enough good wines on the list to make it a thoroughly enjoyable dining experience. Where the list scores heavily, however, is in the gentleness of the prices, with most of his 4- and 5-star wines coming in at under £50 and most of his 3-star wines coming in at under £30. There is a reasonable proportion of half-bottles and a more than reasonable proportion of wines by the glass, although none of the wines available by the glass reach 3-star standard. Apart from Champagnes and sparkling wines and dessert wines, the list is set out by style and grape variety with an introductory heading to each section and useful tasting notes for some of the wines.

The small Champagne section has only non-vintage Champagnes, of which the Laurent Perrier Rosé at £40 looks to be the best value for the quality. 'Chardonnay and Chardonnay blends' has the rare Meursault Meix Chavaux 1998, 4-star quality from Comte Armand, at £38 and 3-star Chablis 1er Cru Lechet 2000 from Bernard Defaix at £28, whilst in the 'Sauvignon Blanc and other dry whites' section, the white Graves Clos Floridène 2000 from Denis Dubourdieu at £22 is also serious wine for the money. Steiger is obviously a fan of the Alsace varietals, from whatever part of the world – **Leeuwin Estate Art Series Riesling 2002** from Western Australia is a giveaway at £18.75, and the **Zind-Humbrecht Tokay-Pinot Gris Clos Windsbuhl 1998** is 5-star quality at only £38.

'Rosés and light reds' has Juliénas Cuvée Prestige from Michel Tête at £22, whilst the more serious 'Cabernet Sauvignon and Merlot' section has the Cabernet/Merlot 2000 blend from C J Pask in New Zealand at only £18 and the 4-star Leeuwin Estate Art Series Cabernet Sauvignon 1999 well priced at £38. There is good value Pinot Noir from the 2001 Fromm Estate's La Strada vineyard at £24 and the 'Syrah, Malbec, Tempranillo, Zinfandel and everything else tasty' section has Alain Graillot's 2002 Crozes-Hermitage at only £22 as well as Château de Pibarnon Bandol 2000 and **Château Montus Cuvée Prestige 1995** from Alain Brumont in Gascony, both 4-star wines and both at £32. Dessert wines include Willi Opitz's Goldackerl Beerenauslese 2003 at £19 the half-bottle – remarkably priced since we have seen this wine at nearly £70 on another list.

The half-bottle list at the end has some quality wines such as Pouilly-Fumé Cuvée des Boisfleury 2003 from Domaine Cailbourdin in the Loire valley at £11 in the whites and Gevrey-Chambertin 2000 from Humbert Frères at £12 and **Hollick Cabernet Sauvignon/Merlot 2001** from Coonawarra, South Australia at £12.25 in the reds. This is a list that has not gone for the top, but is peppered with quality wines at very low prices.

Neville's Best Buy: **Leeuwin Estate** Art Series Riesling 2002 from Western Australia at £18.75

Score: *Quality* 33.55   *Value* 76.98   *Impression* 14.00   *Total* **124.53**

Ranking: *Quality* 86   *Value* 6   *Impression* 81 =   *Overall* **29th**

Recommendations:
NB: 1998 **Zind-Humbrecht** Tokay-Pinot Gris Clos Windsbuhl at £38
DM: 1995 **Château Montus** Madiran Cuvée Prestige at £32
PW: 2001 **Hollick** Coonawarra Cabernet Sauvignon/Merlot (half-bottle) at £12.25

2004

CLOS FLORIDENE

GRAVES

DENIS & FLORENCE DUBOURDIEU

MIS EN BOUTEILLE A LA PROPRIÉTE

40th

MORSTON HALL

Morston Norfolk NR25 7AA
01263 741041

A curious list, this: there are some c r a c k i n g bargains and yet some other wines could be a lot cheaper. It's not that long a list by Top 100 standards, just over 150 bins, but around half are of 3-star quality or more. Of these, around 15% meet our price criteria. The list starts off with Champagnes and then sparkling wines and then is arranged by grape varietals, sub-divided by country, which is quite helpful, as are the useful tasting notes for each wine. At the end of the list there are the pages for half-bottles and wines by the glass, which are reasonable in number but a bit short on quality.

There are no entry-level bargains in the Champagne page, but the super 5-star Taittinger Comtes de Champagne Blanc de Blancs 1995 is listed at £100, which is a lot cheaper than the similarly rated Louis Roederer Cristal 1997 at £265. In the French part of the Chardonnay section Chablis 1er Cru les Vaudevey 2002 from Domaine Laroche at £27 and Meursault Les Tillets 2002 from Patrick Javillier at £50 have the best price/quality ratio, while in Australia the Metier Schoolhouse Vineyard Chardonnay 1999 from the Yarra Valley is also good value at £24. The Beringer Private Reserve Chardonnay 2000 is extremely well priced for a Californian 4-star wine at £40. The Sauvignon Blanc section has Henri Pellé's Menetou-Salon Clos du Blanchais 2003 at £23, and from New Zealand, Hunter's Oaked Winemakers Selection 2002 at £26. In Rieslings Trimbach's Cuvée Frédéric-Emile 1997 offers 4-star quality at £45. Of 4 Semillons listed, all reach the quality criteria, with 2 fine Australians, Meerea Park Epoch 2001 at £18 and Tyrrells Winemaker Vat 1 1997 at £39. In the Chenin Blanc section, the 5-star **Clos de la Coulée de Serrant Savennières Coulée de Serrant 1999** is in at £55. 'Other white grapes' sports 2 good value wines – the Lirac Cuvée de la Reine des Bois 2002 from Domaine de la Mordorée in the Rhône Valley at £20 and Meerea Park's Viognier 2003 at £23 from the Hunter Valley in New South Wales.

The reds kick off with a 'Cabernet Sauvignon, Cabernet Franc and Merlot' section to cover all the Bordeaux blends and the meritage wines from around the world. Château Talbot 1997 looks well priced at £50 and **Château Le Tertre-Rôteboeuf 1986** may well be worth a punt at £117. In Italy, Sassicaia 1990 looks overpriced at £225 and the North American Cabernets also disappoint. There is better value in Australia, where **Plantagenet Cabernet Sauvignon 2001** at £22 and Cape Mentelle Cabernet Sauvignon/Merlot 2001 at £35 once again prove that Western Australian wines have some of the best quality/price ratio wines in the world. There is 4-star value in the South African section, with the Peter Barlow Cabernet Sauvignon 1999 from Rustenberg at £37 and Kanonkop's Paul Sauer 2001 at £44. There are some good quality wines in the Pinot Noir section, but nothing that stands out for value. Syrah fans fare better – Domaine de la Mordorée's red Lirac 2002 is well priced at £20, although their Châteauneuf-du-Pape Reine des Bois 1999 at £90 is decidedly not. The **Gigondas Prestige des Hautes Garrigues 2000** from Domaine Santa Duc is good 4-star value at £43. The Australian wines in this section do not match the value seen in other sections, but you can always try a bottle of Penfolds Grange 1983 if you have £365 to splash out. In the 'Other red grapes' section, La Rioja Alta Gran Reserva 904 1994 at £44 and Seghesio's 1999 Zinfandel at £28 stand out for 4- and 3-star quality and value respectively. The dessert wine section has the interesting red Mas Amiel Maury 2001 at £15 for a half-bottle and another red, the 5-star Amarone della Valpollicella Classico 1998 from Allegrini, at £63 for a full bottle, but whether either of them is sweet enough for English desserts is debatable. The only Sauternes on the list is a half bottle of Château d'Yquem 1998 at £150. Among 17 half-bottles listed, the aforementioned Seghesio Zinfandel is the best value at £15, while of the 17 wines by the glass, the Meerea Park Semillon 2001 is good value at £4.

Neville's Best Buy: 1999 **Clos de la Coulée de Serrant** Savennières Coulée de Serrant at £55

Score: *Quality* 54.12   *Value* 30.95   *Impression* 27.00   *Total* **112.07**

Ranking: *Quality* 57   *Value* 31   *Impression* 8   =   *Overall* **40th**

Recommendations:
NB: 1986 **Château Le Tertre-Rôteboeuf** Saint-Émilion Grand Cru at £117
DM: 2000 **Dom. Santa Duc** Gigondas Prestige des Hautes Garrigues at £43
PW: 2001 **Plantagenet** Cabernet Sauvignon at £22

Find out more about wine and wine producers at *www.winebehindthelabel.com*

15th

THE OLD BRIDGE AT HUNTINGDON

1 High Street Huntingdon Cambridgeshire PE29 3TQ
01480 424300

This is a mature list of around 300 different wines expertly put together over the years by John Hoskins, MW. It has much to be desired – a good selection of first class wines, plenty of choice at all prices, a goodly number of half bottles and a price/quality ratio on most of the wines that should be an example to others. Mind you, John's buying power probably has something to do with it, so it is perhaps not quite as philanthropic as it might first appear. Nevertheless, this is a wine list that brings joy to the beholder and makes a compelling reason to set out on the A1 for Huntingdon.

The list kicks off with an impressive selection of wines by the glass, which cleverly enable both the adventurous to experiment to good effect and the apprehensive to feel at home with some familiar names. A selection of sherries from the driest to the sweetest is an intriguing section – full marks for trying to jazz up this normally rather dull tipple. Next, a dozen or so sparkling wines and Champagnes of all descriptions (NV, rosé, vintage and premium vintage) at the gentlest of prices emphasise John's astute buying prowess.

There is a long list of both white and red wines priced under £20, organised into headings between lightest and heaviest, which are easy on the pocket and could be chosen with confidence, but the serious drinker will find much more satisfaction in the 'Top class' sections, where the prices rise from £20 to £60-plus. These lists are more or less arranged in a combination of varietals and style, which can be a little confusing, so it's best to read the whole list before you make a decision – they won't mind if you take your time – in fact it may be better to order your wine before your food! Any restaurant that offers you larger glasses for the best wines would be happy to see a customer who takes a serious amount of time in making his or her wine choices. White wines that stand out for choice include an Achleiten Smaragd Riesling from Prager in Austria at £33, Condrieu Coteaux de Chéry from André Perret at £39, Chardonnay Sanford & Benedict Vineyard from Au Bon Climat at £19 (don't faint – this is a half-bottle!) and1998 **Chablis Grand Cru Les Clos** from René & Vincent Dauvissat – a super 5-star wine at only £65 (and fine despite the vintage). 'Top class reds' include Alion at £45, Pin from La Spinetta at £55, Clos de Vougeot 1991 from René Engel at £65, Columella Syrah from Eben Sadie in South Africa at £39.50, Ben Nacido Syrah from Qupé at £30, 1997 **Grange des Pères VDP Hérault** at £48 (described as 'expensive but extraordinary' – how right that is),1998 **Viader Estate** (a Bordeaux blend from the Napa Valley) at £58 (£29.50 for a half-bottle of 1997, too) and Domaine de Chevalier 1990 at £59.

The 18-strong selection of pudding wines boasts 2 super 5-star wines – Ch Rieussec in the pretty fine 1989 vintage at £75 and half-bottles of Alois Kracher's Grande Cuvée No. 7 Trockenbeerenauslese 1996 at £40. Two pages of 'exceptional and rare

East Anglia

bottles' complete the list with some pretty impressive wines. Included therein is what must be the bargain of the list: **Kistler Sonoma Coast Chardonnay 1998** – a snip at £55, around a third of the price you would see it in some top London restaurants. Also featured are an impressive range of Coche-Dury Meursaults from 1990 to 1994, priced between £110 and £195, a 1976 (great vintage) Gewurztraminer SGN from Hugel at £75, Ridge Montebello 1995 at £95 or £50 for the half, Guigal's Côte-Rôtie of both La Landonne and La Mouline in the 1985 vintage at £295 (a fair whack less than you would have to pay for them at auction now), Château Palmer 1989 at £145 and Château Ducru-Beaucaillou 1985 at an impressive £98.

This is a grand list – enough to cater for all kinds of pockets and palates, with some very, very serious offerings. If there is to be any criticism, the choice appears to be a bit lightweight in the best of wines from California (particularly reds) and Italy, but that's really nit-picking.

Neville's Best Buy: 1998 **Kistler** Sonoma Coast Chardonnay at £55

Score: *Quality* 78.60 *Value* 38.03 *Impression* 25.00 *Total* **141.63**

Ranking: *Quality* 25 *Value* 27 *Impression* 13 = *Overall* **15th**

Recommendations:
NB: 1997 **Grange des Pères** VDP Hérault at £48
DM: 1997 **Viader** Estate (half-bottle) at £29.50
PW: 1998 **René & Vincent Dauvissat** Chablis Grand Cru Les Clos at £65

Find out more about wine and wine producers at *www.winebehindthelabel.com*

East Anglia

26th

THE OLD FIRE ENGINE HOUSE

25 St Mary's Street Ely Cambridgeshire CB7 4ER
01353 662582

This is one of those establishments that have been under the same ownership for a number of years, giving the proprietor, Michael Jarman, time to develop and fine-tune his list. There are tasting notes on all but the most upmarket of wines and while some of these naturally reach stratospheric prices, there is plenty of good value elsewhere on the list. Indeed, this is one of those lists where you can drink extraordinarily well at very reasonable prices.

The list is conventionally arranged with the opening page of wines by the glass unfortunately pandering to the lowest-common-denominator crowd. Still, there are only half a dozen or so, so you can quickly move on to better things. From a small selection of half-bottles with a 1999 Gevrey-Chambertin from Rossignol-Trapet at £19 looks good value. German and Alsace wines are then pretty much lumped together, with a Rüdesheimer Berg Rottland Riesling Spätlese 1995 from Schloss Schönborn outstandingly priced at £18.80. A short list of red clarets follows, with a note at the bottom of the page stating that 'for fine clarets, please refer to the list of Bin Ends at the back'. Well, the regular list looks pretty fine to us, with the 1997 Clos du Marquis (second wine of Château Léoville-las-Cases) coming in at a very reasonable £30. White Burgundies follow with a toss up as to whether the Chablis Grand Cru Vaudésir 1996 from William Fèvre at £35 is a better bet than the **Puligny-Montrachet 1er Cru Les Folatières 2000** from Gérard Chavy at £42. Depends on how oaky you like your wine. The regular red Burgundy choices do not match the whites, but in both sections we are promised some more fine Burgundies at the end of the list. The Rhône section has **Château de Beaucastel 1996** at a mere £35, but we wonder whether it had lasted the course, being from a rather lightweight vintage. Should you spend double on the blockbusting 1989? Probably, if you have an aversion to risk. A small selection of sparkling wines before the big guns at the end of the list has Pol Roger Reserve Brut White Capsule at £35. After France, the rest of the world doesn't get much of a look in, although **Kumeu River Chardonnay 2000** at £24 looks a real snip as New Zealand's one and only entry.

The supplementary list of really smart wines has some very reasonable prices. Léoville-las-Cases 1982 at £190 is hard to beat, and Pichon Lalande 1983 at £75, Latour 1985 at £120 and Palmer 1986 at £70 are prices one may never see again in subsequent vintages of the same quality, even at this establishment. Burgundies do not fare quite so well, but Chablis Montée de Tonnerre 2000 from Billaud-Simon at £28 is at a very good price. You can continue to pick your way through this list with gems like the **René Rostaing Côte-Rôtie 1995** at £35, Joseph Perrier's vintage 1990 Champagne (disgorged in 2003) at £70 and Ornellaia and Sassicaia 1994 at £50 and £70 respectively (not the best vintage, but not a disaster, so certainly worth a punt). Some good ports round off the list.

Neville's Best Buy: 2000 **Kumeu River** Chardonnay at £24

Score: *Quality* 70.53   *Value* 35.68   *Impression* 22.00   *Total* **128.21**

Ranking: *Quality* 37   *Value* 28   *Impression* 21 =   *Overall* **26th**

Recommendations:
NB: 1995 **René Rostaing** Côte-Rôtie at £35
DM: 1996 **Château de Beaucastel** Châteauneuf-du-Pape at £35
PW: 2000 **Gérard Chavy et Fils** Puligny-Montrachet 1er Cru Les Folatières at £42

Find out more about wine and wine producers at *www.winebehindthelabel.com*

12th

SYCAMORE HOUSE

1 Church Street Little Shelford Cambridgeshire CB2 5HG
01223 843396

This is the shortest wine list we have had to consider in our quest for the Top 100, but certainly one of the most agreeable. Why? Well the prices are unbelievable. Nearly half the wines on the list cost £20 or less, and everything is under £30 – and 21 of the 57 wines listed are wines of 3-star ranking and above. **Ridge Geyserville Zinfandel 2001** is 5-star quality at £29.50, while among 4-star bottles there is Hamilton Russell Pinot Noir 2002 from South Africa at £28 and New Zealand's Isabel Sauvignon Blanc 2004 at an incredible £19.50

In France, Champagne **Veuve Clicquot NV** is £29.50, Sancerre 2003 from Vacheron £19.95, Pouilly-Fumé Château de Tracy 2001 £19.50, Santenay Beauregard 1er Cru 2002 from Domaine Belland £23.50 and 2000 Châteauneuf-du-Pape from Domaine La Roquette £23 – all outstanding value for money.

The New World is not forgotten with two excellent value Chardonnays from Australia – Eileen Hardy 2001 at £20 and Leeuwin Estate Prelude 2001 at £21 – and two good Pinot Noirs from New Zealand: Quartz Reef 2002 at £24.50 and the **Fromm Clayvin Vineyard 2001** at £23.50. There is also the Veritas Heinrich Shiraz/Grenache/Mourvèdre 2002 from the Barossa Valley at an astonishing £16.50. Most expensive of the 11 half-bottles on the list is the **Alois Kracher 2002 Beerenauslese** at £14.95. There are plenty of good, 2-star choices amongst the rest.

All in all, this is a great place for inexpensive imbibing and you should beat a path to Michael Sharpe's door – it's just a shame Sycamore House has no accommodation to crawl upstairs to after such delights.

Neville's Best Buy: 2001 **Ridge** Geyserville Zinfandel at £29.50

Score: *Quality* 36.12 *Value* 105.83 *Impression* 8.00 *Total* **149.95**

Ranking: *Quality* 83 *Value* 1 *Impression* 97 = *Overall* **12th**

Recommendations:
NB: 2002 **Alois Kracher** Beerenauslese (half-bottle) at £14.95
DM: **Veuve Clicquot** Brut NV at £29.50
PW: 2001 **Fromm** Pinot Noir Clayvin Vineyard at £23.50

Find out more about wine and wine producers at *www.winebehindthelabel.com*

31st

THE WILDEBEEST ARMS

82-86 Norwich Road Stoke Holy Cross Norfolk NR14 8QJ
01508 492497

One might be forgiven for imagining that the wine list at this little East Anglian pub would have a propensity for South African wines, but instead we find a balance of fine quality wines from around the world, with South Africa playing a normal part of the total. This is a shortish list – 127 bins in all – with about a quarter of the wines being of 3-star quality or above, but of that quarter nearly all of them meet our value criteria, so you are going to be able to drink some pretty good stuff here at very reasonable prices. There are useful tasting notes on all the wines, so you should be able to tackle this list with confidence.

The House selection has a reasonable number of wines – 13, all available by the bottle at £12.95 or for £3.25 a 175ml glass –but no real excitement. Better to dive into the list proper and for not a lot more money, you could be drinking something of real quality. In the white wine section, for an extra £2, you can drink the Viognier and Chardonnay blend Cuvée Classique 2003 from Domaine de l'Hortus in Pic Saint-Loup in the Languedoc at £14.95 and for another £2, you can graduate to the Vouvray Cuvée de Silex 2003 – an excellent vintage in the Loire Valley – from Domaine des Aubuisières at £16.95. The white Burgundy section has Michel Forest's Pouilly-Fuissé 2002 and Domaine Billaud-Simon's Chablis 1er Cru Vaillons 2001, both excellent value at £22.95. The Italian and Spanish white wines don't really turn us on, although there are some 2-star wines at very reasonable prices – a better bet is to drink the 4-star **2002 Howard Park Chardonnay** in Western Australia at £22.95 again. The rest of the whites do not quite match up to the quality criteria, but in the reds, there are two well priced wines from the Southern Rhône – Les Terrasses 2001 from Château Pesquié in the Côtes du Ventoux at £17.50, and the Gigondas Les Garancières 2001 from Domaine Santa Duc at £19.95. In addition, Alain Brumont's Château Montus Madiran 2000 is good value at £23.95. The rest of the reds also do not quite match up to our quality criteria until you get to the 'Fine wine selection' at the end of the list, with the possible exception of a 2002 Shiraz from Mischa Estate in South Africa at £17.95.

Quality, does however, begin to kick in with the Champagne section, where Dom Pérignon 1996 is priced at a very reasonable £89.95, as is Krug NV at £94.95. In the range of dessert wines, Maculan's Dindarello 2003 is the best of the bunch at £19.95 for a half-bottle. The 'Fine wine selection' has some terrific wines at terrific prices, particularly in the whites. **Wakefield St Andrews Clare Valley Chardonnay 1998** is only £24.95, **Condrieu Les Terrasses du Palat 2001** from François Villard is only £31.95 and Patrick Javillier's **Meursault Les Tillets 2001** is only £35.95. In the reds, again Châteauneuf-du-Pape Les Quartz 2000 from Clos du Caillou is good value at £47.95. Finally, a botrytised Chardonnay 1995 from Helmut Lang in Austria is 4-star value at £29.95 for a 50cl bottle.

Neville's Best Buy: 2002 **Howard Park** Chardonnay at £22.95

Score: *Quality* 20.94   *Value* 82.45   *Impression* 20.00   *Total* **123.39**

Ranking: *Quality* 97   *Value* 5   *Impression* 34 =   *Overall* **31st**

Recommendations:
NB: 1998 **Wakefield** Chardonnay St. Andrews Clare Valley at £24.95
DM: 2001 **François Villard** Condrieu Les Terrasses du Palat at £31.95
PW: 2001 **Patrick Javillier** Meursault Les Tillets at £35.95

Find out more about wine and wine producers at *www.winebehindthelabel.com*

78th

FIRENZE

9 Station Street Kibworth Beauchamp Leicestershire LE8 0LN
0116 279 6260

This is a no-compromise Italian wine list from a no-compromise Italian restaurant. It is fairly short (just over 100 wines) with just under a quarter being of 3-star quality or above, and of those, around a third meet our value criteria. They are not into half-bottles here, but there are 16 wines by the glass, if you are keen to experiment. Wines are just listed in price order, which probably doesn't matter since they are all Italian, but it might have been more helpful for them to have been split into regions. There are useful tasting notes for each wine as well

Sparkling wines include wines from the excellent Bellavista winery in Lombardy but the prices are just a bit over the limit for our price/quality ratio. In the white wine section there is good value in the Veneto with the Soave Classico Superiore Pressoni 2003 from Cantina Castello at £25.10 and in the Marche with the Verdicchio dei Castelli di Jesi Classico 1998 from Villa Bucci at £29.60. For 4-star value go with Silvio Jermann's (Vinnaioli Jermann) classic **Vintage Tunina 2001** at £39.50.

Red wines offer excellent value in the **Aglianico del Vulture Riserva Caselle 1998** from D'Angelo in Basilicata at £21.75 and the Cerasuolo di Vittoria 2002 from Planeta in Sicily at £22 is not far behind. The **Rocca di Montegrossi Chianti Classico 2001** at £28.20 (£7.40 a glass) is also value for money. Other 4- and 5-star wines on the list are the **Castello di Fonterutoli Chianti Classico 1999** from at £45.10, Barolo Vigna Cappella Santo Stefano 1997 from Giovanni Manzoni at £67.60 and Sassicaia 2000 at £130, although the Sassicaia is probably too young to drink at the moment. There is an interesting collection of sweet wines but some are not really sweet enough to take a full-blown dessert. Best to stick to the Moscatos, but you should probably seek advice.

Neville's Best Buy: **D'Angelo** Aglianico del Vulture Riserva Vigna Caselle 1998 from Basilicata at £21.75

Score: *Quality* 20.35 *Value* 46.76 *Impression* 15.00 *Total* **82.11**

Ranking: *Quality* 99 *Value* 11 *Impression* 75 = *Overall* **78th**

Recommendations:
NB: 2001 **Vinnaioli Jermann** Vintage Tunina at £39.50
DM: 1999 **Castello di Fonterutoli** Chianti Classico at £45.10
PW: 2001 **Rocca di Montegrossi** Chianti Classico at £28.20

Find out more about wine and wine producers at *www.winebehindthelabel.com*

47th

HAMBLETON HALL

Upper Hambleton Rutland LE15 8TH

01572 756991

Tim and Stefa Hart's upmarket pile (*Relais and Châteaux* of course) in rural Rutland has been in business for a few years now and the wine list, while constantly evolving, still has that air of grandeur, even if now there is a lot more choice from non-traditional areas. Bordeaux, Burgundy, Champagne and port still dominate – but there are some serious red wine choices from California, in particular, and from Italy and the Rhône Valley.

The list kicks off with a page of ever changing popular wines from the lower reaches of the list, but perhaps one third of them will have 3-, 4- or even 5-star ratings. A page of clarets follows, ranging from 1999 Du Pavillon Canon-Fronsac at £23 to 1982 Cheval Blanc at £645. There's plenty of choice in red Burgundies, too, starting with 2002 Bourgogne Pinot Noir from Jean Grivot at £26 and going right up to 1997 La Tâche at £691. USA reds get a good showing, with Domaine Drouhin Pinot Noir 1999 at £59 and **Ridge Montebello Cabernet Sauvignon 1995** (super 5 stars) at £147 looking infinitely better value than some of their Burgundian and Bordelais counterparts. Some 14 different vintage ports make impressive reading, with Warre's 1983 at £63 looking the best bet. Rhône reds lean towards the south, with older vintages of de Fonsalette and Beaucastel looking a bit pricey. Other wines from the South of France look better value, with La Migoua and La Tourtine 1995 Bandol from Domaine Tempier at £55 and **2001 Le Soula VdP Côteaux des Fenouillèdes** from

Gérard Gauby in the Roussillon at £43. Italy shows innovative choices with Santadi's Terre Brune 1998 outstanding at £55. Spain is not as interesting, but Les Terrasses 2001 from Alvaro Palacios in Priorat at £40 is reasonable enough for the quality. Apart from the USA, other New World red wines from South Africa, Australia, New Zealand, Chile and Argentina are reasonably represented with the **Leconfield Coonawarra Cabernet Sauvignon 1998** at £29 being probably the best value wine on the list.

In whites, Burgundies run the gamut from the entry-level Chablis 2002 from Domaine Vrignaud at £27, right up to 1990 Bienvenues-Bâtard-Montrachet from Ramonet at £300, but the best value would seem to be the 1999 Chablis Grand Cru (presumably Les Clos, but not written) from Gérard Duplessis at £61. The list of Champagnes is a big hitter, with plenty of choice running from halves to Jeroboams. A Jeroboam of Billecart-Salmon NV at £196 looks infinitely better value than a half-bottle of Krug NV at £75. The choice of Californian whites doesn't match the reds – out of 8 wines, 4 are from Au Bon Climat, of which the 1998 Le Bouge d'à Côté Chardonnay at £52 gets the quality/value vote. Australian and New Zealand whites do well, with Giaconda Chardonnay 2000 at £86 (only £11 more than at The Old Bridge at Huntingdon; qv), and one of New Zealand's best Sauvignons, **Isabel Estate Sauvignon Blanc 2004**, on offer at £32 – reasonably priced in the context of the list overall. Other French whites, apart from Burgundy, are not fantastically represented, but François Villard's Condrieu Côteaux de Poncin 2001 at £64 is 5-star quality. Italy's whites definitely need upgrading, while in Spain, the 2 Albariños from Pazo de Señoras look interesting at £30 for the basic and £50 for the Seleccion de Añada. Germany and Alsace are lumped together on one page with nothing really outstanding in either section.

There are nearly 50 pudding wines, with a good spread between Bordeaux, Loire, South-West France, Hungary and Austria, and with Italy, Spain, South Africa and California contributing one wine apiece and Australia a couple. The 1997 Bonnezeaux from Château de Fesles at £45 for 50cl looks to be a good bet from a superb Loire vintage. There is a reasonable spread of both half-bottles and magnums, with a magnum of Duplessis' Chablis Grand Cru Les Clos 1996 at £95 probably being even better value than the 1999 bottle previously mentioned. This is a grand list, but prices are high, which has kept the overall score down. However, if one choses carefully, one can have a superb drinking experience.

Neville's Best Buy: **Leconfield** Coonawarra Cabernet Sauvignon 1998 at £29

Score: *Quality* 84.45   *Value* 12.33   *Impression* 14.00   *Total* **110.78**

Ranking: *Quality* 21   *Value* 74   *Impression* 81   =   *Overall* **47th**

Recommendations:
NB: 1995 **Ridge** Cabernet Sauvignon Montebello at £147
DM: 2001 **Le Soula** VdP Côteaux des Fenouillèdes at £43
PW: 2004 **Isabel Estate** Marlborough Sauvignon Blanc at £32

Find out more about wine and wine producers at *www.winebehindthelabel.com*

50th

HOTEL DU VIN, BIRMINGHAM

25 Church Street Birmingham B3 2NR
0121 200 0600

From one of the group of Hotels du Vin scattered around the country, this comprehensive list is a veritable tome of quality, but alas, the rating is badly hampered by the prices. There are 664 wines on the list, of which 394 are of 3-star quality or above, but of those 394, only 30 meet our price criteria. Of 13 still dry wines by the glass, only one, Stella Bella Margaret River Semillon/Sauvignon 2004, meets the quality criteria. There are many more quality wines in the half bottle choices – but the prices! The list is very comprehensive, but the absence of tasting notes makes it heavy going. Still, there are bargains to be had, and we hope we can help you to find them.

The list starts with two closely typed pages of Champagnes and sparkling wines. They are not listed in price order but in alphabetical order and it takes a bit of searching to find the entry-level Lenoble Blanc de Blancs Grand Cru NV HDV selection (we presume HDV means Hotel du Vin), but it is the best value Champagne on the list from this 3-star house at £34.50. At the other end of the scale the super 5-star Veuve Clicquot La Grande Dame 1995 catches the eye, not just because it is the last wine on this alphabetical list, but also because it is not unreasonably priced at £130. White Burgundies come next but there is nothing of 3-star quality under £30 and of the top wines Bonneau du Martray's Corton-Charlemagne 2000 is the best value, but even that is pretty steeply priced at £140. The 5-star Mas de Daumas Gassac Blanc 2002 is in the Languedoc whites section at £60, but there's better value to be found in the Roussillon section with Domaine des Chênes' Magdaleniens Côtes du Roussillon 2000 at £28. In Rhône Valley whites, the **Château Mas Neuf Costières de Nîmes 2002** is excellent value at £17.50, while the super-5 star white Hermitage 1996 from Jean-Louis Chave is not overpriced at £105. The impressive breadth of the list is emphasised by the inclusion of 3 white wines from the Jura and Savoie, with the **Domaine André & Michel Quénard's Chignin Bergeron 2002** the best value at £28. In the Loire, there is the excellently valued Savennières Clos de Coulaine 2001 from Claude Papin at only £28, whilst Alsace has Seppi Landmann's Vallée Noble Pinot Blanc 2001 at £25. There are white wines from Germany, Austria, Switzerland, England, India and Greece, but only the Austrian whites have any real class, with Emmerich Knoll's Dürnsteiner Smaragd Riesling 1999 delivering 5-star quality at a rather hefty £74.50. Italian whites don't really shine for price and quality, but there is far better value in Spain with Cal Pla's Porrera Priorat 2001 at £22. The price/quality ratio in the Californian whites is pretty poor, too, with Calera Chardonnay 1998 at £43 being as good as you will get. Kumeu River Chardonnay 2002 is 4-star quality in New Zealand at £48.50, but there's nothing to touch it in South Africa or South America. There's always value to be had in the Australian section and it arises here in the shape of the 4-star M3 Vineyard Chardonnay 2003 from Shaw and Smith at £38.

The Midlands

In reds, there is a surprisingly small selection of clarets, with little worth drinking under £100, but you could plump for Réserve de la Comtesse 2000 (the second wine of Château Pichon-Lalande) at £73, or go the extra mile for the reinvigorated Château Lascombes 2000 at £92, but it seems like infanticide to tackle either. In red Burgundies, the best bet would seem to be the super 5-star Gevrey-Chambertin 1er Cru Clos Saint-Jacques 1998 from Louis Jadot at £103, but if you want to save a few pennies, Henri Perrot-Minot's Morey-Saint-Denis En la Rue de Vergy has always been a soft and supple wine and his 2001 at £52 might be drinking already, but don't bank on it. A very impressive list of reds from the Northern Rhône makes choices difficult. At the entry level, Alain Graillot's Crozes-Hermitage 1999 at £37 is good but not particularly cheap – a better bargain would be to go to the top end and choose the super 5-star Hermitage la Chapelle from the excellent 1995 vintage at £102. Southern Rhône choices are almost as good, with 5 vintages of Domaine du Trévallon at prices between £68 and £78 (go for the 1998 at £74), whilst in Provence, Domaine Richeaume's Columelle 2001 is 4-star quality at £48. From South-West France, Domaine Rotier's Gaillac Renaissance 2001 is 3-star quality at £25, whilst in the Languedoc, Aurel from Domaine des Aurelles is 4-star quality at £47, and from Savoie, the savoury Mondeuse Vieilles Vignes 2002 from Quenard at £24.50 is also good value. Italy has some very big names at very big prices in both Piedmont and Tuscany, so it may be wiser to go for Patrizia Lamborghini's Sangiovese/Merlot blend from Umbria, **La Fiorita Lamborghini Campoleone** – 5-star quality in top vintages at £69.50. However, tucked among the Tuscan offerings, the Morellino di Scansano 2003 from Fattoria di Magliano is only £25. There is high quality in the Spanish red section with the 5-star Priorat Clos Mogador 2002 from René Barbier at £73 seemingly the best value on the page. Some very prestigious names appear in the California section, but some of the prices are outrageous, more often than not the fault of the producer. Here, it's probably best to stick with one of the new kids on the block, since they haven't yet learned to be too greedy: try the Brewer-Clifton Clos Pepe Pinot Noir 1999 from the Santa Rita Hills at a very reasonable £69 for the quality. In Oregon, the Columbia Winery Syrah 1999 at £24 is also very good value. The South African section has the fashionable 2002 Shiraz (with a little Viognier blended in) from Homtini at £33, while in New Zealand there is the fashionable Otago Pinot Noir from Mount Edward at £51. A large selection of Australian reds delivers excellent value with the 3-star **Chalkers Crossing Cabernet Sauvignon 2002** at £25, or the Filsell Old Vine Shiraz 2001 from Grant Burge at £26.50. Alternatively, if you feel that these two are a bit too downmarket for you, you can always have a go at the 3 vintages of Penfolds Grange on the list.

On a small list of half-bottles the best value is the Jurançon Sec Cuvée Marie 1999 from Charles Hours at £14. Curiously, of the 8 red halves listed, 4 are from California. A long list of dessert wines has both good and bad value and we were puzzled to see listed under this heading a 'Banyuls Dry'. Also we are a bit unsure about putting some Savennières under this section, although they may be sweet enough. Notwithstanding all this, the Maury MA 2001 from Mas Amiel at £33 and the Banyuls Muté Sur Grains, Mise Tardive 2002 from Mas Cornet at £36 are both excellent value 4-star quality wines. Other value dessert wines are the more-ish Moscato d'Asti Biancospina 2003 from La Spinetta at £24 and if you like a nice sticky end to your meal, a 50cl bottle of Malaga MR 2001 from Telmo Rodriguez would fit the bill at £19. There are ports and Madeiras to really finish you off, but nothing of any great age.

Neville's Best Buy: Costières de Nîmes 2002 from **Château Mas Neuf** at £17.50

Score: *Quality* 86.58   *Value* 8.00   *Impression* 15.00   *Total* **109.58**

Ranking: *Quality* 17   *Value* 87   *Impression* 75 =   *Overall* **50th**

Recommendations:
NB: 1998 **La Fiorita Lamborghini** Campoleone at £69.50
DM: 2002 **Dom. André & Michel Quénard** Chignin Bergeron at £28
PW: 2002 **Chalkers Crossing** Cabernet Sauvignon at £25

53rd

THE OLD VICARAGE

Ridgeway Moor Ridgeway Derbyshire S12 3XW
0114 247 5814

This is one of those lists where style takes precedence over geography – a useful tool, especially when there are no tasting notes for any of the wines. The proprietors here are also wine merchants and they have included wines that you cannot find anywhere else, giving you the chance to experiment. You can also find a number of top class wines in the 'Private reserve' section – at a price. Of course, that's easy enough, but finding wines that meet both our quality and price criteria is trickier. Nevertheless, there are some hidden gems here and we hope that this review will help you to find them. About 70% of the 350 wines on the list are of 3-star quality or above, but only 19 of them meet our price and quality criteria. On the plus side, there are a decent number of dry wines in half-bottles, although they are pretty steeply priced, and 24 'Cheap and cheerful' wines at the end of the list are all available by the glass.

The white wine section kicks off with 'Light, crisp and fresh' with Mulderbosch Sauvignon Blanc 2004 from South Africa at £24 and Henry Natter's Sancerre 2002 at £27. In the 'Aromatic, fruity' style, there is good 4-star value from Alsace with Ernest Burn's Gewürztraminer Grand Cru Goldert 2000 at £43 and Paul Blanck's Riesling Grand Cru Schlossberg 2001 at £41. There is also 4-star value in the 'Dry, fragrant, full-flavoured' style with the white Châteauneuf-du-Pape 2002 from Vieux-Télégraphe at £44. 'Rich, intense, powerful' whites are just that, with a host of top names from Burgundy dominating the page. In cases like this, you might just as well go for the very top and plump for the super 5-star Corton-Charlemagne in the excellent 1996 vintage from Bonneau du Martray at £130.

Red wines kick off with the 'Light and fruity' style. Here there is 3-star value in the Borthwick Estate Pinot Noir 2002 from New Zealand at £27 and the Lemelson Six Vineyards Pinot Noir 2002 from Oregon at £28. The 'Full-bodied, supple' section has C J Pask's Cabernet/Merlot/Malbec 2002 at £27 from New Zealand and Gigondas 2001 from Domaine Les Pallières at £30. There is also 4-star value in Domaine Tempier's Bandol La Tourtine 2000 at £40, but whether it is ready to drink or not is another matter. The style ratchets up a bit with 'Robust, intense, spicy' and there is little of exceptional value there. If we had to make choices we suppose it would have to be between the Tablas Creek Perrin Family Reserve Cuvée 1999 from Paso Robles in California at £56, or Château de Beaucastel Châteauneuf-du-Pape 1998 at £75. Whichever it is, the Perrins won't let you down! 'Rich, powerful' reds come next and deliver exceptional value in Mariano Garcia's very fine and structured **Viña San Román 2000** at £40 – one of the bargains of the list. Another Spanish goodie in this section is Dehesa la Granja 2000 at £26, from Alejandro Fernández of Pesquera fame. On to the 'Elegant, subtle, perfumed' style, which basically means mainly Pinot Noirs from around the world. It's a toss up between New World and Burgundy and we were surprised to see that the prices of the cult Pinot Noirs from Otago in New Zealand were almost as much as those from the more established vineyards in California. On that basis the choice is between the **Lynmar Quail Hill Estate Pinot Noir 2001** from the Russian River Valley at £39, or La Bauge au-dessus Pinot Noir 1994 from Au Bon Climat in Santa Barbara at £55. Ghislaine Barthod's Chambolle-Musigny 1er Cru Les Cras 1996 is 5-star quality over the 4 stars of the other two, but you will need to pay £75 for that. 'Fine, complex, well structured' follows next and seems to be a forerunner for the 'Classy Cabernet from around the world' section which follows, but it could well be worth looking at the super 5-star **Mondavi Napa Valley Cabernet Sauvignon Reserve 1992** at £76, which is as cheap as we have seen it anywhere. In the aforementioned 'Classy Cabernet' section there are lots of overpriced wines such as Opus One, Dominus and Almaviva, but the one to go for here is the super 5-star Ridge Monte Bello Cabernet Sauvignon 1995 at £110. The 'Private reserve' pages list some of the best wines in the world from France, Italy and Spain (but not California). They are all of mature drinking vintages and the choices really depend on the depth of your pocket. Looking at wine under £100 in this section, we would certainly plump for Cos d'Estournel 1983 at £95 in the clarets, **Vosne Romanée 1er Cru Les Brulées 1995** from René Engel at £75 in the Burgundies, Hermitage La Chapelle 1995 at £80 in the Rhône, and Taurasi 1998 from Feudi di San Gregorio in Italy at £50. We would have to cheat a bit for Spain, because the only wine under £100 is the Alenza 1995 from Alejandro Fernández at £90, but we would rather pay the extra to drink his Pesquera Janus of the same vintage at £135. Round that off with a bottle of the super 5-star Taittinger Comtes de Champagne 1995 at £100 and you could have a very happy evening, even if you are financially ruined.

The half-bottle list includes a remarkable selection of sherries from Emilio Lustau at £20. There is not much value in the other halves, however, although you could go for the Domaine Les Pallières Gigondas 2000 at £19. The dessert wine page bristles with quality at pretty high prices, but a full bottle of Château Rabaud-Promis 1996 at £70 is as good as you can get for a Sauternes from this very good vintage. Of the vintage ports, it's probably worth splashing out the extra for a bottle of Warre's from the legendary 1963 vintage at £155.

This is a very interesting list with an obvious eye for quality, and very well laid out. Whilst there are some obvious bargains among the higher priced wines, a few more adventurous purchases of good value wines from regional France, Italy and Spain could well see this list shooting up the table next year.

Neville's Best Buy: The super 5-star **Mondavi** Napa Valley Cabernet Sauvignon Reserve 1992 at £76

Score: *Quality* 74.63   *Value* 9.93   *Impression* 23.00   *Total* **107.56**

Ranking: *Quality* 29   *Value* 81   *Impression* 18   =   *Overall* **53rd**

Recommendations:
NB: 2000 **Viña San Román** at £40
DM: 2001 **Lynmar** Pinot Noir Quail Hill Estate at £39
PW: 1995 **René Engel** Vosne-Romanée 1er Cru Les Brulées at £75

Find out more about wine and wine producers at *www.winebehindthelabel.com*

21st

THE OPERA HOUSE LEICESTER

10 Guildhall Lane Leicester LE1 5FQ
0116 223 6666

This is a short list by our standards (104 bins), but there's plenty of fine quality here. Just under 50% of the list is of 3-star quality or above. Prices are not cheap, but are not over the top either, and some wines offer excellent quality for the price. The list is somewhat unusually divided in to 'Private cellar', Champagne, France, the rest of Europe and the rest of the world, but it is not long and there should be no confusion. There are useful tasting notes on all the wines including those in the half-bottle selection, which also holds some quality wines.

The list opens with the 'Private cellar, specially selected wines from the Opera House cellars', which does, indeed, include some very fine wines. But it is a down-to-earth collection, with no extravagant verticals of top clarets and Burgundies and no super-premium wines from California or Italy. (In fact, there is very little from California and Italy altogether.) There are many 4-star wines hovering around the £50 mark, but probably best value is the **Pavillon Rouge de Château Margaux 1999** at £55 – the second wine of Château Margaux, and quite capable of knocking a lot of other classed growth clarets into a cocked hat, even if this vintage is a little too young to drink just yet. The best value white in this section is the **Savennières Clos du Papillon 2001** from Domaine du Closel in the Loire Valley at £34.50. Champagnes have Roederer Brut Premier NV as their cheapest Grande Marque at £40 and Krug 1990 as their most expensive at £140. Both are reasonably priced. 'The French collection' lists some 8 whites and 10 reds from all parts of France, which presumably are not good enough to go into the 'Private cellar', but we might beg to differ with the **Tokay-Pinot Gris Goldert Grand Cru La Chapelle 1999** from Ernest Burn at £35, which is excellent 4-star value. Gigondas Cuvée Futé 2001 from Domaine de Font Sane in the Southern Rhône at £33.50 is also good value, but may be a little too young to drink. 'The best of the rest of Europe' can hardly be called that, but Prunotto's Barbaresco 1999 from Piedmont at £38 and Theo Haart's (Weingut Reinhold Haart) **Piesporter Domherr Riesling Spätlese 1999** at £27.50 represent good value. 'Classic grapes of the New World' has some good selections, but as one has found so often, the wines from Western Australia represent the best value and there is no exception here, with Vasse Felix Cabernet/Merlot 2001 at £27 and the 4-star Howard Park Riesling 2003 at £28 taking the honours.

'A small selection of half-bottles' has Châteauneuf-du-Pape Domaine du Vieux-Télégraphe 1998 at £27.50 and Chablis 1er Cru 2002 from Domaine des Marronniers at £21.75, but neither of them is particularly good value. A 3-star rating is achieved by just 1 of the 6 dry wines available by the glass – the Sancerre Domaine de Montigny 2002 from Henry Natter at £5 for a small glass and £6.50 for a large – but the sizes are not specified on the list. Dessert wines include the 4-star Château Rabaud-Promis at £27 (£6 the glass) but it is not clear as to whether this is for a full bottle or a half, nor are we sure of the size of the glass.

Neville's Best Buy: Tokay-Pinot Gris Goldert Grand Cru La Chapelle 1999 from **Ernest Burn** at £35

Score: *Quality* 74.33 *Value* 38.81 *Impression* 16.00 *Total* **129.14**

Ranking: *Quality* 30 *Value* 25 *Impression* 67 = *Overall* **21st**

Recommendations:
NB: 1999 **Château Margaux** Pavillon Rouge at £55
DM: 2001 **Domaine du Closel** Savennières Clos du Papillon 2001 at £34.50
PW: 1999 **Weingut Reinhold Haart** Piesporter Domherr Riesling Spätlese at £27.50

Find out more about wine and wine producers at *www.winebehindthelabel.com*

45th

THE CHESTER GROSVENOR – ARKLE RESTAURANT

Eastgate Chester Cheshire CH1 1LT
01244 324024

As one would expect from a property owned by the richest man in Britain, this is a very high quality list, and as one would also expect, prices are excruciatingly high. There are though a few value wines to be found among the 500-odd that make up the list and we hope that this little appraisal will point you in the right direction. Just under three-fifths of the wines listed are of 3-star quality or above, but only 10 of them meet our price/quality criteria. There are a fair number of half-bottles listed and almost one in two of these are quality wines and even those offered by the glass have quality amongst them.

Of these, the 3 Ruinart Champagnes are certainly fine, with the 5-star Dom Ruinart 1990 vintage at £16.50 for 175ml offering a foretaste of what is to come. Also by the glass is a good array of fortified wines, with Warre's 1970 Vintage Port at £17.50 the 100ml glass infinitely better value than the Yalumba 50-year-old Museum Tawny at £20. The list is then conventionally arranged by country and region and starts off with Champagne, where 'R' de Ruinart NV is the entry-level wine at £45. There is a dazzling display of top names, including 6 vintages of the Dom Pérignon Cuvée Oenothèque from the 1959 vintage at £1,500 a bottle to the 1990 at a mere £325. You might instead consider the super 5-star Taittinger Comtes de Champagne 1995 at a not terribly overpriced £140. There is nothing of value in Alsace or the Loire, but Didier Dagueneau's Pur Sang Pouilly-Fumé 2002 at £105 is 5-star quality even if it is not yet ready to drink. Château Tour des Gendres Cuvée des Conti 2001 is definitely a fine value white Bergerac at £20.50, while the Domaine les Aurelles Aurel 1997 from the Côteaux du Languedoc is 4-star value at £48. The red Lirac 2002 from Château Saint-Roche is excellent value at £26.50 in the surprisingly short Rhône Valley section. Of course, there are pages and pages of wines from Bordeaux, in all sizes, none of which offer value for the quality, but you might just try **Domaine de Chevalier,** still in its glory days in the fabulous 1982 vintage at £120. We were surprised, considering the name of the restaurant, to find only two vintages of Château Cheval Blanc listed – for choice we preferred the glorious 1949 vintage at £1,200 to the more mundane 1996 at £285. There are magnums, double magnums, Jeroboams and Imperials – in fact an Imperial (8 bottles) of Léoville-Barton 1983 at £1,000 is probably quite good value. White Burgundy has Louis Michel's 4-star Chablis 1er Cru Montée de Tonnerre 2001 at £48, but value, of course, is harder to find in the Côte d'Or, although Puligny-Montrachet 1er Cru Champs-Canet 1997 from Domaine Ramonet, is not bad value for the list at £75. In red Burgundies, there is a stunning collection of wines from the Domaine de la Romanée-Conti in several crus and in several vintages, from the entry-level Romanée-Saint-Vivant 1972 at £300 to the 1985 La Romanée-Conti at £5,000. Lesser mortals may have to be content with Clos de la Roche 1986 from Domaine Dujac at £75, but since the wines then weren't exactly blockbusters, it may be wise to enquire if the sommelier team think it is still drinking. The same would apply to some of the 1976s listed, it was a very good vintage and if the wines are still going strong, there are real bargains to be had. The page of red Burgundy magnums is not as exciting as the clarets, with too many wines in dodgy vintages such as 1992 and 1994, and some of the wines of the 1980s will also have to be carefully evaluated. A magnum of Roumier's muscular super 5-star Bonnes-Mares 1983 at £395 ought to have stood the course.

For the rest of the world, the Italian section has a few overpriced wines such as the 1988 Sassicaia at £400, but the real bargain of the whole list must be the **Teroldego Rotaliano 1998** from Elisabetta Foradori in Trentino at only £25. Another well priced wine is the 4-star Barolo Cerretta 1996 from Ettore Germano at £66. In Spain, Alejandro Fernández's Condado de Haza Crianza 2001 is value at £25.50 in the reds, whilst the Albariño 2002 from Pazo de Señoráns is just off the value cusp at £35. There is nothing exciting in the German, Swiss or English sections, but there is plenty in the North American section – at a price, of course. There is a large selection of practically every vintage of the overpriced Opus One, but serious students of Californian wines will note some relatively good value (as far as this list goes) in Delia Viader's 5-star 1995 Napa Valley Estate Red at £80 and, on a lesser note, John Kongsgaard's **Luna Vineyards 1998 Napa Valley Sangiovese** at £44. There's no great value in the wines listed from Oregon or from South America, but there is some value to be had in the Australian listings. First and foremost, the Katnook Odyssey Cabernet Sauvignon 1997 comes just under the frame at £49.50, whilst Charlie Melton's 2000 Barossa Valley Shiraz is as good as you will get here for £65. New Zealand has the 4-star Craighall Riesling 2002 from the Dry River Estate right on the button at £50, whilst in South Africa the Rustenberg Chardonnay 2002 is in at £30.50.

There is an interesting list of sweet wines, with 4 vintages of Château d'Yquem listed, ranging from the 1969 at £400 to the 1921 at £3,500. At the other end of the scale, the Muscat de Beaumes de Venise 2002 from Domaine Durban is only £29.50. In vintage ports Warre's 1970 looks good at £170, as does the **Niepoort Colheita 1987** at £65. There is a fairly long half-bottle list – mainly of clarets and Burgundies, but there is value to be found in the Crozes-Hermitage 2001 from the Domaine des Entrefaux at £18 and the Rioja Crianza 1999 from Sierra Cantabria at £15. A little more adventure with some well chosen wines outside France and less of a reliance on the cosy world of claret and Burgundy could well see this list increasing its ranking substantially, despite the prices.

Neville's Best Buy: Teroldego Rotaliano 1998 from Elisabetta **Foradori** at £25

Score: *Quality* 87.98   *Value* 4.15   *Impression* 19.00   *Total* **111.13**

Ranking: *Quality* 16   *Value* 97   *Impression* 43 =   *Overall* **45th**

Recommendations:
NB: 1982 **Domaine de Chevalier** £120
DM: 1998 **Luna Vineyards** Napa Valley Sangiovese at £44
PW: 1987 **Niepoort** Colheita Port at £65

Find out more about wine and wine producers at *www.winebehindthelabel.com*

HOLBECK GHYLL

Holbeck Lane Windemere Cumbria LA23 1LU

015394 32375

There are civilised places that have civilised wine lists and this is certainly one of them. Just over 200 wines are listed of which nearly half meet our quality criteria, and of these, a little over one eighth meet our price criteria, too. That's not a lot and we suppose that had the prices been a little gentler, the list would have finished several places up the table. There are 33 dry half-bottles listed, of which 13 are of great quality, and 8 wines by the glass, which do not rise above 2 stars, so it's probably best to stick to the halves if you want to experiment. There are no tasting notes except for the House wines.

The Champagne and sparkling wines section has a lot of quality wines, but only the Cloudy Bay Pelorus 1999 meets our price/quality criteria at £29.50. However, at the top of the range, the super 5-star Taittinger Comtes de Champagne 1995 is not expensive for what it is at £110. The white wine section starts off with the only full bottle of Sauternes listed (there is a separate list of half-bottles of dessert wines, which does include Château d'Yquem 1998 at £140), but you are far better off to run with Château Lafaurie-Peyraguey 1983, 5-star quality at £77.50. There are some good quality white Burgundies, too, but they are pretty pricey. There is nothing to excite in the Loire, but in Alsace, Marc Kreydenweiss has 2 value entries in his Wiebelsberg Grand Cru Riesling 2000 at £39 and his Moenchberg Grand Cru Pinot Gris at £45.

The North West

In the French regional section, Château Val Joanis Les Aubépines Côtes du Luberon 2002 is 3-star quality at £30. There is nothing to meet our criteria in Germany, Italy or Spain, but in South Africa, the Hamilton Russell Chardonnay 2003 is 3-star quality at £28.95. Australia, too, has the Leeuwin Estate Art Series Riesling 2003 at £24.75 and the Sauvignon Blanc at £29.50, whilst in New Zealand, Vavasour Sauvignon Blanc 2003 and **Vavasour Chardonnay Awatere Valley 2003**, are both right on the button at £30.

Red wines kick off with Burgundies and as one would expect, there are no bargains to be found here. However, the 5-star **Volnay Santenots-du-Milieu 2000** from Domaine des Comtes Lafon, is certainly worth a punt at £64.75, and you could always go for the super 5-star Richebourg Grand Cru 1997 from Anne Gros, but at £280 you might want to think twice about it. There is 3-star quality in the Moulin-à-Vent, Clos du Tremblay 2001 from Paul Janin at £25, while in the Rhône, Jaboulet's Hermitage La Chapelle 1996 is not overpriced at £87.50, even if it's not the most exciting vintage. Clarets come next, and whilst there are wines of undoubted quality, better value can be found elsewhere on the list. No more so, perhaps, than in the Italian section, where the rare and impressive **Montevetrano 2000** from Silvia Imparato in Campania is as good as anything you will get on this list for £95. In Spain, La Rioja Alta 904 Gran Reserva 1995 is 4-star value at £47.50, as is the Hamilton Russell Pinot Noir 2002 from South Africa at £42. South Africa also has the 3-star Reserve Selection Shiraz 2002 from Vergelegen at £29. In Australia, Leeuwin Estate scores again with the Art Series Cabernet Sauvignon 2000 at £45 and there are other top quality wines from there culminating with the super 5-star Hill of Grace Shiraz 1994 from Henschke at £280.

There is 3-star value in the **Merlot Cuvée Alexandre 2000** from Casa Lapostolle in Chile at £29.50, and while none of the North American wines reached our price/quality ratio, the 1995 Oregon Pinot Noir from Domaine Drouhin at £57.50 was not far off. The half-bottle list finishes off the list and offers enough choice, but perhaps not enough value. Again, it's best to look at top of the quality scale, and here a half-bottle of the 5-star Château de Beaucastel 1999 at £35 is not that much more expensive than some of the 3- and 4-star wines listed.

Neville's Best Buy: The 5 star Volnay Santenots-du-Milieu 2000 from **Domaine des Comtes Lafon**, at £64.75

Score: *Quality* 60.76 *Value* 17.03 *Impression* 15.00 *Total* **92.79**

Ranking: *Quality* 47 *Value* 59 *Impression* 75 = *Overall* **69th**

Recommendations:
NB: 2000 **Montevetrano** at £95
DM: 2000 **Casa Lapostolle** Merlot Cuvée Alexandre at £29.50
PW: 2003 **Vavasour** Chardonnay Awatere Valley at £30

Find out more about wine and wine producers at *www.winebehindthelabel.com*

60th

THE LIME TREE

8 Lapwing Lane West Didsbury Manchester M20 8WS
0161 445 1217

A tried and tested formula has maintained this West Didsbury establishment for many years. One of the features that helps it do so well is the wine list, which incorporates good value all round with some wines of real quality. There are just over 100 different wines on the list, although many of them are also grouped together as 'Wines of the month', all of which are available by the glass. Almost a third of the wines meet our quality criteria, and of those, around a third meet our price criteria. After the 'Wines of the month' pages there is a short list of House white and red wines, but these are geared very much to price rather than quality. The main list is conventionally arranged by country and region for Europe, with a page of sparkling wines and Champagnes. New World wines are all lumped together in one section.

In the Champagne section Dom Pérignon 1996 is very fairly priced at £95, as is **Krug 1988** at £120, but there is nothing at the cheaper end that screams value. Loire whites include Henri Pellé's Ménétou-Salon Clos des Blanchais 2003 at a very reasonable £21.95 and there are 2 wines in the Alsace section from Grand Cru Brand – one Pinot Gris 2001 and one Gewürztraminer 2000 at £22.95 – which look appealing, but the name of the producer is not mentioned. White Burgundies include **Domaine de la Soufrandière Pouilly-Vinzelles 2000** from Bret Brothers at £28.95 and Chablis 1er Cru 2002 from Louis Moreau at £29.95 as well as the 4-star Chassagne-Montrachet 1er Cru Boudriottes 2001 from Blain-Gagnard at £49. There is no outstanding value in the red Burgundy section, but the Volnay 2000 from Comtes Lafon at £45 may be worth a look. The clarets have the 4-star Château Haut-Marbuzet 1999 at £49, while in the Rhône section, the Brunel's **Châteaude la Gardine 1998 Châteauneuf-du-Pape** is also 4-star value at £42.50. There is a reasonable selection of Spanish wines, but nothing offering any real value; neither is there in Italian section, but Castello di Ama's Chianti Classico 1999 at £35 is probably the best choice.

There is better value in the New World whites section with Rustenberg 2002 Chardonnay from South Africa, exceptional value at £18.75. Craggy Range Estate Sauvignon Blanc 2004 from New Zealand at £22.50 is good value, too. In the reds, Rustenberg scores again with the Peter Barlow Cabernet Sauvignon 1999 – 4-star quality at £35. There is a good selection of half-bottles, but nothing of outstanding quality. All in all, this is a good little list, nicely priced, with quality choices to be had, particularly by the glass – all of which could lead to some happy experimentation.

Neville's Best Buy: **Rustenberg** 2002 Chardonnay from South Africa at £18.75

Score: *Quality* 37.08 *Value* 40.74 *Impression* 23.00 *Total* **100.82**

Ranking: *Quality* 82 *Value* 22 *Impression* 18 = *Overall* **60th**

The North West

Recommendations:

NB: 1988 **Krug** Champagne at £120

DM: 1998 **Châteaude la Gardine** Châteauneuf-du-Pape at £42.50

PW: 2000 **Dom. de la Soufrandière** Pouilly-Vinzelles at £28.95

75th

LINTHWAITE HOUSE HOTEL

Crook Road Bowness-on-Windemere Cumbria LA23 3JA
015394 88600

This is a very neatly presented list, arranged by style with clear and concise tasting notes for each wine and featuring a number of half-bottles and wines by the glass of good quality. Prices aren't exactly cheap, which is probably why it isn't further up the ratings, but you can't have everything. There are over 150 wines on the list, of which just over a quarter are of 3-star quality or higher. Of these, around a sixth reach the price criteria, too.

The list kicks off with the Champagne section, but since most of the NV Grandes Marques start at around the £50 mark, it seems to us that it would make better sense to go for the **Dom Pérignon 1996** at £96. There is a long list of Sauvignon Blancs from around the world, but the only one to achieve 3-star status is the Cloudy Bay 2004, outside our quality/price criteria at £35. There's better value in the Chardonnays, with the **Roger Lassarat Saint-Véran Cuvée Prestige 2002** coming in at £28.50.

The 'Light red wines' section has the 3-star Moulin-à-Vent Vieilles Vignes 2003 from Jacky Janodet at £23.50. Opening 5 pages of 'Medium to full red wines' is the **Casa Silva Reserve Carmenère 2002** from Chile, excellent value at £22. There is also Billi-Billi Creek Shiraz/Grenache/Cabernet 2001 from Mount Langhi Ghiran in Australia at £26.50 (£13.75 the half) and the outstanding if still youthful **2000 Dead Arm Shiraz** from D'Arenberg in South Australia at just £35.50. From South Africa, Warwick Estate's Bordeaux blend Trilogy 2001 is 3-star quality at £30 (£16.75 the half) and is also available by the glass. In the 'Fine claret' section Château Montrose 1989 looks best at £109.

Neville's Best Buy: The Dead Arm Shiraz 2000 from **D'Arenberg** in South Australia at £35.50

Score: *Quality* 42.66 *Value* 15.93 *Impression* 27.00 *Total* **85.59**

Ranking: *Quality* 72 *Value* 61 *Impression* 8 = *Overall* **75th**

Recommendations:
NB: 1996 **Dom Pérignon** at £96
DM: 2002 **Casa Silva** Reserve Carmenère at £22
PW: 2002 **Roger Lassarat** Saint-Véran Cuvée Prestige at £28.50

Find out more about wine and wine producers at *www.winebehindthelabel.com*

The North West

96th

THE LOWRY HOTEL

50 Dearmans Place Chapel Wharf Salford Greater Manchester M3 5LH
0161 827 4000

For an international restaurant in a Rocco Forte hotel, the Lowry's River Restaurant wine list is a pretty minimalist affair, although they have managed to cram nearly 130 choices onto 2 sheets of paper. Around 25% are of 3-star quality or higher and of these, around 15% meet our price criteria. There are no tasting notes and the list is arranged conventionally by country and region. One of the best things about the list is fact that 23 wines are available by the glass and 14 wines available in half-bottle format, although these are not geared to the quality end of the list.

There is a good selection of Champagnes, but they are pretty pricey; for example Dom Pérignon 1996 is on at £160, whereas you can buy it for half that price at the Hotel du Vin in Tunbridge Wells (qv). There are some stellar wines in the white Burgundy section, but none of these offer value. The super 5-star Corton-Charlemagne 2001 from Bonneau du Martray is still no give away at £145, as well as being too young to drink. There is 3-star value in the **Caves de Turckheim Grand Cru Brand Gewürztraminer 2000** from Alsace at £30 as well as in the Loire whites, with the **Henry Natter Sancerre 2002** at £29. Australia and New Zealand have **Stella Bella Semillon/Sauvignon Blanc 2004** at £23 from the former and the Craggy Range Avery Vineyard Sauvignon Blanc 2003 at £29 from the latter. There are no 3-star wines or above in either the South American or South African but in the USA, the 5-star Mon Plaisir Chardonnay 2000 from Peter Michael is a cool £100.

In the reds, practically all the clarets are poor value for money, with some outlandish prices being asked for some of the mature classed growths – and 3 of them have been placed in the Burgundy section! In that section Faiveley's 5-star Mazis-Chambertin 1999 is in at £145, but it's far too young to drink. Italy, Spain and Portugal do not pass the price/quality ratio test, but in Australia, the **Balgownie Cabernet Sauvignon 2000** just makes it at £30. In USA reds the super 5-star Bordeaux blend Les Pavots 1999 from Peter Michael twins the Chardonnay at £185. Finally there is a good selection of vintage ports, but they are a bit pricey, so it may be wiser to stick to the 'off' vintage wines such as Taylor's Quinta da Vargellas 1988 at £55 (£12 a glass), or Fonseca-Guimaraens 1986 at £65.

Neville's Best Buy: **Stella Bella** Semillon/Sauvignon Blanc 2004 at £23

Score: *Quality* 40.03 *Value* 13.89 *Impression* 10.00 *Total* **63.92**

Ranking: *Quality* 76 *Value* 70 *Impression* 96 = *Overall* **96th**

Recommendations:
NB: 2000 **Caves de Turckheim** Grand Cru Gewürztraminer Brand at £30
DM: 2002 **Henry Natter** Sancerre at £29
PW: 2000 **Balgownie** Cabernet Sauvignon at £30

Find out more about wine and wine producers at *www.winebehindthelabel.com*

The North West

64th

NORTHCOTE MANOR

Northcote Road Langho Lancashire BB6 8BE
01254 240555

This is an impressive list, with over 450 entries, of which some 40% are at least of 3-star quality, but sadly, of those, only 9 wines in the whole list meet our price criteria. There are 36 dry wines available in half-bottles, of which 26 reach our quality criteria, but there are none in the 7 wines listed by the glass. The list is arranged conventionally by country and region with the added joy of having the white wines printed on yellow paper and the red wines on pink paper.

The Champagne section kicks off with some non-vintage wines, of which the 4-star Vilmart Grande Réserve and **Vilmart Grand Cellier** are listed at £42.95 and £49.95 respectively (£26.95 for a half of Grande Réserve). There is no great value in any of the other Champagnes, although the super 5-star Taittinger Comtes de Champagne Blanc de Blancs 1995 is not wildly overpriced at £134.50. Australian whites follow and here the 4-star Shaw and Smith M3 Vineyard Chardonnay 2002 just squeezes under the bar at £49.95. There is nothing to meet our price/quality ratio in the white wines from New Zealand, America (North and South), South Africa, or Germany, and in Italy Silvio Jermann's 'Dreams' 2001 is pretty outrageously priced at £97.95. The same could be said for the white wines from Portugal and the Loire Valley, but the 5-star white from Mas de Daumas Gassac 1994 is not far off the cusp at £53.50. There is just one Sauternes listed, the 5-star Château Lafaurie-Peyraguey 1995 – not cheap at £81.50, but not over the top, either. There is quality but not value in the Rhône whites, but in Spanish whites, the Rioja Gran Reserva Capellania 1997 from Marqués de Murietta is reasonable value at £30.50. With the pattern of prices on this list, one can expect no real bargains in the white Burgundy section, but Bonneau du Martray's super 5-star Corton-Charlemagne 1999 at £125 is not the most expensive we have seen this wine by a very long chalk. The rare **Clos Blanc de Vougeot 2000** from Domaine de la Vougeraie may be worth looking at, but it is heftily priced at £93.95. White half-bottles are listed at the end of the white wine section, and of these, the Pinot Blanc/Auxerrois 1998 from Domaine Albert Mann at £14.95 looks to be the best value.

Red wines start with Australia and here Dean Hewitson's Barossa Valley Old Garden Mourvèdre 2001 is 4-star quality at £50.75. However, the rest of the New World scores poorly on value. In Italy the Immensum Negroamaro/Cabernet blend 1999 from Francesco Candido at £30.50 should be worth drinking, if better in more recent vintages, and the 5-star Barolo Sorì Ginestra 1998 from Conterno-Fantino is not badly priced for a top Barolo at £85.95. There is a long and interesting list of red wines from Portugal with the top of the range Batuta 2000 from Dirk Niepoort coming in at £98.50. The range of Spanish reds is good, too – Viña Alberdi Reserva 1999 from La Rioja Alta is reasonable value at £32.95, while Vega Sicilia Unico 1989 at £150 is not overpriced in the context of this list. In the Rhône reds, the 4-star **Rasteau Cuvée Prestige 2000** from Domaine de la Soumade is good value at £45.75. Côte-Rôtie La

Mordorée from Chapoutier is a super 5-star wine, but the vintage offered is the poor 1993, so you may need to ask the sommelier whether it's worth risking £101.95 on it. There are some fine reds from Burgundy, but again, picking out value for money here is nigh impossible. René Engel's Grands Echezeaux 2000 is super 5-star quality and even at £95 is well worth considering if relatively youthful. The red Bordeaux list is a little disappointing with a number of minor clarets of little consequence and few of the big guns, but of these, the super 5-star Château Ducru-Beaucaillou 1989 looks the best bet at £120.

In the dessert wine section, a half-bottle of the **Anselmi I Capitelli 1995** at £21.75 looks good value, as does a full bottle of Côteaux du Layon St-Aubin de Luigné 2000 from Domaine des Forges at £23.60. And for the 50cl fan, Chapoutier's Banyuls 1997 at £26.40 is good value, too. There are some good Madeira's available by the glass, but not such good ports. However, you could buy a bottle of Graham 1966 for £143, which should be terrific. There is a short list of 'Limited selection' wines, which we presume changes from time to time, but on the list we were sent the Roussanne 2002 from Giaconda in Victoria, Australia, was the most interesting, but a bit pricey at £87.50. Finally, there is a list of sherries sold by the glass, mainly from Lustau, which are well worth a look.

Neville's Best Buy: a half bottle of **Anselmi** I Capitelli 1995 at £21.75

Score: *Quality* 72.19 *Value* 5.78 *Impression* 18.00 *Total* **95.97**

Ranking: *Quality* 45 *Value* 94 *Impression* 13 = *Overall* **64th**

Recommendations:
NB: 2000 **Dom. de la Vougeraie** 1er Cru Clos Blanc de Vougeot at £93.95
DM: 2000 **Domaine de la Soumade** Rasteau Cuvée Prestige at £45.75
PW: **Vilmart** Grand Cellier Champagne at £49.95

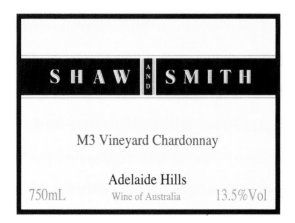

Find out more about wine and wine producers at *www.winebehindthelabel.com*

4th

SHARROW BAY HOTEL

Ullswater Cumbria CA10 2LZ
01768 486301

This is a terrific list with over 60% of the entries rating 3 stars or more. Nicolas Chièze, the head sommelier, has built on the solid foundations begun by his predecessor to produce one of the most intriguing wine lists in the country. Prices are pretty much up to London levels, but certainly not outrageous, and whilst there are many fine establishments in the land where you could find some of the wines at a considerably cheaper price, there are few which could beat the Sharrow Bay for sheer balance.

The 626-strong list kicks off with some 60 wines in magnums or larger formats – a magnum of René Barbier's Clos Mogador 1999 from Priorat at £95 looks good value for money. There follows a list called 'The Sharrow selection', some 27 wines available by the glass and not confined to the lowest common denominator. Domaine de la Soumade Rasteau 2001 is excellent value at only £4.95 the 175ml glass. The Champagne list is impressive, ranging from Billecart-Salmon NV at £39.95 right through to Dom Pérignon Œnothèque 1988 (disgorged in 2002) at £210 or Roederer Cristal Rosé 1995 at £305, but there is plenty of good drinking between these extremes.

White wines commence with Bordeaux – it's good to see a reasonable range of dry white Bordeaux for once – with 1994 Château de Fieuzal Blanc at £75 being the pick of the bunch; although the vintage is not one of the greatest, it should still be drinking well. Sweet Bordeaux boasts 3 vintages of Yquem, but it is the **Château Rieussec 1988** (a great Sauternes vintage and a super 5-star wine) that catches the eye at £75. South-West France has 2 offerings from Domaine Cauhapé: the Sec 2002 at £21 and the Moelleux 2001 at £33. The list is strong in white Burgundies, particularly in Chablis and the Côte de Beaune, with Chassagne-Montrachet 1er Cru les Vergers 1997 from Marc Morey at £69.50 looking good value and Joseph Drouhin's Montrachet Grand Cru Marquis de Laguiche 1993 at £215 weighing in with super 5-star quality. Loire Valley whites lean towards the Sauvignons from the east rather than the Chenins from the centre, but Huët's Le Mont Première Trie Moelleux 1996 is 5-star stuff at £49. Rhône whites has Condrieu 2002 from Domaine Niero Pinchon at £42 as well as good value white Saint-Joseph 1998 from André Perret at £25.50. Alsace is well represented with a plethora of wines from Zind Humbrecht, but the Riesling Muenschberg Grand Cru 2000 from Ostertag at £42 drinks better with food. In Germany, there are 3 wines from the Reichsgraf von Kesselstatt estate, amongst others, with the 2001 Piesporter Goldtröpfchen Spätlese looking good value at £27.15. Spanish whites are graced by the rare Clos Nelin 2001 from René Barbier, a wine blended from Garnacha Blanca, Viognier, Pinot Noir (vinified as white), and a little Roussanne, Marsanne and Macabeo – and at only £22.50 this shows the innovative enterprise of the sommelier. Italian whites shine with Jermann's 'Were dreams, now it's

just wine!' 2002 at £78.50, although expensive, one of the top Chardonnays emanating from Italy. There's a good selection of Californian whites, with lots of choices other than Chardonnay, such as Cline Cellars Marsanne 1999 at £34.50 and John Alban's 2001 Roussanne at £50. Two Reserve Chardonnays from South Africa, Glen Carlou 2002 and Hamilton Russell 2003, both rate 3 stars, so you might as well go for the significantly cheaper one, Glen Carlou at £28 against the Hamilton Russell at £38.50. New Zealand whites are dominated by Sauvignon Blancs, with Isabel Estate 2004 far and away the best value at £27.55. Australian whites have some of the usual suspects, with Cullen's Chardonnay 2001 looking good at £48. There are also 4 vintages of half-bottles of De Bortoli's Noble One Botrytis Semillon, at prices between £28.50 and £34.50 per half.

In the red wine sections, Bordeaux is heavily represented and it is difficult to choose a best buy. All the wines are pretty expensive and some of them are pretty old. If we were really prepared to take a chance we would probably go for the **Château Léoville-las-Cases** from the legendary 1961 vintage at £215, rather than the Lafite-Rothschild from the same vintage at twice the price. Perhaps we should come down to earth and choose one of the most consistent Saint-Estèphe's, Château Haut-Marbuzet, which is a mere £49.50 for the 1998 vintage. There is also some good kit in the Burgundies, but nothing that screams 'value'. The Volnay 1er Cru Santenots de Milieu 2000 from Comtes Lafon is real 5-star class, but at £115 it is not cheap for such a young wine.

The North West

In the Rhône Valley, Jaboulet's super-5 star Hermitage La Chapelle 1995 should be mature enough to be enjoyable even at £85, but if you really want to go for value, try the Domaine de la Soumade Rasteau 2001 at a mere £23.55. There are some gems from South-West France and the Languedoc – Madiran Château Montus Cuvée Prestige 1996 at £37.50 and Mas de Daumas Gassac 1996 at £47.50, respectively. These wines are not cheap, but they are worth the money. Italian choices are fairly conservative, try the entry-level Barbera d'Asti 2000 Ca' di Pian from La Spinetta at £27, or the remarkable, unoaked Cabernet Sauvignon 1996 from the Terre Rosse Vineyard near Bologna at £36 if you want a change from Gaja or Antinori. There is a nice selection of dry reds from the Douro in Portugal, with Dirk Niepoort's Redoma Tinto 1999 at £30 being a good buy. Australian reds are packed with good wines from Grant Burge and Henschke, but if you want something less well known, try the Bindi Pinot Noir 1998 from the Macedon Ranges in Victoria at £58. Although New Zealand Pinot Noirs are all the rage these days, it's good to see New Zealand's best Cabernet blend on the list – Larose from Stonyridge Vineyards on Waiheke Island. The 1999 vintage comes in at a hefty £74, but in the context of the list, it is good value. A cheaper alternative is **Te Mata 2000 Bullnose Syrah** from Hawkes Bay at £31.50, who also make an excellent Cabernet, the Coleraine at £56.50. In the South African section the Hamilton Russell Pinot Noir 2001, £39, is a reliable 4-star performer. You could do no better for quality and value by diving in to the impressive USA red selection, with either Cline Cellars Small Berry Vineyard Mourvèdre 1998 at £37.50, or Ridge Geyserville Zinfandel 2001 at £42 (£21.50 for a half). You could be intrigued by the Pinot Noir Cuvée Laurène 1997 from Domaine Drouhin in Oregon at £58.50, or you can go the whole hog and take the 1997 Hillside Select Cabernet Sauvignon from Shafer at £175. There's a good range from Chile, Argentina and Uruguay, with **Nieto Senetiner's Cadus Tupungato Malbec 1999** at £41 from the Mendoza region of Argentina.

A long list of dessert wines (some already mentioned above) by bottle, half and glass, together with ports and digestifs, completes this very comprehensive list – well worth the effort and a complementary asset to the rest of the services offered by this establishment.

Neville's Best Buy: **Château Rieussec** 1988, a great Sauternes vintage and a super 5-star wine, at £75

Score: *Quality* 107.74   *Value* 22.64   *Impression* 33.00   *Total* **163.38**

Ranking: *Quality* 7   *Value* 43   *Impression* 4 =   *Overall* **4th**

Recommendations:
NB: 1961 **Château Léoville-las-Cases** at £215
DM: 1999 **Nieto Senetiner** Cadus Malbec at £41
PW: 2000 **Te Mata** Bullnose Syrah at £31.50

Find out more about wine and wine producers at *www.winebehindthelabel.com*

The North West

72nd

60 HOPE STREET

60 Hope Street Liverpool Merseyside L1 9BZ
0151 707 6060

This is one of Liverpool's new wave restaurants with a wine list to match. It's not very long – around 90 wines, but it is well balanced with nearly 40% being of 3-star quality or higher, of which around a quarter reach our price criteria. There is a short selection of half-bottles of dry wines and 7 wines come by the glass but are decidedly not geared to the quality end of the spectrum. The tasting notes for each wine are useful and the list is divided simply into white and red wines, in price order with the country of origin noted by the side of each entry. Half-bottles are listed at the end of each section. We do not seem to have been given details of any dessert wines – maybe they are on a separate list, but it wasn't sent to us.

Before that, of course, there is a list of Champagnes and sparkling wines and at the very end there is a list of 4 wines under the heading 'Connoisseur's choice', but more of that later. In sparkling wines, the **Nyetimber Classic Cuvée 1996** is well priced at £29.95 and may well be preferred to some of the NV Champagnes listed. There seems to be a polarisation between the NV Champagnes and the selection of prestige cuvées, with no ordinary vintage Champagnes listed at all. In the white wine section, Henry Pellé Menetou-Salon Clos des Blanchais 2002 from the Loire is good value at £26.95, but better still is the 5-star **Pouilly-Fumé Buisson Renard 2003** from Didier Dagueneau at £39.95. Another adequate value is the Pouilly-Fuissé 2002 from Michel Forest in Burgundy at £30.95.

In the reds there is 4-star value with **Alain Voge Cornas 2000** from the Rhône Valley at £34.50, the Rioja Gran Reserva 1996 from Sierra Cantabria at £34.75, Benton Lane Pinot Noir 2001 from Oregon at £38.75 and Châteauneuf-du-Pape 2001 from Château de la Gardine at £39.50, although that may be a bit on the young side. The 4 wines in the 'Connoisseur's choice' include Opus One 1999 at £195 and Henschke's Hill of Grace 1995 at £295, but also Condrieu 2000 from Saint Cosme at £49.95 and Château Lascombes 1996 (a much better property since 2000), also at £49.95. We wonder why these have been singled out, seeing as there are some equally fine wines on the main list. We would have thought, for instance that the **Volnay Santenots 1er Cru 1997** from Domaine Darviot-Perrin at £68.50 would have qualified for this honour.

Neville's Best Buy: **Alain Voge** Cornas 2000 from the Rhône Valley at £34.50

Score: *Quality* 44.22   *Value* 25.83   *Impression* 21.00   *Total* **91.05**

Ranking: *Quality* 68   *Value* 38   *Impression* 29 =   *Overall* **72nd**

Recommendations:
NB: 1996 **Nyetimber** Classic Cuvée at £29.95
DM: 2003 **Didier Dagueneau** Pouilly-Fumé Buisson Renard at £39.95
PW: 1997 **Darviot-Perrin** Volnay Santenots 1er Cru at £68.50

Find out more about wine and wine producers at *www.winebehindthelabel.com*

The North West

99th

THYME RESTAURANT

32-34 Sandygate Road Crosspool Sheffield S10 5RY
0114 266 6096

This is a shortish, 100-strong list with useful tasting notes to help in one's choices. Just over a quarter of the wines are of 3-star quality or greater, but unfortunately, very few meet our price criteria. The list is arranged into white wines and red wines in ascending price order without any division for country or style, so you do have to read it all the way through if you are seeking out anything in particular. The main body of the list is preceded by a page of wines by the glass which are clearly geared towards the lowest priced wines, followed by a list of Champagnes. There do not appear to be any half-bottles available in dry wines although there are sweet wines in halves at the end of the list, together with the ports.

The very good Champagne selection has the 5-star **Krug NV** at £99 and the super 5-star Bollinger RD 1990 at £120, neither of which are bargains, but not overpriced either. In the white wine section, the **Diamond Valley Estate Chardonnay 2001** from the Yarra Valley in Australia is exceptional value at £26, but nothing else has a good price/quality ratio. However, there are some good, if not great wines listed, and Saint-Aubin 1er Cru Murgers Dents du Chien 1999 from Hubert Lamy at £42 is certainly worth a look.

There is a similar pattern in the reds, with a raft of downmarket wines before you get to anything of interest. After some good 2-star wines, there is value in the 3-star Estate Cabernet/Merlot 2000 from Diamond Valley again, at £29. Among the big boys, there is Château de Beaucastel 1994 at £70, although it's not a great vintage,and the super 5-star **Clos du Tart 1996** at £90 and Château Palmer 1990 at £140. In the dessert wine section, a half-bottle of the **De Bortoli Black Noble** from Australia at £22.50 (£5.50 a 75ml glass) looks good value, whilst a whole bottle of Château d'Yquem 1994 will set you back £190, although this was a dismal year for Sauternes. Finally, Graham's 1983 Vintage Port looks very interesting at £40 'per decanter'– if the decanter contains half a bottle or more, that's not too bad, and excellent if it contains a whole bottle.

Neville's Best Buy: **Diamond Valley** Estate Chardonnay 2001 from the Yarra Valley in Australia at £26

Score: *Quality* 24.65 *Value* 16.07 *Impression* 16.00 *Total* **56.72**

Ranking: *Quality* 94 *Value* 60 *Impression* 67 = *Overall* **99th**

Recommendations:
NB: 1996 **Clos du Tart** at £90
DM: **Krug** NV at £99
PW: **De Bortoli** Black Noble at £22.50

Find out more about wine and wine producers at *www.winebehindthelabel.com*

The North West

66th

WHITE MOSS HOUSE

Rydal Water Grasmere Cumbria LA22 9SE

015394 35295

There are almost 250 different bins on this wine list, many of them very reasonably priced. Just over 30% of the wines are of 3-star quality or above and of those, around a third meet our value criteria. There are around 40 half-bottles listed, of which over a quarter are of good quality. The 8 dry wines listed by the glass have some good 2-star options among them. The list is somewhat unusually arranged: French wines are listed conventionally by regions, but at the end of each section wines from other countries that are similar in style or make up are listed.

The list starts off with Bordeaux reds, with some wines being of very mature vintages, for example a 1928 Château Carbonnieux at £195. How this is drinking is probably within the knowledge of the proprietor, so it's best to ask. Less risk for £195 is probably the **1982 Château Pichon-Longueville-Lalande** – it was superb when we had the chance to drink this wine 3 years ago. The sole wine listed here that meets our price/quality ratio is Château La Tour de By 1996 at £26.90 (£13.50 for 1998 halves). The non-French 'Other Cabernets and Merlots' section has better value with the 4-star **Cape Mentelle Cabernet Sauvignon 2000** from Western Australia very well priced at £20.50 and Leeuwin Estate Art Series Cabernet Sauvignon 1999 less so at £35.25, but nevertheless well inside our price/quality ratio for a 4-star wine. In Beaujolais, Moulin-à-Vent 2002 from Jacky Janodet is only £17.95 and there's value too in the red Burgundies with Girardin's Santenay 1er Cru La Maladière 1999 at £28.25. 'Other Pinot Noirs from around the world' do not fare as well as the Cabernets and Merlots and there is nothing here to meet our criteria. Rhône reds too, fail to impress, but in 'Other Rhône style wines from around the world', Taltarni Shiraz 2000 from Australia is only £19.95, whilst the 5-star Henschke Mount Edelstone Shiraz 1995 should be a beautiful drink at £42. Spanish reds come next and here there is a pair of 3-star wines from La Rioja Alta – Viña Alberdi Reserva 1999 at £19.50 (£11.55 for a 1998 half) and Viña Ardanza Reserva 1996 at £29.30 (£16.10 for a 1998 half). In Italy, 4-star **Antinori Tignanello 1997** comes in at £49.50

There is also good value in the white Burgundies, with the 4-star Chablis 1er Cru La Forêt 1996 from Dauvissat at £36.90 and in the Mâconnais there is the Mâcon-Milly 2001 from Les Héritiers du Comte Lafon at £20.75. And, citing Comte Lafon, there is a nice little run of Meursaults from 1994 to 1999 at very reasonable prices. 'Other Chardonnays from around the world' include the 3-star Leeuwin Estate Prelude Chardonnay 1998 at £20.50 and the 5-star Art Series Chardonnay 2000 at £49.50. Loire whites don't thrill but among 'Other Sauvignon Blancs from around the world' Craggy Range Sauvignon Blanc 2003 from New Zealand is only £17.90. There is good quality in Alsace with **Hugel Gewürztraminer VT** from the superb 1983 vintage at only £49.50 and for £59.50 you can drink a bottle of the equally superb 1976. If you are a real Alsace freak, then the super 5-star Riesling SGN 1976 at £85 is probably not too much to pay for this phenomenal wine. Bordeaux dessert wines have a half-bottle of Château Rabaud-Promis 1996 at £19.75 and 'Other dessert wines' includes a half-bottle of Symphonie de Novembre 2001 from Domaine Cauhapé at £14.50. The German selection is not a thrill, but from Western Australia, the Leeuwin Estate 1996 Riesling probably is at £17.50. In Spain, the white Rioja 1995 from Marqués de Murietta is £16.50, while in the Italian whites, Vintage Tunina 1992 from Jermann is 4-star value at £34.50, but you should check as to whether it hasn't become a bit long in the tooth. The list finishes up with a list of Champagnes with Charles Heidsieck NV at £29.90 looking best value here.

Neville's Best Buy: **Cape Mentelle** Cabernet Sauvignon 2000 from Western Australia at £20.50

Score: *Quality* 40.17   *Value* 38.86   *Impression* 16.00   *Total* **95.03**

Ranking: *Quality* 75   *Value* 24   *Impression* 67 =   *Overall* **66th**

Recommendations:
NB: 1982 **Château Pichon-Longueville-Lalande** at £195
DM: 1983 **Hugel** Gewürztraminer Vendange Tardive at £49.50
PW: 1997 **Antinori** Tignanello at £49.50

Find out more about wine and wine producers at *www.winebehindthelabel.com*

The North West

1st

THE DEVONSHIRE ARMS
BURLINGTON RESTAURANT

Bolton Abbey   North Yorkshire BD23 6AJ

This is one of the most serious and imposing wine lists we have ever come across. Over 2,000 wines are listed, with over 1,300 being of at least 4-star quality and almost another 400 of 3-star quality. The sheer volume of the list can be daunting, so a selection of the less expensive wines are grouped together at the beginning of the list as a shortcut. But it would be a pity to stop there, as there are many hidden gems within the main body of the list, some at quite affordable prices: there are 63 4-star and 5-star wines at £50 or less (including 5 at under £30) and 57 3-star wines at £30 or less (including 4 under £20) so you have got 120 quality wines to play with, which is more than some establishments' entire list. What we like, too, are the 128 choices in small formats (half-bottles or 50cl), of which almost 100 are of 3-star quality or above. There are 13 dry wines by the glass and 5 of these are quality wines.

The list opens with the selection of wines by the glass. If you are fairly abstemious you could do a lot worse than going for 125ml of the 3-star Gravitas Sauvignon Blanc from New Zealand at £5.60 (£7.50 for 175ml) followed by a glass of the 4-star Ridge Lytton Springs Zinfandel at £7.50 for 125ml or £10.50 for 175ml. The 'House white wines and sparkling' section offers11 vintages of Schramsberg Blanc de Blancs and only 2 Champagnes! The House wines are then divided into price bands, whites from £14.25, then from £18.50, then from £25, then from £40, with Pazo de Señoráns Albariño 2003 at £19.50 looking to be good value here. House reds are banded as from £13.50, from £18.50, from £25 and from £40. Château de Beaucastel 1999 is 5-star quality at £40. There follows a page of 1997 clarets and a page of 2000 red Burgundies, minor vintages in their respective regions that represent exceptional drinking value. Clos Fourtet 1997 is a steal at £45 in an establishment of this class, as is the **Domaine Henri Gouges Nuits-Saint-Georges 1er Cru Les Pruliers 2000** at £47.50.

The list then swings on to the selection of small formats – included therein is an impressive selection of Alsace wines from Trimbach, but what caught our eye was the 3-star Jurançon Camin Larredya Selection des Terrasses 2001 – a 50cl bottle at £20. The Champagne section lists anybody who is anybody, from NV House Champagnes, of which Billecart-Salmon at £33.50 is the best quality, to a magnum of Taittinger Comtes de Champagne 1991 – a super 5-star wine and good value at £175.50. Laurent-Perrier NV Ultra Brut at £45 looks good value, too. Chablis always seems to produce good value and here a magnum of Louis Michel's 4-star 1er Cru Montée de Tonnerre in the excellent 1999 vintage is well priced at £62.50. A long list of white Burgundies from the Côte d'Or includes some of the top producers –Comtes Lafon, Coche-Dury, Domaine Ramonet and Domaine Leflaive being especially well represented with a range of vintages and wines. There are so many good wines here at all prices, but Patrick Javillier's Meursault les Tillets Cuvée Speciale 2001 at £49.75 looks to be the best value and Bâtard-Montrachet 1999 from Domaine Leflaive is also good value for a super 5-star wine from an excellent vintage at £165, although probably not yet ready to drink.

The list continues with white wines from Bordeaux, both sweet and dry. There are 11 vintages of Château d'Yquem going back to 1947 at £1,455, but Château Filhot from the excellent 1996 vintage is more affordably priced at £41. In the dry whites, Pavillon Blanc de Château Margaux 1997 at £67.50 should be drinking well now. The Alsace section is dominated by wines from Trimbach, Hugel and Zind-Humbrecht, but Riesling Harth Cuvée Caroline 1999 from Domaine Schoffit looks excellent value at £29, whilst an impressive range of magnums from Zind-Humbrecht has their Riesling Clos Hauserer Vendange Tardive from the legendary 1983 vintage, which at £166 is one of the least expensive. The white Loire section has impressive ranges from Moulin Touchais and Huët, but Nicolas Joly's straight Savennières 2001 at £38.75 probably represents the best value here. There is nothing that can be called outstanding value for money in the white Rhône section, but for seekers of rare wines with deep pockets, why not try a half-bottle of Jean-Louis Chave's extraordinary Hermitage Vin de Paille 1990 at £250? There's a lot better value in the white wine section from the Languedoc, with Domaine de l'Hortus 2001 at £27.50 looking the best bet.

The small selection of Italian whites has Capitel Foscarino 2000 from Anselmi at £21.50 and the Spanish whites includes Pazo de Señoráns 2001 Albariño at £26.50, but you would be better off to go for the 2003 vintage which is listed in the House wines section at the beginning of the list at £19.50. Mulderbosch Chardonnay 1999 at £19.50 is by far and away the best value white in the South African section. The best price/quality Australian white is Knappstein's Lenswood Sauvignon Blanc 2002 at £24.50, while for the curious, the Chardonnay and Roussanne Nantua les Deux 2001 from Giaconda may be worth a look, even at the relatively high price tag of £45. It is good to note that Cloudy Bay Sauvignon Blanc 2004 is only £29.50 on a list of this calibre, whilst Alpha Domus 1999 Oaked Chardonnay at £22.50 represents the best value in the New Zealand white section. There is a large selection of top quality whites from North America, but hidden among the famous names is the Lynmar Russian River Chardonnay 2000 – 4-star quality at only £36.50. At the other extreme, who is going to be the one who takes up the single bottle of Three Sisters-Sea Ridge Meadow Chardonnay 1999 from Helen Turley's Marcassin Vineyard at £425? South American whites don't really thrill although there are downmarket choices at under £20. German whites are difficult to assess – it depends a lot on individual tastes – for quaffing value the best seems to be the Erdener Treppchen Auslese 1990 from Robert Eymael at £39.25, although we would be at a loss to suggest what you would eat with it.

The red sections starts off with a listing of 302 bins of clarets, in all shapes and sizes including 84 in large formats of up to a Salmanazar (9 litres). There are runs of several vintages of all the first growth wines and if you are feeling really flush and are prepared to risk your money by choosing a very mature claret, then look no further than a magnum of Château Lafite-Rothschild 1870 at £10,000. However, for ordinary mortals the Léoville-las-Cases 1981 at £63 is probably a risk well worth taking. It's not the greatest vintage, but it's not a bad one at all and a château of this calibre should be able to provide fine drinking. In Burgundy, too, there are great runs from top producers including Leroy and DRC, but the pick of the bunch for us for price and quality is the **Domaine Jean Grivot Vosne-Romanée 1er Cru Aux Brulées 1995** at £55, which should be drinking beautifully now. So should Romanée-Conti 1990, but that's £4,000! In the Rhône, again, there are runs from the great producers, both north and south, but value stands out with Auguste Clape's Cornas 1999 at £50, even if it may be a little too young to drink. In this case, you may consider Jamet's Côte-Rôtie 1994 at £60, which should be drinking very well now. Languedoc-Roussillon and Provence figure with some good value wines, notably two wines from Domaine Canet Valette in Saint-Chinian – the Mille et Une Nuits 1999 blend of Syrah, Grenache, Carignan and Cinsault, wonderfully priced at £21, and the outstanding Maghani 1999, a blend of Grenache, Syrah and Mourvèdre at £35.

Italian reds follow with a marvellous selection of wines from Tuscany, with most of the top names and runs of vintages in the Antinori top wines. The Piedmont selection is very much dominated by the wines from Angelo Gaja although the small number of other wines are very good. Surprisingly, there is only one wine from outside these regions. Best value here would seem to be Luciano Sandrone's Nebbiolo Valmaggiore 1999 at £42.50. The Spanish section, as one would suspect, is dominated by the wines from Vega Sicilia and there are lots of vintages in lots of sizes at pretty steep prices. For the more down to earth, Bodegas Mauro's Viño de Mesa 1998 is a better bet at £36, whilst in Portugal, the 4-star Vinha Maria Teresa 1998 from Quinta do Crasto is also good value at £47 the bottle or £94 the magnum.

In South Africa, the impressive **Boekenhoutskloof Syrah 1999** stands out at £49.50 in a short selection, but Australian reds have a better showing with, of course, a range of vintages of Penfolds Grange and Henschke's Hill of Grace. For a less exalted Shiraz, you could do a lot worse than to plump for the Blue Pyrenees Estate Shiraz 2000 at £24. The California section is very impressive, with 7 vintages of Harlan Estate and 6 vintages of Screaming Eagle at fairly stratospheric prices. In our quest for value we did find buried amongst the 3- (and 4-) figure prices in this section, 3 wines of outstanding value, all from Cline Cellars – Ancient Vines Mourvèdre and Carignan 1997, both at £24, and the single-vineyard **Small Berry Vineyard Mourvèdre 1998** – 4-star value at £29.50. The quality of the South American section is still evolving, although there is a selection from Catena – at a price.

Dessert wines from Austria and Hungary are pretty much from Willi Opitz and The Royal Tokaji Company, but the Oremus Late Harvest Furmint 2000 at £18.50 for a 50cl bottle looks good value for money. The list concludes with a selection of fine vintage ports, with Warre's 1983 at £75 being the least expensive

Neville's Best Buy: **Cline Cellars** Small Berry Vineyard Mourvèdre 1998 at £29.50

Score: *Quality* 135.84   *Value* 10.51   *Impression* 44.00   *Total* **190.35**

Ranking: *Quality* 2   *Value* 78   *Impression* 2   =   *Overall* **1st**

Recommendations:
NB: 1995 **Dom. Jean Grivot** Vosne Romanée 1er Cru Aux Brulées at £55
DM: 1999 **Boekenhoutskloof** Syrah at £49.50
PW: 2000 **Dom. Henri Gouges** Nuits-Saint-Georges 1er Cru Les Pruliers at £47.50

Find out more about wine and wine producers at *www.winebehindthelabel.com*

61st

HOTEL DU VIN, HARROGATE

Prospect Place Harrogate North Yorkshire HG1 1LB
01423 856800

This is one of the monster lists from the Hotel du Vin group – over 700 wines listed with just under 300 reaching our quality criteria, and of those, around a quarter reaching our value criteria. As is the pattern with the group, the wines are listed conventionally by country and region and there are no tasting notes, so you will have to ask the sommelier team for further information about the wines. Although there was a list of half bottles sent to us, we did not receive any details about wines available by the glass; the rating might have been higher had we done so.

The Champagne section has the Hotel du Vin group's House Champagne, from Lenoble, as good as any NV, for £32.50, whilst at the other end, Pol Roger's Cuvée Sir Winston Churchill 1993 at £120 is well priced, too. Surprisingly, there is not a lot of value in the white Burgundy section, but in white Bordeaux, Vieux Château Gaubert 2001 looks good at £28. There is better value in the whites from South-West France – the Gaillac Mauzac Vert 2001 from Domaine Robert Plageoles at £21.50 is well priced, as is the Jurançon Sec Cuvée Marie 2000 from Charles Hours at £24.50. In Alsace, the Riesling Cuvée Théo 2000 from Domaine Weinbach looks good at £36.50. Two 3-star Savoie wines from Domaine Quénard follow – the Vin de Savoie Cuvée Speciale Abymes 2002 at £15.50 and the Roussette de Savoie Altesse 2002 at £23.50. From the Languedoc, Domaine de l'Hortus Grande Cuvée 2001 at £26.50 is also good value. There are some good prices in the Loire, with Didier Champalou's 2002 Vouvray at £22.50 and Jean-Claude Châtelain's Pouilly-Fumé Les Chailloux 2003 at £28. Domaine de Bellivière's Côteaux du Loir Vieilles Vignes Eparses 2002 at £45 is 4-star quality, as is Château Simone's Palette 2000 at £49.50 from Provence. There is nothing to excite in either Austria or Germany, but in Italy the Tocai Friulano Toh! 2003 from Di Lenardo at £21 is good value. Other good value whites from Italy include the Chardonnnay Sant'Antimo 2003 from Banfi at £29.50 and the Verdicchio dei Castelli di Jesi Riserva Plenio 2000 from Umani Ronchi at £24. Spanish whites have the Rias Baixas O Rosal 2003 from Bodegas Terras Gauda at £27, whilst in Greece, the **Santorini 2003** from Hatzidakas looks a snip at £18.50. There is a good selection of Californian whites – the best price/quality ratio coming from La Crema, whose Sonoma Coast Chardonnay 2001 comes in at £26. There is more 3-star value from South Africa with the Sauvignon Blanc Life from Stone 2003 from Springfield Estate at £21 and the Rustenberg Chardonnay 2003 at £23, while in New Zealand, the 4-star Kumeu River Chardonnay 2002 is good value at £44. There are 2 value Semillons from Australia – the 3-star Fermoy Estate 2003 from Margaret River at £26.50 and the 4-star 1997 Vat 1 from Tyrrell's in the Hunter Valley at £42.50.

Clarets come next and most of the classy wines are pretty expensive, even some that are not so classy, so maybe it's best to concentrate on the top end of the range if you have the money. The same applies to the red Burgundies. Looking for value certainly means looking at the lesser appellations and the Chignin/Mondeuse 2002 from Domaine André & Michel Quénard in Savoie at £22.50 fits the bill here. In the Northern Rhône there is the Crozes-Hermitage Papillon 2003 from Gilles Robin at £27 and in the Southern Rhône, the Rasteau 2001 from Domaine du Trapadis at £23 – both good value. More outstanding value from the South of France comes in the shape of the Côtes du Roussillon-Villages Tradition 2001 from Domaine des Schistes at £19.50 and the Madiran Vieilles Vignes 2000 from Domaine Capmartin at the same price. Not far behind in value is the Saint-Chinian Causse de Bousquet 2001 from Mas Champart at £26 and the **Château du Cèdre Cahors Le Prestige 2001** at £29. In the Loire, the Anjou-Villages 2000 from Domaine Ogereau at £21 is also good value. Away from France the **Quinta de Cabriz Dão Colheita Seleccionada 2000** from Portugal is excellent value at £14, as is the Atrium Merlot 2002 from Torres in Penedès, Spain at £17.50. There is a large selection of Italian reds, with value coming from the Vertigo Merlot/Cabernet Sauvignon blend 1999 from Livio Felluga in the Veneto at £29.50; and in the super 5-star department, Roberto Voerzio's Barolo Cerequio 1995 is not overpriced at £95. The long list of Californian reds has some good value wines: Ravenswood Amador County Zinfandel 2001 at £25 and Cline Cellars Ancient Vines Mourvèdre 2001 at £29.50 supply 3-star value, while 4-star quality is there with Au Bon Climat's La Bauge au-dessus 2000 at £49.50. There is always value in Australian reds and here the 4-star Leconfield Coonawarra Cabernet Sauvignon at £32.50 looks exceptionally good. There are plenty of other 4-star wines under £50 including Charlie Melton's Nine Popes 2000 at £49.50, Greenock Creek's Seven Acre Shiraz 2001 and Dutschke's St Jakobi Shiraz 1999 at £44.50, all from the Barossa Valley. Best value New Zealand red is the 3-star **Redmetal Merlot/Cabernet Franc Basket Press 2002** from Hawkes Bay at £36.50, whilst there is also 4-star value from South Africa in The Foundry's Double Barrel 2001 at £42.50.

Good dessert wines include the 4-star Château Rayne-Vigneau 1er Cru Sauternes 1997 at £39.50, the Jurançon Clos Lapèyre Sélection 2000 at £36.50 and R L Buller's Premium Fine Old Tokay at £29.50. In ports, Fonseca-Guimaraens 1986 is good value at £41.50 as is Sandeman's 1970 at £89.50. In the half-bottle list, there are a number of NV Champagnes at £19.50, Pinot Grigio Le Zuccole 2002 from Puiatti at £14.50 in the whites, and the Bandol Domaine de la Suffrène 2001 at £15 in the reds.

Neville's Best Buy: Dão Colheita Seleccionada 2000 from **Quinta de Cabriz** in Portugal, at £14

Score: *Quality* 59.91   *Value* 24.01   *Impression* 14.00   *Total* **97.92**

Ranking: *Quality* 48   *Value* 39   *Impression* 81 =   *Overall* **61st**

Recommendations:
NB: 2001 **Château du Cèdre** Cahors Le Prestige at £29
DM: 2003 **Hatzidakas** Santorini at £18.50
PW: 2002 **Redmetal** Vineyards Merlot/Cabernet Franc Basket Press at £36.50

58th

THE STAR INN, HAROME

High Street Harome North Yorkshire YO62 5JE
01439 770397

There are some pretty impressive choices on this shortish wine list (just shy of 120 bins, of which almost half meet our quality criteria, with two-fifths of those meeting our price criteria). The selection of House wines just falls short of including anything of 3-star quality or above – there are some pretty good 2-star wines – but the rest of the list shows some bold choices to suit all pockets. One minus point, however, seems to be the complete absence of half-bottles, which does restrict experimentation during a meal. After the House wines and 'Star choices' (which we presume change on a regular basis), the list is arranged conventionally on a country and regional basis.

The white Burgundy section kicks off with a well-priced wine from Domaine de la Croix Senaillet, their Saint-Véran Les Rochats 2001 at £21.95, and for 4-star value the same section has the Meursault 1er Cru Charmes 2000 from Domaine Drouhin at £49. There is also 4-star value in the red Burgundy section with Bruno Clavelier's Vosne-Romanée Les Hauts de Beaux Monts 2000 at £46.50, and the 5-star Grand Cru **Clos des Lambrays 1999** is not overpriced at £64. There is not so much value in Bordeaux but the classed growths listed are reasonably priced for what they are. In the South of France, Château de la Liquière's 3-star **2001 Faugères** is very attractively priced at £19.75, while Domaine Rimauresq's Cuvée 'R' Syrah/Cabernet blend 2001 is still 3-star value at £29.50. There is not a lot of excitement in the Alsace section but in the Rhône, Château de Beaucastel's 1999 Châteauneuf-du-Pape at £46 is impressively priced for a 5-star wine. Hermitage La Chapelle 2000 is a super 5-star wine and the price tag of £80 is not excessive, but it is far too young to drink. In the Loire Valley, Didier Champalou's Vouvray Cuvée des Fondraux 2003 is reasonably priced at £26.50 and Château de Tracy's Pouilly-Fumé 2002 just gets in under the wire at £29.50, but we have seen both wines cheaper elsewhere. Germany and Austria don't shine, but in Italy, the Brunello di Montalcino 1999 from La Fiorita at £50 is a 4-star wine. There is a good value Spanish white – the 3-star Albariño 2004 from Pazo de Señoráns at £24.50 – and in the reds Alvaro Palacios's Les Terrasses 2001 is just off the value cusp at £32.50.

The New World starts off with South Africa, where the reds have an outstanding value wine in the shape of Vergelegen's Mill Race Cabernet/Merlot 2002 at only £18.50 and Fairview's SMV Shiraz/Mourvèdre/Viognier 2002 is not far behind at £21.50. The John X Merriman 2002 Bordeaux blend from Rustenburg at £27.50 completes a value treble in this section. The same can't be said about South America, although there is Montes Estate Alpha Syrah 2002, but it's a bit pricey at £32.50. In California, the ubiquitous Ridge Geyserville Zinfandel 2000 is 5-star value at £45, whilst the New Zealand section boasts the 4-star Mount Edward Pinot Noir 2002 at £40. Australia has the excellent **Dalwhinnie Moonambel Chardonnay 2001** and Shiraz 2001 at

£32.50 and £35.50 respectively, as well as the super 5-star Torbreck RunRig Shiraz 2002 at £150, although it seems a shame to spend so much on a wine that is still 6 to 8 years off being ready to drink.

In Champagne and sparkling wines the one to go for is definitely the **Nyetimber Classic Cuvée 1996** at only £21.50. Bollinger Grande Année 1997, however, at £65 is also very reasonably priced for its 5-star quality. In the dessert wine section it is not very clear whether some of the wines listed are full bottles or halves. If Château Coutet 1998 at £38.95 is a full bottle, then it is indeed outstanding value, but even if it is a half, it's not too bad. Alternatively, there is Campbell's Rutherglen Muscat from Australia at £18.75 a bottle (we assume), but if it's only a half, then don't bother. In ports, Taylor's Quinta de Vargellas 1988 at £45 is 4-star value, while in declared vintages, Dow's 1985 at £80 is looking good, too.

There are some pretty good bargains on this list, but it is not consistently cheap. Perhaps too much reliance on sourcing from local, rather than national, wine merchants has led to some middleman's profits increasing the prices of these wines.

Neville's Best Buy: **Nyetimber** Classic Cuvée 1996 at £21.50

Score: *Quality* 38.82   *Value* 46.29   *Impression* 16.00   *Total* **101.11**

Ranking: *Quality* 80   *Value* 17   *Impression* 67 =   *Overall* **58th**

Recommendations:
NB: 1999 **Domaine des Lambrays** Clos des Lambrays at £64
DM: 2001 **Château de la Liquière** Faugères at £19.75
PW: 2001 **Dalwhinnie** Chardonnay Moonambel at £32.50

Find out more about wine and wine producers at *www.winebehindthelabel.com*

The North East

90th

SWINTON PARK

Masham   North Yorkshire HG4 4JH
01765 680900

Samuel's is Swinton Park's fine dining restaurant. For an upmarket country house hotel, the wine list is a little more geared to wines at the lower end of market than one would expect. Not that there is any lack of quality – of the 200-plus wines on the list, around 30% meet our quality criteria, and of these, some 15% meet our value criteria as well. You can drink quite well for under £30 – even under £20 – but most of those wines reach no further than 2 stars at best. There are 14 dry wines by the glass, none of which reach our criteria, and 10 half-bottles, of which 3 reach our criteria. The list is usefully arranged by style with a brief tasting note for each wine, and at the end of the list is a section titled 'The Castle Cellars – a selection of fine wines'.

The list starts off with 'Clean and crisp – dry whites', but we found nothing here that reached 3-star quality. In 'Tangy and creamy – medium whites' there is 3-star value in the Albariño Pazo de Señoráns 2003 at £25.50 and the 4-star Chablis 1er Cru Vaillons 2002 from Joseph Drouhin at £43.50. It was always unlikely that 'Rich and succulent – full bodied whites' would produce anything to meet our price/quality ratio, and this has proved to be correct, but the Puligny-Montrachet 1er Cru La Garenne 2002 from Olivier Leflaive at £59.50 is probably worth a punt. There is a better price/quality

ratio in the 'Fragrant and fruity – aromatic whites' section, with the **Plantagenet Mount Barker Riesling 2003** from Western Australia offering excellent value at £19.95. Another 3-star value wine in this section is the Grüner Veltliner Langenloiser 2002 from Weingut Bründlmayer at £22.95. For 4-star quality look no further than the **Trimbach Riesling Cuvée Frédéric-Emile 1998** at £47.00 from Alsace.

'Light fruity reds' comes next, with the Fleurie La Madone 2002 from Jean-Marc Despres at £22.95 (£13 the half-bottle) and the **Sancerre Rouge 2000** from Domaine Vacheron at £27 showing good value for money. In 'Soft and juicy reds' there is the 4-star **Mount Edward Pinot Noir 2002** from Central Otago in New Zealand at £40.50, but in the 'Full and fruity reds' section, the best value appears to be the 4-star Château Léoville-Poyferré 1998 at £61.50, although it may be a bit on the young side to drink. 'Spicy fruity reds' has the 5-star Châteauneuf-du-Pape 1998 from Château de Beaucastel at £67.50. Champagnes comes next, with the super 5-star Taittinger Comtes de Champagne Blanc de Blancs 1995 reasonably priced for what it is at £115, as well as the super 5-star Krug 1988 at £147.50. There is value in the sparkling wines with Pelorus Reserve 1998 from New Zealand at £26.50, but there is not so much value among dessert wines, where a half-bottle of Stanton and Killeen's Collectors Muscat NV from Australia at £27 (£3.75 for a pretty mean 50cl glass) seems the best. Still, there's always a bottle of Château d'Yquem – £299.50 for the 1996 or £400 for the 1986. There is a selection of 6 different vintage ports, 4 of which seem to be available only by the 50ml glass, which is strange. Of the bottles, 1963 Cockburn's would seem to be the best bet at £146.50. There are some decent sherries from Emilio Lustau available by the glass only, at prices between £3.20 and £3.60, and various different glasses of Madeira from Barbeito between £3.50 and £5.95 should also be worth trying. Finally, in the 'Castle Cellars' there are top clarets and Burgundies in mature vintages. We would go for the Clos de Tart Grand Cru 1995 at £125 (although better since 1996), or the super 5-star Château Léoville-las-Cases 1986 at £167 – they are probably both just about ready to drink.

Neville's Best Buy: Mount Barker Riesling 2003 from **Plantagenet** in Western Australia, at £19.95

Score: *Quality* 42.73 *Value* 14.82 *Impression* 16.00 *Total* **73.55**

Ranking: *Quality* 71 *Value* 66 *Impression* 67 = *Overall* **90th**

Recommendations:
NB: 1998 **Trimbach** Riesling Cuvée Frédéric-Emile at £47
DM: 2000 **Domaine Vacheron** Sancerre Rouge at £27
PW: 2002 **Mount Edward** Pinot Noir at £40.50

80th

THE WEAVERS SHED

88 Knowl Road Golcar West Yorkshire HD7 4AN
01484 654284

This is an interesting list with the emphasis definitely on the wines from the South of France, where quality has risen enormously over the past few years. It's not a long list at just over 100 entries, of which some 25% are of 3-star quality or higher, and of these, around 40% meet our price/quality ratio. There's not much in the way of half-bottles, nor wines by the glass of quality, but prices are pretty gentle and there are good tasting notes to assist you in your choices. The list is arranged conventionally by country and region.

The white wine section starts off with wines from Southern France, and while there are a number of 2-star entries, the one to go for is undoubtedly the 5-star **Mas de Daumas Gassac 2003** at £36.95. As usual, white Burgundies don't show up any value choices, but in Alsace, 2 wines from Seppi Landmann get the nod – the 3-star Gewürztraminer Grand Cru Zinnkoepflé 2001 at £28.95 and the 4-star Riesling Vallée Noble, Hospices de Strasbourg 1997 at £31.95. Outside France, there is little to meet our criteria, with the exception of the Rías Baixas O Rosal 2003 from Bodegas Terra Gaudas in Northern Spain at £23.95, and **Barolo La Serra 1998** from Marcarini at £55 which is well priced for a cru Barolo.

There are some good choices in the red wines from Southern France, with 3-star value in the Cahors Cuvée Prestige 2002 from Château du Cèdre at £23.95, Bandol 2002 from Domaine La Suffrène at £24 and the Domaine de la Rectorie Collioure La Coume Pascole 2002 from the Parcé brothers in Roussillon at £27.95. And, of course, there is the red Mas de Daumas Gassac 2002 at £36.95. Nothing excited us in the more conventional regions of France, and we are quite happy to stick to the south for our drinking, but in Italy, the **Poggio Argentiera Morellino di Scansano Bellamarsilia 2003** from Tuscany is good value at £15.95. Two good buys in the USA are the 3-star Petite Rousse Syrah 2001 from Clos Mimi in Paso Robles at £25.50, and the 4-star Le Cigare Volant 2000 from Bonny Doon Vineyards, also in Paso Robles, at £47.50. It's easy to see how the proprietors favour these wines since Paso Robles is so similar to the Midi in climate and terrain. We are a little puzzled by the description of Eben Sadie's Columella 2000 as a Pinot Noir. This is in fact mainly Syrah, so maybe you had better check before you order this delicious 5-star wine from South Africa – one of the best to come from that country, but it will set you back £62.50. In the Champagne section, the refined and rare Grand Siècle – La Cuvée Champagne from Laurent-Perrier comes in at £110. Finally, there is a good selection of dessert wines, with the Muscat de Beaumes de Venise 2001 from Domaine Durban at £17.95 the half-bottle (£4.50 a glass) and the **Dom. de la Rectorie Banyuls Le Muté sur Grains 2002** from the Parcé brothers at £31.95 for a 50cl bottle (£6.50 a glass) looking best.

Neville's Best Buy: Morellino di Scansano Bellamarsilia 2003 from **Poggio Argentiera**, in Tuscany, at £15.95

The North East

Score: *Quality* 20.59   *Value* 41.67   *Impression* 19.00   *Total* **81.26**

Ranking: *Quality* 98   *Value* 20   *Impression* 43 =   *Overall* **80th**

Recommendations:
NB: 2002 **Dom. de la Rectorie** Banyuls Le Muté sur Grains (50cl) at £31.95
DM: 2003 **Mas de Daumas Gassac** V d P l'Hérault Blanc at £36.95
PW: 1998 **Marcarini** Barolo La Serra at £55

92nd

THE YORKE ARMS

Ramsgill Pateley Bridge North Yorkshire HG3 5RL

01423 755243

This is a serious wine list with good quality choices. Some 40% of the 200-strong selection meet our quality criteria, but the prices are a bit on the high side and only just over 10% of these qualify for our value criteria. There are 16 wines by the glass and 17 halves of dry wines, mainly geared towards the lower end of the spectrum, but with some quality choices among them. The list is arranged conventionally by country and region and there are no tasting notes except in the House selection, where there is excellent value in the Sierra Cantabria white Rioja 2003 at only £15.50 a bottle, but unfortunately, it is not available by the glass as so many of the others are.

The House Champagne, Louis Roederer Brut Premier NV, is fairly priced at £39.50 (£8 a 125 ml glass). The same cannot really be said for the other Champagnes, though, especially the prestige Champagnes, which are particularly pricey. There is a longish white Burgundy section without any great value and the only 5-star entry, the Criots-Bâtard-Montrachet 2000 from Blain-Gagnard, comes in at £151. It may be better to go with the 4-star Chassagne-Montrachet 1er Cru Les Boudriottes 2001 from Domaine Ramonet at £66. The same may be said for the red Burgundies, although the Clos Vougeot 1988 from Georges Roumier should be mature enough to be a peach of a wine at £160. Some high quality wines come in mature vintages in the clarets, and the one to go for is probably the Léoville-Barton 1989 at £128. There is nothing to excite in Alsace, but there is good 3-star value in the Loire with Didier Champalou's Vouvray Cuvée des Fondraux 2002 at £28. The red Rhône section offers value in the **Côtes du Rhône-Villages 2001** from Château La Gardine at £26.50 and the Lirac 2002 from Château Saint-Roche at £27 (£5.40 a glass), while there's 5-star quality in the **Jean-Michel Gerin Côte-Rôtie Les Grandes Places 1996** at £81.60.

Outside France, Italian whites have Verdicchio Classico Riserva Plenio 2000 from Umani Ronchi at £26.50 and in the Spanish reds, the Sierra Cantabria Tempranillo 2002 is £22.50 (£4.35 a glass). There is nothing to meet our 3-star criteria in either South Africa or South America, but in Australian reds the **Parker Coonawarra Estate Cabernet Sauvignon 2001** is 5-star quality in this vintage at £47, matched in the New Zealand whites by the Kumeu River Chardonnay 2000 at £46.50. Finally, there are several vintage ports available by the glass but not by the bottle.

Neville's Best Buy: the Tempranillo 2002 from **Sierra Cantabria** at £22.50

Score: *Quality* 47.86   *Value* 11.06   *Impression* 13.00   *Total* **71.92**

Ranking: *Quality* 63   *Value* 76   *Impression* 87   =   *Overall* **92nd**

Recommendations:
NB: 1996 **Jean-Michel Gerin** Côte Rôtie Les Grandes Places at £81.60
DM: 2001 **Château La Gardine** Côtes du Rhône-Villages at £26.50
PW: 2001 **Parker Coonawarra Estate** Cabernet Sauvignon at £47

Find out more about wine and wine producers at *www.winebehindthelabel.com*

The North East

44th

THE ALBANNACH

Baddidarroch Lochinver Sutherland IV27 4LP

01571 844407

nother remotely situated establishment getting 3 cheers for the restraint in
pricing despite the cost of delivering the wines there. Colin Craig's policy earns
him a pretty high place in this Top 100, even if only around a third of the 300-
strong wine list meets our quality criteria. This is amply made up by the prices and the
53 half-bottles of dry wines on the list, as well as a 40% hit rate for value on those
quality wines. Wines by the glass are scant, but are usually offered daily according to
what Colin thinks will go well with what is cooking, and they do not obviously come
from the bottom end of the list. The list is conventionally arranged by country and
region, whites first and then reds, although curiously, Champagnes are listed after the
reds and before the half bottle selection.

White Bordeaux kicks off the list and value is found right away with Château Brousted
1999 at £18.50 and **Château Thieuley Cuvée Francis Courselle 2001** at £23. In the
Mâconnais, the Saint-Véran Hauts de Leynes 2002 from Verget is also good value at
£20.50. In the Côte de Beaune, Meursault Clos de Cromin 2000 and Chassagne-
Montrachet Les Blanchots 2002 are both good value wines at £40 from the *négociant*
house of Olivier Leflaive. There is better value in Chablis, with Mont de Milieu 1er
Cru 2001, 4-star quality from Billaud-Simon at £29.50, and super 5-star **René et
Vincent Dauvissat Grand Cru Les Clos 1998** at £49. The Loire has Didier
Champalou's Vouvray Cuvée des Fondraux 2000 at only £19, whilst in Alsace,
Gewürztraminer Grand Cru Furstentum 2002 from Albert Mann is 4-star quality at
£28. Californian whites has Frog's Leap Sauvignon Blanc 2003 at only £22, while
from Australia, Crawford River Riesling 1999 is in at £23. New Zealand has **Staete
Landt Marlborough Sauvignon Blanc 2004** at £19 and Fromm's La Strada
Chardonnay 2001 at £23, both excellent 3-star value.

The red wine section starts off with some pretty impressive clarets, with Château
Talbot 1997 looking the best value at £50. There are, rather disproportionately, 7
Beaujolais listed, of which the Côtes de Brouilly 2002 from Domaine de la Voute des
Crozes at £17 is the one to go for. It's more difficult to find value in the Côte d'Or,
even in this list, so it may be better to go for the Nuits-Saint-Georges 1er Cru Les
Vaucrains 1998 from Nicolas Potel, just on the cusp at £52. There are some tempting
grand cru wines at tempting prices from older vintages, but we would be concerned as
to whether they are still standing up to the test of time – particularly the 1987s. Best
to ask. There's more clear cut value in the red Rhône section, with Gigondas Vieilles
Vignes 2000 from Domaine du Grand Montmirail coming in at £22 and the excellent
Châteauneuf-du-Pape 1997 from Domaine du Pegaü at £46. In the French country
wines, the Saint-Chinian Côte d'Arbo 2000 is outstanding value at £15. In Italy,
Angelo Gaja's Tuscan Promis IGT 1997 is good 3-star value at £27. There are some
nice choices in the Californian reds, with the honours taken by the 4-star Ridge

Scotland

Cabernet Sauvignon 1999 at £38. **Heitz Cellars Napa Valley Cabernet Sauvignon 1994** is also worth a try at £35, especially from such a great vintage in the Napa. Antipodean wines do well, too, with New Zealand providing value in the shape of C J Pask's Cabernet/Merlot 2002 at only £18 and Escarpment Pinot Noir 2001 at £26, while Australia provides 4-star value with Grant Burge's Shadrach Cabernet Sauvignon 1996 at £36 and Parker Coonawarra Estate Terra Rossa First Growth 2000 Bordeaux blend at £42. Champagnes follow, but there is nothing to match our price/quality criteria, although the 5-star Bollinger Grande Année 1983 should be absolutely delicious and well worth the £90 asked for it.

The lengthy half bottle list has some good value wines, thus allowing the 3-halves drinker (as opposed to the 1-bottle drinker) the chance to experiment a bit. Chablis 1er Cru Montmains 2001 from Domaine de Vauroux at £13 the half and Pouilly-Fumé 2002 from Château de Tracy at the same price takes care of the value whites, whilst Fleurie Clos de la Roilette 2004 at £10 and Savigny-les-Beaunes Les Fournaux 2000 from Simon Bize at £18, hold sway with the reds, but there are also other higher priced halves worth drinking. There is a bit more quality to the dessert halves than in the full bottle section (where you will, however, find the super 5-star Condrieu Quintessance 1999 from François Villard at £56 for 50cl), with Huët's 5-star Clos de Bourg Moelleux 1999 at £22 having the best price/quality ratio. Ports are not forgotten and Dow's 1983 is reasonable value at £65, but if you really want to push the boat out, why not have the legendary Warre's 1963 at £175?

The list is not an easy read, and there are no tasting notes and some irritating spelling mistakes, but the wines speak for themselves, and when you have driven all the way to Lochinver, why should you care?

Neville's Best Buy: **René et Vincent Dauvissat** Chablis Grand Cru Les Clos 1998 at £49

Score: *Quality* 51.90   *Value* 42.33   *Impression* 17.00   *Total* **111.23**

Ranking: *Quality* 58   *Value* 19   *Impression* 61 =   *Overall* **44th**

Recommendations:
NB: 1994 **Heitz Cellars** Napa Valley Cabernet Sauvignon at £35
DM: 2001 **Château Thieuley** Cuvée Francis Courselle at £23
PW: 2004 **Staete Landt** Marlborough Sauvignon Blanc at £19

Find out more about wine and wine producers at *www.winebehindthelabel.com*

Scotland

48th

BRIAN MAULE

176 West Regent Street Glasgow G2 4RL
0141 248 3801

---

he cities of Glasgow and Edinburgh seem to be fighting it out as to which has the best short quality list and there's not a lot to choose between them. Brian Maule's Glasgow establishment is only 0.45 points behind Edinburgh's Fishers in the City (qv), but the approach is quite different. There is a bigger concentration on quality here rather than price, although the price/quality ratio on a lot of the wines is exemplary. Another factor is that here there are 2 quality wines by the glass out of 4 options, whereas none of Fishers' wines by the glass meet our quality standard out of a range of 16. There are nearly 150 wines on this list, of which just over a quarter meet our quality criteria and of those, almost a third meet the value criteria, too.

The list is arranged conventionally by country and region and there are brief tasting notes on most of the wines. The Champagnes are a bit overpriced at the entry level, but higher up the quality scale the 4-star **Ruinart Blanc de Blancs NV** at £59 is excellent value, as is the 5-star Bollinger Grande Année 1995 at £89. The four House wines include a red and a white from the 3-star Château Tour de Mirambeau, the 2004 Bordeaux Sauvignon and the 2002 Bordeaux Supérieur, both at £22.50 the bottle and at £4.95 the glass (size unspecified). Alsace has Schoffit's Cuvée Caroline Riesling 2002 at £29.50 and in the Beaujolais section the **2003 Domaine de la Madone Fleurie** at £26 also represents value. There are several 3-star wines under £30 in the Loire section, including **Henri Bourgeois Pouilly-Fumé 2003** and red, white and rosé Sancerre from the same producer – the red being from the 2002 vintage, white and rosé from 2003. The claret section boasts some fine names, with the best being in mature drinking vintages; but of course, these come at a price. If we had the money, we would plump for the **1970 Château Ducru-Beaucaillou** at £191.50, beautiful when we first tasted it in the late 70s and still going strong when we last tasted it in the late 90s, and there's no reason to doubt it now. There is also the white Domaine de Chevalier 1989 at £95, which is powerful enough to still be drinking well. In Burgundy reds, René Engel's 5-star Clos Vougeot is listed as being in either the 1997 or the 1998 vintage at £80. Certainly the 1997 will be more approachable now, but the 1998 is perceived as the better vintage. The wines from the Rhône Valley are dominated by négociant offerings from Guigal, with the 3-star Condrieu 2002 and Côte-Rôtie (00/01) both not wonderful value at £65.

There is not a lot of value in the Italian or Spanish sections, either, but Australia has Willow Bridge Estate Shiraz 2002 at £26. New Zealand, South America and California don't thrill (particularly California), but there are some good quality South African wines, with the 4-star Hamilton Russell Pinot Noir 2001 at £45 taking the honours for value. There are a fair number of quality wines among the half-bottles, with Fleurie Domaine de la Madone 2003 at £15 and Château Tour de Mirambeau red 2002 at £11.50 looking to be the best value. In dessert wines, half-bottles of

Château de Fesles Bonnezeaux 1998 at £27 and Château Tour de Mirambeau Sémillon Noble 1999 at £30 would both be worth a try.

There are a few irritations about the list, such as insufficient information about a producer or a region, and there is also the very bad habit of listing alternative vintages for the same wine at the same price. Also, if we are getting wines by the glass, it would be nice to know the size of the glass. Apart from these few minor quibbles, we rate this as a very well thought out list.

Neville's Best Buy: 4-star **Ruinart** Blanc de Blancs NV at £59

Score: *Quality* 66.77   *Value* 26.78   *Impression* 17.00   *Total* **110.55**

Ranking: *Quality* 44   *Value* 37   *Impression* 61   =   *Overall* **48th**

Recommendations:
NB: 1970 **Château Ducru-Beaucaillou** £191.50
DM: 2003 **Pouilly-Fumé** Henri Bourgeois £26.95
PW: 2003 **Domaine de la Madone** Fleurie at £26

Find out more about wine and wine producers at *www.winebehindthelabel.com*

Scotland

42nd

CHAMPANY INN

Champany Corner Linlithgow West Lothian EH49 7LU
01506 834532

his is a massive list with nearly 650 bins, of which nearly 400 are of high quality. The rating, however, is a little let down by the pricing, but because of its size, you can still find plenty of wines with a good price/quality ratio. There are 25 half-bottles offered, of which 15 meet our quality criteria, but alas, there seems to be no wines offered by the glass (which might also have pushed up the score). The list is conventionally arranged by country and region (even in the dessert wine section) but there are no tasting notes

Every wine in the Champagne section is of at least 3-star quality and the bargain here is undoubtedly the 1996 vintage Champagne from Charles Heidseick at £50 – look no further. The white Burgundy section follows, with Louis Michel's Chablis 1er Cru Montée de Tonnerre 1999 good 4-star value at £35. There are a host of good names from the Côte de Beaune, but some of the wines are not from terribly good vintages – 1995, 1996, 1999, 2000 and 2002 are best, 1997 and 2001 at a pinch. There is good quality but not terribly good value from the white wines in the Rhône Valley and Southern France, but in dry white Bordeaux, Vin Sec de Château Coutet 1997 is interesting at £28. There's more value in the Alsace section, with Trimbach's Reserve Gewürztraminer 1998 looking good at £30, but **Domaine Weinbach's Cuvée Theo Riesling 1997** at £36 may be an even better bet. Two mature Vendange Tardive Gewürztraminers are worth looking at – one from Hugel in the superb 1983 vintage at £80 and the other a Trimbach bottle in the equally superb 1976 vintage at £90. There's no great value in the German whites, but in South Africa the Springfield Estate Methode Ancienne Chardonnay 1997 and the Boekenhoutskloof Semillon 2001 look good value at £30. There is good quality in the Australian whites, with Cape Mentelle Semillon/Sauvignon 2000 at £26.50 and Leeuwin Estate Art Series Riesling 2001 providing the best value here. American whites have the 4-star Jade Mountain Paras Vineyard Viognier 1997 in at £48.50, whilst the 1998 Kistler Chardonnay is well priced at £70.

In the red Burgundy section, Paul Janin's Moulin-à-Vent Clos du Tremblay 2000, is good entry-level value at £30, but you will need to go to £70 before you can find a 4-star wine (Vosne-Romanée 1er Cru Les Suchots 1999 from Confuron-Cotétidot). For nor a lot extra, you might as well go for the super 5-star Ruchottes-Chambertin Clos du Ruchottes 1991 from Armand Rousseau at £105, which should be drinking beautifully now. At the very top end, Domained Dujac's best shot, the super 5-star Bonnes Mares 1998, may be broached now but you will have to pay £190 for the privilege. The Rhône and Southern France have Mas Mortiès Pic-St-Loup 1995 at £23 and Alain Graillot's top cuvée, La Guiraude Crozes-Hermitage 1999, 4-star value at £42.50. There are also several vintages of the 5-star Domaine de Trévallon – the 1993 should be drinking well at £45, although this was not one of the greatest vintages. You may be more assured with the 1996 vintage at £60, but it is probably only just about ready to be broached. At the top end again, the

Scotland

166

Hermitage 1997 from Jean-Louis Chave may still need a while to show at its best, but it is fairly priced at £145. Maybe if you are staying at the hotel, you could ask them to open it for you the day before. Alternatively, another super 5-star wine, the Hermitage La Chapelle 1983, should be drinking superbly at £195. There are some great Bordeaux wines listed, but none of them meet our price/quality ratio. Of the top names in mature vintages, Château Cos d'Estournel 1983 at £135 looks fair value, but if you want to see just how well the very top clarets can mature, then take a chance on Château Lafite-Rothschild 1957 or 1958 at £200. There is a lot of good value in the extensive South African red section, but many wines are of mature vintages and it would be best to ask advice about their current drinkability. Warwick Farm Cabernet Franc has always been one of the best emanating from South Africa, but is the 1991 still holding up? If so, it's a bargain at £25. Their Cabernet Sauvignon 1994 at £28.50 may be a safer bet. In more recent vintages, and all at £45, you have the 4-star Paul Sauer 1998 blend from Kanonkop, the **Boekenhoutskloof Shiraz 1999**, the Hamilton Russell Pinot Noir 2000, and the 5-star Boekenhoutskloof Cabernet Sauvignon 1999 – all excellent value. The Australian section has The Custodian Grenache 1999 from D'Arenberg at £30, while there is 4-star value with **Hollick Ravenswood Cabernet Sauvignon 1998** and Leeuwin Estate's Art Series Cabernet Sauvignon 1996, both at £45. There are 5 straight vintages of Penfolds Grange from 1993 to 1997, all at £250, so if you want an amusing comparative tasting, this is your chance! New Zealand reds has the Unison Selection blend 1998 at £45 and Ata Rangi Pinot Noir 2000 at £50, both 4-star quality. The value wine in the North American reds section is undoubtedly Bonny Doon's 1995 Le Cigare Volant Grenache and Syrah blend at £42.50. The Spanish section has the Alion Reserva 1996 at £42.50, well priced for a 4-star quality wine. Italy has the 1998 Barbera d'Asti Ca' di Pian from La Spinetta as good 3-star value at £25.50, whilst the 5-star **Barolo La Serra 1995** from Roberto Voerzio is remarkable value at £90.

Ports are well represented here, with the non-declared vintage Quinta de Vargellas from Taylor at £45 for the 1987 and £50 for the 1986 and 1984. In declared vintage years, Graham's 1983 at £80 and Warre's 1977 at £160 look the best bets. There is a long list of dessert wines with several offerings in the excellent 1996 vintage for Sauternes. Château Guiraud is the cheapest at £38.50 for a half-bottle, but any of the others would do. In the Loire, a 50cl bottle of Château de Fesles Bonnezeaux 1996 is £40. There are quality wines in the dry half-bottle list, the best value being Viña Ardanza Reserva 1995 from La Rioja Alta at £18 and Châteauneuf-du-Pape, Domaine du Vieux-Télégraphe 1997 at £25.50.

Neville's Best Buy: **Boekenhoutskloof** Shiraz from South Africa 1999 at £45

Score: *Quality* 83.52 *Value* 13.93 *Impression* 14.00 *Total* **111.45**

Ranking: *Quality* 23 *Value* 69 *Impression* 81 = *Overall* **42nd**

Recommendations:
NB: 1995 **Roberto Voerzio** Barolo La Serra at £90
DM: 1997 **Domaine Weinbach** Cuvée Theo Riesling at £36
PW: 1998 **Hollick** Ravenswood Cabernet Sauvignon at £45

Find out more about wine and wine producers at *www.winebehindthelabel.com*

Scotland

65th

THE CROSS, KINGUSSIE

Tweed Mill Brae Ardbroilach Road Kingussie PH21 1LB
01540 661166

his is a rather idiosyncratic list with a very personal, warm feeling. It is certainly interesting, for example, to see a host of second wines from famous Bordeaux châteaux, but none of the château wines themselves! This is certainly not a conventionally arranged list and each section heading creates an air of expectancy. There are over 200 wines in all, of which about 40% are of 3-star quality or more, and of these, around 20% meet our price/quality criteria as well. There are 34 half-bottles listed, a pretty good percentage, of which almost half meet our quality criteria, but only 3 wines are offered by the glass. Prices are not that cheap, but generally fair, considering the distance the wines have to travel from the importers' cellars

The list starts off with a section called 'The short list', which is very much geared to price. There are some good 2-star wines among them but none of 3-star quality or higher. Champagne comes next with Billecart-Salmon NV Brut Réserve at £40 not being overtly cheap, but providing the best price/quality ratio. There follows a list of a dozen Bordeaux second wines in varying vintages, with La Dame de Montrose 1996

Scotland

(second wine of Château Montrose) looking to be the one to drink at £48. A 'Classic French' section comes next, divided into red and white. In the white section, there is little to excite in Chablis, Burgundy or the Loire, but there is 4-star value in the **Zind-Humbrecht Pinot Gris Herrenweg de Turckheim 2001** at £40 from Alsace. In the white Rhônes, André Perret's 5-star **Condrieu Côteau du Chéry 2002** comes in at just £48. Classic French red wines brings up no bargains in Burgundy but in the Rhône section, the Vacqueyras 2001 from Domaine Le Clos de Caveau is reasonably priced at £30. There are some well priced French country wines, with the 5-star Mas de Daumas Gassac looking good at £47, although the vintage (2003) is far too young to drink.

'Personal selection' comes next and the first sub-division here is Tuscan reds, with the **2001 Villa Pillo Syrah** IGT looking reasonably priced at £33. Riojas follow, 7 of them, with La Rioja Alta's Reserva 904 1992 looking to be the best quality but a bit pricey at £51. Of 6 wines from Quinta do Crasto in Portugal the Reserva Douro 2002 at £30 is arguably the best value if not a top vintage. In the Western Cape sub-section, South African pride is upheld with the **Fairview Single Vineyard Primo Pinotage 2001** delivering 3-star value at £27.

'Selection of New World wines' has some 4-star whites at good prices – Fromm's La Strada Chardonnay 2000 from New Zealand at £33 and Jeffrey Grosset's Polish Hill Riesling 2003 from South Australia at £41. There's also Cabernet/Merlot/Petit Verdot The Clan 2001 from Capercaillie in the Hunter Valley in Australia at £29. Best value on a good and varied list of half-bottles comes from the 5-star Ridge Geyserville Zinfandel 2001 at £26. There is a good list of pudding wines, too, mainly in half-bottles – Samos Muscat NV from Greece at £13 looks good value, as does Alois Kracher's Eiswein 2001 at £30. In ports, Graham's 1991 should be approachable already at £68 and there is a selection of older 'off' vintages from various producers for something more mellow.

Neville's Best Buy: Pinot Gris Herrenweg de Turckheim 2001 from **Zind-Humbrecht** at £40

Score: *Quality* 56.80   *Value* 21.09   *Impression* 18.00   *Total* **95.89**

Ranking: *Quality* 53   *Value* 48   *Impression* 53 =   *Overall* **65th**

Recommendations:
NB: 2002 **Dom. André Perret** Condrieu Côteau du Chéry at £48
DM: 2001 **Fairview** Single Vineyard Primo Pinotage at £27
PW: 2001 **Villa Pillo** Syrah at £33

13th

DARROCH LEARG

Braemar Road Ballater Aberdeenshire AB35 5UX

013397 55443

---

his is a *very* civilised wine list, with helpful tasting notes and a good spread of wines from around the world at very reasonable prices indeed. The only criticism is the poor selection of Californian wines, when there are so many world class wines from that area, but no doubt this will be rectified in due course. There are over 200 bins on the list, with almost half being of 3-star quality or above, and of those, over 60% meet our value criteria. There is also a goodly number of half-bottles on the list, although the price/quality ratio here is less apparent. The 5 dry House wines by the glass are sound, but not exciting

At the beginning of the list a section entitled 'Brief encounters! – a House selection' lists some interesting wines 'which you may not find on other lists'. Well, this is probably true – there are wines from Luxembourg, Switzerland and the Jura, an English sparkling wine (Nyetimber 1995 at £31 – one of the best from the UK), a white Nuits-Saint-Georges, an Australian Cabernet Sauvignon made like an Italian Amarone, and from the Rhône Valley, Hermitage Les Bessards 1994 from Délas, cheap at £32, if not on a par with later years of this wine which are super 5-star. The list is then conventionally arranged by country and region with Champagnes and sparkling wines at the front and half-bottles and dessert wines at the back. The Champagne section is good, with Dom Pérignon 1996 a bargain at £85. The clarets follow, with Château Canon de Brem at £25 and Vieux Château Gaubert 1999 at £23 both excellent value for the quality. Château Léoville-Barton 1995 is also good value at £54. There are some very fine red Burgundies with Robert Chevillon's Nuits-Saint-Georges 1er Cru 1998 at £29 and Louis Jadot Pommard Les Epenots 1998 looking to be the best value at £42. In white Burgundies, Patrick Javillier's Meursault Les Tillets 2001 is very well priced at £32, as is the super 5-star Corton-Charlemagne 1993 from Bonneau du Martray at £77. Fleurie Clos de la Roilette 2003 from Coudert at £22 and Chablis 1er Cru Mont de Milieu 2002 from William Fèvre at £32 are the best value wines in the Beaujolais and Chablis sections respectively, and Henry Natter's Sancerre Cuvée François de la Grange 2000 at £24 takes the honours in the white Loire section (there are no Loire reds listed). In the Rhône, the super 5-star **Châteauneuf-du-Pape Domaine du Vieux-Télégraphe 1999** is listed at a remarkable £28 in the reds, whilst their white Châteauneuf La Crau 2002 comes in at £26.30. Look no further. Alsace has both Marcel Deiss's Riesling Beblenheim 2002 and Blanck's Pinot Gris 2001, both listed at £24. In the French country section, the Bandol 1999 from Domaine Tempier is very fairly priced at £24.

There is nothing higher than 3-star quality in the Italian section, with Palazzo della Torre 2001 from Allegrini in the Veneto and Santadi's Carignano del Sulcis Riserva Rocca Rubia 2001 from Sardinia, both at £26, being the ones to choose. The pick of the bunch in Spain are Finca l'Argata 2000 from Bodegas Joan d'Anguera 2000 at £23 and the **Marqués de Murietta Gran Reserva Castillo Ygay 1994** at £33. Australian reds show good value in Parker First Growth Cabernet Sauvignon 1999 from Coonawarra at £34 and the 5-star Henschke Mount Edelstone Shiraz 1999 at £45. New Zealand whites include Cloudy Bay Sauvignon Blanc 2004 at a reasonable £28, but the solitary red on the list, the Escarpment Pinot Noir 2001 at £26, is cheaper. Kanonkop Pinotage 2001 at £27 is a good price for one of the better wines from South Africa, whilst the Bouchard Finlayson Chardonnay 2002 is also very well priced at £22. The classy Argentinian Achaval Ferrer Malbec/Cabernet Sauvignon/ Merlot 2001 at £34 is the best bet in South American and in California, the only wine worth considering is the Ridge Geyserville Zinfandel 1998 at £35. There is a fairly substantial list of half-bottles with Domaine Tempier Bandol 2000 at £14 in the reds and Chablis 1er Cru Vaillons 2000 from Louis Michel at £12 being far and away the best value. A short list of dessert wines has **Doisy-Daëne 1981 Sauternes**, outstanding value at £24 for a mature vintage. There is also the superb **Graham's 1985 Vintage Port** at a very reasonable £45 a bottle. Nigel Franks has put a lot of effort into producing this very user-friendly list – one of the best in the country.

Neville's Best Buy: The super 5-star Châteauneuf-du-Pape, **Domaine du Vieux-Télégraphe** 1999 at a remarkable £28

Score: *Quality* 48.14 *Value* 73.73 *Impression* 24.00 *Total* **145.87**

Ranking: *Quality* 625 *Value* 8 *Impression* 15 = *Overall* **13th**

Recommendations:
NB: 1994 **Marqués de Murietta** Gran Reserva Castillo Ygay at £33
DM: 1981 **Doisy-Daëne** Sauternes at £24
PW: 1985 **Graham's** Vintage Port at £45

Find out more about wine and wine producers at *www.winebehindthelabel.com*

Scotland

54th

ÉTAIN

The Glasshouse Springfield Court Glasgow G1 3JX
0141 225 5630

he Glasgow outpost of the Conran empire naturally has some pretty smart wines on the list – with just about half of the 250 bins achieving 3-star quality status or higher. Of these, however, less than a fifth can be singled out as offering a good price/quality ratio. That said, there are enough bargains to choose from, including some in the upper echelons. The list is conventionally arranged by country and region with a short selection of wines by the glass at the beginning and half-bottles, magnums and dessert wines at the end.

Nothing stands out among the wines offered by the glass except 150ml of Billecart-Salmon Rosé Champagne at £11.50, although Blandy's 10-year-old Malmsey at £7.25 the 100ml glass and Warre's 1983 Vintage Port at £9.75 are worth noting in the fortifieds. In the Champagne section, the 5-star Billecart-Salmon Cuvée Nicolas-François 1997 is £75, which is about as good a price you will pay for this quality. There are a couple of value wines in the Alsace section from **Paul Blanck – Tokay Pinot Gris Patergarten 2001** at £26.50 and Gewürztraminer Altenbourg 2001 at £27.75 – while Henry Pellé's Ménétou-Salon Clos des Blanchais 2002 at £29.50 is the best value wine in the Loire section. The Rhône has the super 5-star Hermitage Blanc 1997 from Jean-Louis Chave, and at £110 it is probably not overpriced in a restaurant of this class. On the other hand, the top Rhône red, the Hermitage La Chapelle 1983 is a bit excessive at £140. A shortish list of clarets has no heartstoppers, but there's some real value in the reasonably extensive range from regional France. Top value here is Alain Brumont's Gros Manseng Côtes de Gascogne 2002 at only £15, whilst Domanie Cauhapé's Jurançon Sec 2001 at £25.50 and Domaine de l'Hortus Grande Cuvée 2002 at £30 are not that far behind. The white Mas de Daumas Gassac 2003 is 5-star quality at £47.50, but it's probably a bit too young to drink. In the reds Château l'Euzière's Pic Saint-Loup 2001 at £21.50 and Château de la Negly's Coteaux de Languedoc La Falaise 2001 at £26.50 represent the value end of the spectrum and at the top end there's the 5-star Domaine de la Grange des Pères 2001, which should just about be broachable at £75. If you prefer maturity there is always Mas de Daumas Gassac 1982 at £115, or Domaine de Trévallon 1988 at £95. Burgundy, alas, does not get into the price/quality frame but from Beaujolais there's the Morgon 2001 from Domaine de la Chaponne at £21.50. At the top end Domaine Drouhin's Grands Echezeaux 1999 is 5-star quality at £175, but is almost certainly too young to drink, while Bonneau du Martray's Corton-Charlemagne 1996 is horribly overpriced at £250, even if it does rate super 5 stars.

Away from France, Italy doesn't offer any great bargains either. The 1999 Barolo from Matteo Ascheri at £52 is reasonably enough priced for the appellation, but is probably not yet ready to drink. Some of the other 5-star offerings are either too young or too expensive. The same may be said for Spain, but here at least, there is Pesquera Gran

Scotland

Reserva 1996 representing super 5-star quality at a reasonable £95. In Germany, Leitz Weingut's Rudesheimer Riesling Spätlese 2002 is good value at £24.50, whilst the **Joh Jos Prüm Wehlener Sonnenuhr Riesling Auslese 1993** is 4-star quality at £47.50 and should be impressively mature. Hungary has Tokaji Dry Furmint 2002 from Disznoko at £24.50 and a pat on the back must be given to this Scottish restaurant for listing three English wines, with Nyetimber Classic Cuvée 1999 on the value cusp at £32.50. The North American section is not as comprehensive as at some of the other Conran restaurants, and there is nothing of any great value here either, but the 5 star **Joseph Phelps Insignia 1996** might be considered at £145, seeing as it retails  for around £100. In South America, the Argentinian Quimera Malbec/Merlot blend 1999 from Achaval Ferrer is worth a look but it's not cheap at £60. There is always value to be found in the Australian section and this list is no exception. Grosset's Polish Hill Dry Riesling 2003 at £42, **Cullen Margaret River Chardonnay 2000** at £45 and Tyrrell's Vat 47 Chardonnay 2001 at £46 are all 4-star wines that meet our value criteria in the whites, whilst Charlie Melton's Shiraz 2000 at £48.50 and Nine Popes 1999 at £50 do the same in the reds. Plantagenet's Omrah Shiraz 2001 from Western Australia is 3-star value at £26.50, whilst in New Zealand, there is 4-star quality in Mount Edward's Central Otago Pinot Noir at £46.50. There are 15 half-bottles of dry wines listed, of which 8 are of 3-star quality or better, but none of them meet our price criteria. In the magnums, however, Viña Alberdi 1999 from La Rioja Alta in Spain looks excellent value at £45. Dessert wines on the whole look pricey, but a half-bottle of the 5-star Quarts de Chaume from Domaine Baumard at £25 should be good value, although the vintage, 1999, is only average. Finally, in vintage ports, Dow's 1983 at £60 looks very reasonable indeed.

Neville's Best Buy: **Joh Jos Prüm** Wehlener Sonnenuhr Riesling Auslese 1993 – 4-star quality at £47.50

Score: *Quality* 76.99   *Value* 17.99   *Impression* 11.00   *Total* **105.98**

Ranking: *Quality* 27   *Value* 55   *Impression* 94 =   *Overall* **54th**

Recommendations:
NB: 1996 **Joseph Phelps** Insignia at £145
DM: 2001 **Paul Blanck** Tokay Pinot Gris Patergarten at £26.50
PW: 2000 **Cullen** Margaret River Chardonnay at £45

Find out more about wine and wine producers at *www.winebehindthelabel.com*

Scotland

46th

FISHERS IN THE CITY

58 Thistle Street Edinburgh EH2 1EN
0131 225 5109

his is a neat little list – just 125 bins – and on the face of it not particularly interesting, but at the end of the white and red sections there are supplementary lists headed 'Fishers fine wines'. Here is where the quality really begins and, because the prices are very reasonable, where this list earns its top-50 ranking. The regular list is annotated with tasting notes and customers are invited to ask the staff for tasting notes on any of the fine wines. Just over 40% of the wines meet our quality criteria, but of those, almost half meet the value criteria, too. Several wines are available by the glass, but they do not reflect the overall quality of the list, so are best left alone. There are also a few half-bottles of dry wines with a couple of quality choices there. The regular list is conventionally divided by country and region, but the fine wine lists are completely mixed – they are not even in price order, so you will just have to read through them all in order to make your choice; it makes quite pleasant reading.

On the regular list, from New Zealand, the Villa Maria Reserve Clifford Bay 2004 at £23.95 is a good value Sauvignon Blanc. In the USA whites, Stag's Leap Wine Cellars (we presume it is 'Wine Cellars' and not 'Winery' – these are two completely different producers) Napa Valley Chardonnay 2002 is well priced for this wine at £36, even if it doesn't meet our price criteria for the quality. The **Meerlust Estate Chardonnay 2001** from Stellenbosch in South Africa is good 3-star value at £27. There is also good 3-star value in the French whites. Rolly-Gassmann's Gewürztraminer 1996 at £25.50, Chablis 1er cru Fourchaume 2003 from Adhémar Boudin at £26.95 and Saint-Romain, Domaine des Forges 1996, also at £26.95. The 4-star value kicks in with the excellent VdP Côteaux des Fenouillèdes Le Soula 2001 from Gérard Gauby at £36. The fine white wine list follows, with some good 4-star value wines, including **Tyrrell's Vat 1 Hunter Semillon 1997** at £37.50, Pouilly-Fuissé Ménétrières Hors Classé 1998 from Domaine Ferret at £37 and Grüner Veltliner Durnsteiner Kellerberg Smaragd 2000 from F-X Pichler in Austria at £48. There is also a bottle of the super 5-star Château Climens Barsac 1991 at only £49; but beware, it's a poor vintage.

The regular red wine section has excellent value in **Kilikanoon Cabernet Sauvignon 2001** from South Australia at £27, as well as St Francis Old Vines Zinfandel 1998 from California at £27.95. Other good value wines are Esporão Reserva 2002 from Alentejo in Portugal at £19.95 and **Moulin-à-Vent Vignes du Tremblay 2003** from Dom. Paul et Eric Janin at £16.95. There is 4-star value in the Bandol 2000 from Domaine Tempier at £30. The red fine wines show a dazzling display of quality, from the 4-star Clos l'Eglise 1996 Pomerol at only £45 to some super 5-star giants, such as Penfolds Grange 1997 at £160, Château Latour 1986 at £225 and Château Cheval Blanc 1988 at £200. If you want to spend a bit less, then Domaine de Chevalier 1970 at £100 is worth a look. There is quality but no great value in the Champagne section, but a half-bottle of Krug NV at £55 would do very nicely before you tackle the Cheval

Blanc. Among dry half-bottles, Châteauneuf-du-Pape Château de Beaucastel 1997 at £21 looks to have the best price/quality ratio. At the end of the list is a page devoted to the wines of the Dry River Estate in Martinborough in New Zealand. We don't know if there is some connection between the restaurant and this estate, but certainly the wines are some of the highest quality you can find coming out of New Zealand, particularly the Riesling and the Gewürztraminer. The tasting notes that accompany the wines refer to the 2002 Craighall Riesling, although only the 1997 is listed at £55.

This is a list full of hidden gems – a little more quality in the wines by the glass could see this shooting up the table next year.

Neville's Best Buy: Moulin-à-Vent Vignes du Tremblay 2003, from **Dom. Paul et Eric Janin** at £16.95

Score: *Quality* 44.77   *Value* 48.23   *Impression* 18.00   *Total* **111.00**

Ranking: *Quality* 67   *Value* 15   *Impression* 53 =   *Overall* **46th**

Recommendations:
NB: 1997 **Tyrrell's** Vat 1 Hunter Semillon at 37.50
DM: 2001 **Meerlust Estate** Chardonnay at £27
PW: 2001 **Kilikanoon** Cabernet Sauvignon Blocks Road at £27

Find out more about wine and wine producers at *www.winebehindthelabel.com*

Scotland

KILLIECRANKIE HOUSE

Killiecrankie Perthshire & Kinross PH16 5LG
01796 473220

his enthusiastic and anecdotal wine list by ex-wine merchant Tim Waters scores highly in our opinion, mainly for the large number of good 3-star quality wines at very reasonable prices. Tim takes you through his list with a blow-by-blow commentary on every wine except for the few clarets and ports which he bought from a private cellar, declaring 'caveat emptor'. Well, you can't be fairer than that, although we suspect that Tim is a canny buyer.

The list is conventionally arranged by country and region and kicks off with a modest selection of clarets boosted by the list of fine and rare ones purchased from the famous private cellar. Of the 11 wines in this section, there are 3 vintages of Clos du Marquis (second wine of Château Léoville-las-Cases), 1997, 1996 and 1998 at £49, £55 and £59 respectively, which are probably too young for you to have any worries as an *emptor* – we wouldn't! A small selection of red Burgundies and Beaujolais is followed by a much larger selection of wines from the Rhône Valley and southern France, where the Syrah/Cabernet blend Cuvée de la Stèle 2000 from the Mas de la Dame estate in Les Baux de Provence is good value at £25.90. Spanish and Italian reds are relatively mundane, but the list is enhanced by a really good value section of Australian wines dominated by D'Arenberg and Veritas, with the **Veritas Heysen Vineyard Shiraz 2001** at £28.90, although still young, looking to be superb drinking value. New

Scotland

Zealand red choices are not quite up to the same standard and Californian reds are confined to just 2 Zinfandels from Ravenswood, the Old Vine Lodi County 2002 at £21.90 being well worth the extra 2 quid over the regular Zin. South America gets a reasonable look in, but only the relatively pricey and too young Casa Lapostolle Merlot Cuvée Alexandre 2003 (£32.90) is really worth looking at. There are better choices elsewhere on the list. South Africa scores heavily with a number of efforts by Neil Ellis and Vergelegen, but it's the **Saxenburg Private Collection Shiraz 2000** at £24.90 that stands out as a top red at a very friendly price.

In whites, there are a few gaps in the Côte d'Or Burgundies, but there's a good collection of Chablis, culminating in **Domaine Pinson Grand Cru Les Clos 2001** – really fine drinking for under £40, well - £39.90 – compare that with Grand Cru Chablis on other lists, where you will be hard pressed to find anything under £60. Loire Valley wines are pretty straightforward, but there is a fine collection of Alsace wines with top-of-the-range Tokay Pinot Gris, Clos Windsbuhl 1999 from Zind Humbrecht (£39.90 again) adding 5-star quality to the list. White Rhônes include Guigal's Condrieu 2001 at (you've guessed it) £39.90, but the German and Italian sections that follow are thinner. Australian whites are not as powerful as the reds, with Henschke's Louis Semillon 2002 at £25.90 being the best of the bunch. There is a goodly selection of New Zealand whites all drinking well for less than £25, but nothing of outstanding merit. There is an even longer selection of South African whites, all reasonably priced with the Vergelegen Reserve Chardonnay 2001 at £22.90 taking the honours. Small selections from Chile and Champagne have some good value prices.

There are not a lot of dessert wines, but the **Banyuls Domaine de la Mas Blanc 2003** from Dr Parcé (£36.90) is an innovative and outstanding choice, particularly for chocolate lovers. Bravo Tim, for this. There are some ports and Madeiras available by the bottle or the glass and a *caveat emptor* selection of vintage ports from 'a private cellar'. A good selection of half-bottles includes Gewürztraminer Clos Windsbuhl 1998 from Zind Humbrecht (£19.90), but there are only 5 dry wines sold by the glass. However, with the prices on the list being what they are, they can safely be ignored.

If there is a major criticism of the list it is in its reliance on too many wines from the same producer, which does make it a less exciting read. On the other hand, the introduction of wines that you won't see in very many other places, such as the Banyuls, greatly enhances the overall impression and hopefully this will be a continuing trend.

Neville's Best Buy: Banyuls **Domaine de la Mas Blanc** 2003 at £36.90

Score: *Quality* 40.22   *Value* 71.27   *Impression* 19.00   *Total* **130.49**

Ranking: *Quality* 74   *Value* 10   *Impression* 43 =   *Overall* **24th**

Recommendations:
NB: 2001 **Domaine Pinson** Chablis Grand Cru Les Clos at £39.90
DM: 2001 **Saxenburg** Private Collection Shiraz at £24.90
PW: 2001 **Veritas** Shiraz Heysen Vineyard at £28.90

Find out more about wine and wine producers at *www.winebehindthelabel.com*

Scotland

25th

THE PEAT INN

Peat Inn Cupar Fife KY15 5LH
01334 840206

avid Wilson has been ploughing his gastronomic furrow in Scotland for over 30 years now and this wine list is an accumulation of his experiences over that period. He states in his introduction to the list that he is not a traditionalist – and it shows when Mourvèdre from California, Pinot Noir from New Zealand and Viognier from Australia sit side by side with the more familiar offerings from France although, strangely enough, there are no Italian wines on the list. Nearly two thirds of the wines on the list merit 3 stars or more and the prices are on the whole pretty reasonable. There is a good selection of quality halves but wines by the glass are almost non-existent.

The Champagne section sets the tone with Krug NV at a very reasonable £75. In vintage Champagnes Pol Roger's Cuvée Sir Winston Churchill 1990 is well priced, too, at £85. Alsace has the 5-star Riesling Grand Cru Schlossberg 1996 from Domaine Weinbach at £40, whilst in the Loire section there is an interesting 2003 Sancerre Le M D de Bourgeois from Henri Bourgeois at £30. There is some decent white Bordeaux with Domaine de Chevalier 1997 at £58 looking best. On the same page we find a trio of Semillons from Australia, with Tyrrell's Vat 1 Hunter Sémillon 1997 providing excellent 4-star value at £36. On a long list of white Burgundies Dauvissat's Chablis 1er Cru Vaillons 2000 at £38 looks good value and Bonneau du Martray's Corton-Charlemagne 1995 at £110 adds super-5 star quality to the list. Chardonnays from other countries include the 5-star Leeuwin Estate Chardonnay 2000 from Western Australia at £48. Condrieu 2001 from Pierre Gaillard at £45 is the best of the 'other white wines from France', whilst the best value German wine on the list is the Niederhäuser Hermannshöhle Riesling Auslese 1989 from Dönnhoff in the Nahe at £36. There is a good selection of quality white half-bottles with Krug NV at £42 and Chablis 1er Cru Montée de Tonnerre from Louis Michel at £16 providing the best price/quality ratio here.

On the red side, there is a good list of clarets, many of which are in mature, drinkable vintages. Château Léoville-Barton 1982 at £140 and **Château Palmer 1990** at £120 are certainly not overpriced, but if the budget doesn't stretch that far, then Clos du Marquis 1995 (the second wine of Château Léoville-las-Cases) at £45 is well worth looking at. 'Cabernet Sauvignons and Merlots from other countries' has Stag's Leap Wine Cellars SLV 1999 at £45 and Shafer Merlot 1997 at £40 at the value end of the Californian section and the super 5-star Ridge Montebello in 3 different vintages to score at the top quality level at prices between £170 and £185. Australian Cabernets include the Coldstream Hills Briarston Cabernet Sauvignon/Merlot/Cabernet Franc blend 1999 at only £20, whilst the Leeuwin Estate Art Series Cabernet Sauvignon 2000 at £40 is also worth drinking. A list of 7 Beaujolais precede the red Burgundies, of which the Morgon 2002 from Jean Descombes at £20 looks to be the best value.

Scotland

The red Burgundies themselves include some remarkable wines, particularly from Armand Rousseau. The straight Gevrey-Chambertin 1995 at £40 is well priced, but for around double that you can get the super 5-star Grand Cru Clos des Ruchottes for £75 in the 1991 vintage and £85 in the 1988 vintage. Fine drinking indeed. There are other big names such as Dujac, Roumier, Barthod and J J Confuron from the Côtes de Nuits, but the selection from the Côtes de Beaune is less impressive, with the 1993 Pommard 1er Cru Clos des Epeneaux from Comte Armand at £52 looking the best bet. The Rhône selection is certainly not as impressive as Bordeaux or Burgundy (or even California, for that matter). Vacqueyras Cuvée des Templiers 1999 from Clos des Cazaux at £24 is good 3-star entry-level wine and from Provence the **Bandol Cuvée La Tourtine 1998** from Domaine Tempier is one notch up at £38, but the French selection is outperformed by **Cline Cellars Ancient Vines Mourvèdre 1997** from California at £30 and Clarendon Vineyard Old Vine Grenache 1997 from Clarendon Hills at £40. From a striking array of California Zinfandels, Ridge Geyserville 2000 and Cline Cellars Live Oak Vineyard 1997, both at £38, take the honours. A couple of good dry reds hail from the Douro region in Portugal, with the **Quinta do Crasto Vinha da Ponte 1998** at £48 being the best quality. Finally, the page of red half-bottles has as its best shots Shafer Napa Valley Cabernet Sauvignon 1997 at £20 and Châteauneuf-du-Pape 1998 from Domaine du Grand Tinel at £17. This is a slightly idiosyncratic list, but David certainly knows what he likes and it's odds-on that you will like what he has to offer, too.

Neville's Best Buy: **Cline Cellars** Ancient Vines Mourvèdre 1997 at £30

Score: *Quality* 85.70 *Value* 22.08 *Impression* 22.00 *Total* **129.78**

Ranking: *Quality* 19 *Value* 44 *Impression* 21 = *Overall* **25th**

Recommendations:
NB: 1990 **Château Palmer** Margaux at £120
DM: 1998 **Domaine Tempier** Bandol Cuvée La Tourtine at £38
PW: 1998 **Quinta do Crasto** Douro Vinha da Ponte at £48

Find out more about wine and wine producers at *www.winebehindthelabel.com*

Scotland

34th

SANGSTER'S

51 High Street Elie Fife KY9 1BZ

01333 331001

his is another small, quality wine list with a superb price/quality ratio on many of the bottles. There are only 57 bins on the list, but 20 are of 3-star quality or above, of which 13 meet our value criteria. The only drawback is that there is little in the way of wines by the glass and no half-bottles of dry wine except for one Champagne. The Champagne in question is **Deutz NV**, which is very fairly priced at £30 a bottle and £15 for the half. After the Champagnes, dessert wines are listed and here the best choices are either the Noble Sémillon 2003, or the Museum Muscat NV, both from Yalumba, in South Australia and both priced at £19.75 for the half-bottle. The whites are divided into French, Italian, Austrian and New World. France has a Sancerre of outstanding value – **Lucien Crochet Le Chêne Marchand 2003** at £19.95 – and Saint-Aubin Le Charmois 2000 from Bernard Morey at £29.95 is also good value. The undoubted choice from Italy is Antinori's Cervaro della Sala 2003 from Umbria – 4-star quality at £33.50. The Austrian choice of Willi Bründlmayer's Grüner Veltliner Alte Reben 2003 is superb value at £22.50. Best value in the New World whites are the 2003 Pinot Gris from Matakana Estate in the North Island of New Zealand at £21.95 and the 2003 Riesling The Mesh from the Grosset/Hill-Smith partnership in South Australia at £24.50.

French reds have Chambolle-Musigny 1er Cru Les Feusselottes 2001 from Mugneret-Gibourg at £39 and in Italy there is the **2000 Antinori Guado al Tasso** at £39.50, both of 4-star quality. In New World reds, best value comes from **Matakana Estate Moko** Merlot/Cabernet 2000 at £21.50.

As we have said – the list is short, but there is plenty of good drinking value there. There are also useful tasting notes for each wine, which should help you make informed decisions. There are a number of good restaurants in the area, but this is one not to be missed.

Neville's Best Buy: **Lucien Crochet** Sancerre Le Chêne Marchand 2003 at £19.95

Score: *Quality* 29.82 *Value* 76.67 *Impression* 12.00 *Total* **118.49**

Ranking: *Quality* 91 *Value* 7 *Impression* 92 = *Overall* **34th**

Recommendations:
NB: 2000 **Antinori** Guado al Tasso at £39.50
DM: **Deutz** NV Champagne at £30
PW: 2000 **Matakana Estate** Moko at £21.50

39th

SUMMER ISLES HOTEL

Achiltibuie Ross shire IV26 2YG

01854 622282

his hotel is a long way from anywhere, so it's not surprising that prices are not quite as cheap as they could be, what with the cost of transportation. Nevertheless, the Irvines have done a remarkable job in putting together such a very good list, and whilst our value criteria applies only to around 15% of the 3-star and upwards wines on the list, the quality criteria applies to some 40% of the whole. Additionally, there is a goodly number of half bottles available, although you will have to look at the end of each section of the list to find them. A complete list of half-bottles would be useful. Wines by the glass are indicated as going with the food available each day, but these are only taken from the list of wines available from the bar by the glass anyway, so there is no real incentive for experimentation. Notwithstanding this, the nearly 500-strong list makes fascinating reading and holds many hidden gems.

Unusually, the list doesn't start off with Champagnes, but with red Bordeaux. There is good value on the first page in the shape of Château Cap de Faugères Côtes de Castillon 1998, an excellent vintage in the Right Bank, at only £21.50, and at the top end Château Lafite-Rothschild 1979 shouldn't be drinking badly at £145, although there are a number of other wines you can pay a lot more money for. On a fair list of Bordeaux half bottles Château Malescot-St.-Exupéry 2000 at £22 looks best and might just about be ready to drink. In white Bordeaux, Clos Floridène 2002 from the Graves at £30 should be drinking well. The best quality/price ratio wine on the red Burgundy list is undoubtedly Jean-Noël Gagnard's Chassagne-Montrachet l'Estimée 1999 at £29.50, and at the other end of the list, the Latricières-Chambertin 1998 from Domaine Rossignol-Trapet at £79.50 is probably a better bet than the Grands Echézeaux 1985 from Domaine de la Romanée-Conti at £545. Also from DRC is the 1991 Richebourg for only £330. There are some good value Beaujolais on the list, not always easy to find, with Hubert Lapierre's Moulin-à-Vent Vieilles Vignes 2002 at £18 and Michel Tête's Juliénas Cuvée Prestige 2002 at £22 standing out. In white Burgundies, the Mâcon-Milly Lamartine 2003 from Les Héritiers du Comte Lafon 2003 is 3-star value at £26.50, while the super 5-star Corton-Charlemagne 1991 from Bonneau du Martray is not unreasonably priced at £105. There are quality choices in half-bottles for both red and white Burgundies, but nothing of outstanding value. In the Côtes-du-Rhône whites, Châteauneuf-du-Pape Blanc 2002, from Château Mont Redon, is on the value cusp at £30.50, but there is outstanding value in the reds in the shape of the **Domaine du Vieux-Télégraphe Châteauneuf-du-Pape 1999**, super 5-star quality at only £36.50 (£19 the half bottle). The Hermitage 1996 from Domaine du Colombier is also good value at £49. Loire Valley wines include Lucien Crochet's white and rosé Sancerres (2002 for the white and 2003 for the rosé) both at £23 and his 2002 red at only £20. Gaston Huët's Le Mont Sec Vouvray 2002 is in at £28.50, while the super 5-star Savennières Coulée de Serrant 1999 from Nicolas Joly should just about be ready to drink at £59.50. Yannick Amirault's Bourgeuil La Petite Cave

Vieilles Vignes 2000 is a well priced Loire red at £25.50. In Alsace, the Faller sisters' Domaine Weinbach 1997 Riesling is in at £30. The French section finishes off with Champagnes – there is nothing really good value there, but for lovers of rarities, the super 5-star 1995 **Salon Le Mesnil** is tempting at £148.

Away from France, there are some good value reds from Spain with the Viña Pedrosa Crianza 1994 and **La Rioja Alta's Viña Alberdi Reserva 1998** looking the best value at £25.50, but for just a little more there is the Bodegas Duron Crianza 1999 from Ribera del Duero at £27.50 and Alvaro Palacios's Les Terrasses 2001 from Priorat at £30. Portugal has the Quinta de Chocapalha Touriga Nacional 2000 at £28.50 and the European trio of Germany, Austria and Switzerland have some interesting listings, but nothing of outstanding value. Italy has a Nero d'Avola 2002 from Do Zenner in Sicily at £29.50 and the best price any 4-star wine can muster is the Barbaresco Brich Ronchi 1998 from Albino Rocca at £65. There ought to be scope for quality in the USA selections and we were not disappointed, although the prices are relatively steep. Saintsbury Carneros Unfiltered Chardonnay 1997 comes in reasonably at £30, but after that, better value can be found elsewhere in the list unless you simply have to go for the 1999 Screaming Eagle at £1,455. Which brings us to Australia. **Crawford River Riesling 2001** at £28.50 and Colonial Estate's L'Explorateur Shiraz 2003 at £26.50 represent 3-star quality at under £30, but better value can be found in the Redbank Sally's Paddock 1997 at £33. New Zealand has three 3-star wines at under £30, Fromm's La Strada Chardonnay 2000 at £26, Vavasour Sauvignon Blanc 2003

Scotland

at £29 and Dry River Chardonnay 2001 at £29.50. There is some good value to be found in the Argentinian section, with the Malbec Altos Las Hormigas 2001 at £21 and Malbec Grande Reserve 2001 from Alta Vista at £22, as well as Achaval-Ferrer's Quimera 2001 blend of Malbec, Cabernet Sauvignon and Merlot – 4-star quality just outside the line at £52. The choices from Chile do not excite us but there are some good value wines from South Africa, notably the Oaked Chardonnay 2000 from Cordoba Vineyard at £18, the Saxenburg Private Collection Pinotage 2000 at £19 and the Private Collection Shiraz 2000 at £25.

There is a fair selection of dessert wines – Château Coutet 1995 seems fair value at £28 for a half-bottle, but it is in a poor vintage for Sauternes. A better bet would be to go for Domaine Weinbach's Tokay-Pinot Gris Vendange Tardive in the excellent 1997 vintage at £39 the half-bottle, or you could really go for broke and have their rare Riesling Cuvée d'Or, Quintessence de Sélections Grains Nobles 2001 at £127.50 for the half. Alternatively, you could try a full bottle of 1996 Château Climens at £109 in an excellent year for Sauternes. Vintage ports are well represented with Fonseca 1983 at £75 but this is not notable vintage for this great port shipper, better to go for a half-bottle of Graham's 1980 at £34.

This is a very well thought out list with a number of good value wines as well as some naturally pricey rarities and we presume that there must also be enough single malt whiskies to keep you going for a very long time. A little shading of some of the prices would do wonders for the list's ratings in future years.

Neville's Best Buy: **Domaine du Vieux-Télégraphe** Châteauneuf-du-Pape 1999, super 5-star quality at only £36.50 (£19 the half bottle)

Score: *Quality* 76.76 *Value* 17.18 *Impression* 20.00 *Total* **113.94**

Ranking: *Quality* 28 *Value* 58 *Impression* 34 = *Overall* **39th**

Recommendations:
NB: 1995 **Salon-le-Mesnil** Champagne at £148
DM: 1998 **La Rioja Alta** Rioja Viña Alberdi Reserva at £25.50
PW: 2001 **Crawford River** Riesling at £28.50

68th

THE THREE CHIMNEYS

Colbost Dunvegan Isle of Skye IV55 8ZT

01470 511258

t's always nice to find a quality wine list in a remote area such as the Isle of Skye and we suppose we must excuse the Three Chimneys for its poor showing in the value section (84th out of 100) due to the cost of transporting the wines to such a location. Over 200 wines are listed, of which almost a third are of 3-star quality or more, but of those, less than 10% meet our value criteria. There is a good list of half-bottles available and 9 dry wines come by the glass, of which the only 3-star wine is the Billecart-Salmon NV Champagne at £8.50 for a 125ml glass. The list is arranged conventionally by country and region and there are short tasting notes for most of the wines, which is a useful adjunct in making your choices.

Apart from the Champagne mentioned above, there are no 3-star wines in the House wine selections, but nevertheless there are a few 2-star choices. The Languedoc has the 3-star white 2001 and the 4-star red 2002 from Domaine Gauby, pretty heftily priced (particularly the white) at £54.95 and £52.95 respectively. In Champagne the 5-star **Pol Roger Cuvée Sir Winston Churchill 1995** is well priced at £99.95. There's better value in the Alsace section, with a pair of 4-star Gewürztraminers – Kappelweg de Rorschwihr 1998 from Rolly-Gassmann at £42.95, and **Grand Cru Furstentum Vieilles Vignes 2002** from Albert Mann at £36.95. In the Loire, the 4-star Clos du Bourg Demi-Sec 1996 at £46.25 and the 3-star **Le Haut-Lieu Sec 1998** at £29.95 from Huët represent value for money, but the same cannot be said for any of the choices, red or white from Bordeaux: although Château l'Evangile is a 5-star wine, you would have to think twice about paying £99.95 for the average 1997 vintage. It's the same in Burgundy, although you would pay less for 5-star quality here – £72.95 for Ghislaine Barthod's Chambolle-Musigny 1er Cru les Cras, but from the pretty weak 1994 vintage. The red Rhône section has the 4-star Châteauneuf-du-Pape Vieilles Vignes 2000 from Domaine de Villeneuve just off the value cusp at £53.95, but if you want to go for 5 stars, Jean-Luc Colombo's Cornas La Louvée 1997 is available at a fairly substantial £70.95. There's nothing exciting in Austria, Spain or in Italian whites, but in the reds the Aglianico Donnaluna 2003 from De Conciliis in Campania at £29.95 is fair value for the quality.

There are wines from Greece and California, but in neither case are our criteria met. New Zealand, however, has the 4-star **Stonecroft Hawkes Bay Syrah 1999** at a good value £47.95. Cloudy Bay Sauvignon Blanc 2004 is a pretty outrageous £49.95. There is nothing in Australia that meets our price/quality ratio for wines, although there certainly are wines of quality listed. South African and South American entries don't particularly excite us, either, but there is a good deal of quality among the half bottles – at a price, of course. It's the same story with the pudding wines, although a bottle of Riesling Auslese 1989 from Schloss Schönborn at £39.25 is acceptable.

Scotland

Neville's Best Buy: Gewürztraminer Grand Cru Furstentum Vieilles Vignes 2002 from **Albert Mann** at £36.95

Score: *Quality* 58.69   *Value* 9.27   *Impression* 26.00   *Total* **93.96**

Ranking: *Quality* 49   *Value* 84   *Impression* 11 =   *Overall* **68th**

Recommendations:
NB: 1995 **Pol Roger** Cuvée Sir Winston Churchill at £99.95
DM: 1998 **Huët** Vouvray Le Haut-Lieu Sec at £29.95
PW: 1999 **Stonecroft** Hawkes Bay Syrah at £47.95

43rd

UBIQUITOUS CHIP

12 Ashton Lane Glasgow G12 8SJ
0141 334 5007

---

long-standing purveyor of quality wines to Glaswegians, this restaurant has a somewhat rambling list that contains a number of hidden gems from around the world. Over 50% of the 339 wines listed are of 3-star quality or better and a good selection of half-bottles and wines by the glass, particularly in the Upstairs Restaurant are most welcome. Prices are not cheap, but this should not inhibit one from making deep explorations into the list.

The list kicks off with Champagne and sparkling wines, including a good selection of somewhat pricey vintage Champagnes. Probably the best value is the Roederer Brut NV at £47.80. There is a long list of Bordeaux wines, many of which are of very high quality, and in quite drinkable vintages, with Château Lafon-Rochet 1988 at £56.20 worth a try. In recent vintages, the 1997 Château Certan de May at £49.50 looks reasonable, too. For top end buyers, Château Latour 1983 at £265 would fit the bill nicely. White Bordeaux, both dry and sweet, are high quality choices with Pavillon Blanc du Château Margaux 2000 at £96.50 and Château Suduiraut 1996 at £69 standing out. White Burgundies have Leflaive's Puligny-Montrachet Clavoillon 1988 at £198 for a magnum and 1999 Chablis Grand Cru Les Clos from Duplessis at £63 as our 4-star choices. Red Burgundies are a veritable *tour de force*, with **Armand Rousseau Gevrey-Chambertin 1er Cru Clos Saint-Jacques 1997** flying the flag for super 5-star quality at £129. Loire whites shine with best value coming from Domaine des Baumard's Savennières Clos du Papillon 1998 at £28.40 and their **Côteaux du Layon Clos Sainte-Catherine 1995** at £27.80 – both 4-star quality at under £30. The quality of the Alsace section doesn't match that of Bordeaux and Burgundy, but **Rolly Gassmann Riesling Kappelweg de Rorschwihr 1995** at £28.50 should be worth drinking. Northern Rhône whites have Georges Vernay's Condrieu Les Terrasses de l'Empire 2001 at £58.50, while the reds have a magnum of Hermitage La Chapelle 1985 at £325 which should be drinking well. There is top quality red Châteauneuf-du-Pape (at a price) – Château du Beaucastel 1990 at £132 and Château Rayas 1989 at £376.95. In French country wines, Domaine de Trévallon 1996 is £52 and should be drinking well now. Italian whites do not match the quality of the Italian reds, where Arnaldo Caprai's Sagrantino di Montefalco 1998 is the pick of the bunch for value at £44. Gaja's 1999 Barbaresco provides super 5-star quality at £134. There are some good Spanish choices with La Rioja Alta's Reserva 904 1994 vintage looking to be an excellent choice at £57 and Vega Sicilia Unico 1985 at £115 not looking overpriced.

The New World kicks off with some fair offerings from California, with Rochioli's Russian River Valley Sauvignon Blanc 2003 looking value at £26.80. At the other end of the spectrum, the Niebaum-Coppola Rubicon 1993 at £97.80 looks a far better deal than Opus One 1996 at £185. From a long list of Australian wines the value stakes go to Yering Station's Marsanne-Viognier/Roussanne 2003 at £28.95 and the quality stakes to Torbreck's super 5-star RunRig 2001 at £173, although it may be too

Scotland

young to drink. Grant Burge's Meshach Shiraz 1998 is only a notch down at 5 stars and may be a better drinking bet for now at £95.50. There's surprisingly little of top quality from New Zealand but in South Africa, Hamilton-Russell's 2003 Chardonnay at £28.95 looks good value. In the short South American selection Clos de los Siete 2003 from Argentina at £33.30 is the best quality wine listed.

There is a long list of German wines, particularly from the Mosel, with **Dr. Loosen Wehlener Sonnenuhr Riesling Spätlese** from the excellent 2001 vintage at £26.85 at the value end and the Eitelsbacher Karthäuserhofberg Riesling Auslese 1997 from Weingut Karthäuserhof at £43.50 at the higher end. The Austrian selection is pretty much dominated by Willi Opitz's stickies, with the Goldackerl Beerenauslese 2001 looking the best value at £26.95 the half-bottle, although the Roter Eiswein Cuvée 1998 (a red Eiswein) looks intriguing, even if it will set you back £78.25 for a half. The list finishes off with some impressive sherries and ports, not the least of which is the super 5-star Amontillado Coliseo from Valdespino at £31.75. There are some ports from great vintages, but Graham's 1966 will set you back £150 and Warre's 1963, £198. There is also an enormous selection of Scotch whiskies, as you would expect from such a serious Scottish list. This is one of the best lists in Scotland and a great complement to the casual dining experience at 'The Chip', although it's not an easy one to read.

Neville's Best Buy: **Domaine des Baumard** Côteaux du Layon Clos Sainte-Catherine 1995 at £27.80

Score: *Quality* 71.95   *Value* 21.45   *Impression* 18.00   *Total* **111.40**

Ranking: *Quality* 34   *Value* 47   *Impression* 53 =   *Overall* **43rd**

Recommendations:
NB: 1997 **Armand Rousseau** Gevrey-Chambertin 1er Cru Clos Saint-Jacques at £129
DM: 1995 **Rolly Gassmann** Riesling Kappelweg de Rorschwihr at £28.50
PW: 2001 **Dr Loosen** Wehlener Sonnenuhr Riesling Spätlese at £26.85

Find out more about wine and wine producers at *www.winebehindthelabel.com*

Scotland

35th

WITCHERY BY THE CASTLE

Castlehill Royal Mile Edinburgh EH1 2NF
0131 225 5613

his list of nearly 500 wines has been skilfully put together by John Power and is a masterpiece of clarity of presentation. The 138-page list, bound in a hard cover, may appear daunting at first glance, but there are no more than about 7 wines on any page, all of which are amply described with comprehensive tasting notes. The list is conventionally arranged by country and region and would certainly have enjoyed a higher rating had the prices not been so fierce. That doesn't mean to say that there are no bargains to be found on the list, but they need to be dug out and we hope that this appraisal will help you to find some of them. Some 60% of the wines on the list are of 3-star quality or more and there are a reasonable number which meet our price criteria.

The list starts off with the 'Witchery selection', 13 wines available by either the bottle or the glass, but there is nothing of any real interest here. Pol Roger White Foil Brut NV at £40 starts off a very good list of Champagnes. Among vintage Champagnes Krug 1988 at £180 gives an indication of the general price levels of this list. Bordeaux comes next, with a comprehensive list of clarets, but there is nothing in there to meet our price/quality criteria. However, Clos Fourtet 1995 at £60 seems good value for the list, but bear in mind that this was before the recent change in ownership, so the wine may not possess the same finesse as is now apparent from the 2001 vintage onwards. Other wines to consider pricewise are Château Cissac 1996 at £45 and Château La Lagune 1983 at £85. There is quite a lot of top drawer stuff, Château Latour 1982 at £825, Mouton-Rothschild 1982 at £875 and Château Margaux 1982 at £675 from the Left Bank; and Château Pétrus 1989 at £1750 and Château Le Pin 1990 at £2000. In the Sauternes section, Château La Tour Blanche 1989 at £55 is good value in an excellent vintage and Château d'Yquem 1983 is £410, but there is not much in between. In Burgundy, Charmes-Chambertin 1997 from Armand Rousseau at £80 and Gevrey-Chambertin 1er Cru Clos Saint-Jacques 1997 from Bruno Clair at £85 are the best drinking value, although you could splash out £835 on a bottle of La Tâche 1996 from the Domaine de la Romanée-Conti. White Burgundies has Chablis 1er Cru Fôret 1999 from Raveneau at £70 and Chassagne-Montrachet 1er Cru Les Chenevottes 1996 from Jean Noël Gagnard at £80, both 4-star wines. If you want super 5-star quality, then Chevalier-Montrachet 1997 from Domaine Leflaive at £250 is your wine.

There's better value to be had in the Rhône, with the Vinsobres Côtes du Rhône 2001 from Chaume-Arnaud at only £22. In the Northern Rhône section, Bernard Chave's Crozes-Hermitage 2001 is also good value at £24.50. At the other end of the spectrum, the Hermitage 1985 from Jean-Louis Chave is super 5-star quality at £155, as is the Côte-Rôtie La Turque 1990 from Guigal at £275. Domaine Chave's Hermitage Blanc 1994 is another super 5-star wine at £110. In the Loire Valley

Scotland

section, Nicolas Joly's **Savennières Coulée de Serrant 1996** is a super 5-star wine at a reasonable £60 and there is also Henry Pellé's Ménetou-Salon Clos des Blanchais 2003 at £28.50 and Pierre-Jacques Druet's Bourgueil Cent Boisselées 1996 at £28. Regional France has the 5-star Domaine du Trévallon Rouge 1996 at £60. There is nothing of outstanding value in the Alsace section, but Trimbach's Cuvée Fréderic-Émile Riesling Vendange Tardives 1990 is quality at £75. There is some value drinking in the Italian sections, with the Merlot and Sangiovese blend Belcore 2001 at £29 from I Giusti & Zanza in Tuscany and a Verdicchio dei Castelli di Jesi Classico 2002 at £26 from Bucci in the Marche. Of course, there are super wines from Piedmont and Super-Tuscans at super prices: Gaja's Barbaresco Costa Russi 1988 is £230 and Antinori's Solaia 1997 is £260, although the latter is definitely too young to drink. At a more reasonable level, Romano Dal Forno's Valpolicella Superiore 1998 at £70 is good value for this rather expensive cult winemaker. There is an excellent Spanish selection, with Gotim Bru 2002, a blend of Cabernet, Merlot and Tempranillo from Castell del Remei, excellent value at only £20, while both the Rioja Gran Reserva 904 1994 from La Rioja Alta at £52.50 and Castillo Ygay Gran Reserva Especial 1989 from Marqués de Murietta at £55 are mature enough to be really enjoyed. In Portugal, Dirk Niepoort's Redoma Red 1996 from the Douro at £33.50 is excellent value for a 4-star wine. Austrian choices include **F-X Pichler Loibner Berg Grüner Veltliner Smaragd 2000** from the Wachau at £55 and Alois Kracher's super 5-star Nouvelle Vague Trockenbeerenauslese 1996 at £60 the half-bottle.

There is a very big selection of wines from California, some of them belying the notion that these wines are expensive. Leading the value wines are the usual suspects, Cline Cellars and Ridge, with Cline Zinfandel 2001 coming in at £24.50 and Ridge York Creek Petite Sirah 1999 at £35. There are other value wines from Ridge – Cabernet Sauvignon Santa Cruz Mountains 1996 at £40 and Geyserville Sonoma County Zinfandel 2001 at £45. Alban Vineyards Estate Viognier 1998 at £50 and the Côte-Rôtie lookalike, Alban Vineyards Lorraine Syrah 1997 at £55 are also value for money in the context of this list. Kistler Chardonnay Les Noisetières 2002 is respectably priced at £80, while Sanford Barrel Select Pinot Noir 1998 is good 4-star Pinot at £55. The big guns are here, too. Harlan Estate Cabernet 1997 is a whopping £425, Dalla Valle's Maya 2000 is £350 and Opus One 1997 is £250, but you will probably do better with the Caymus Special Select Cabernet Sauvignon 1997 at only £185. Oregon does pretty well, too, with Duck Pond Pinot Noir 2003 good value at £22.50 and **Cristom Marjorie Vineyard Pinot Noir 2000** bringing a 4-star quality Pinot Noir at £55. Argentina has a couple of quality wines from Catena, but these are pretty heavily priced. South Africa offers better value, with the **Welgemeend Estate Red 1997** at £26 and Martin Meinert's Merlot 2000 at £29.50. There are some good value wines in the extensive Australian section with Hollick Chardonnay 2002 and Shiraz/Cabernet 2003 coming in at £26 and £26.50 respectively. Henschke's Louis Semillon 2001 at £28.50 and Cape Mentelle Semillon/Sauvignon 2003 at £23.95 are also good value. There are, of course, the top names, such as Penfolds Grange and Henschke Hill of Grace in various vintages at prices ranging from £275 to £500, but if you are after at least 4-star quality, you should look at either the Cape Mentelle Cabernet/Merlot 2001 at £32, or the cult Virgin Hills 1993 red at £40. New Zealand has Stonecroft Syrah 1999, 4-star value at £43, and Dry River Craighall 2002 Riesling

Scotland

at £45. Finally there is a fair selection of half-bottles with Bernard Chave's Crozes-Hermitage 2001 at £13.95 looking the best value.

Neville's Best Buy: **Clos de Coulée de Serrant** Savennières Coulée de Serrant 1996 at £60

Score: *Quality* 78.23 *Value* 15.47 *Impression* 24.00 *Total* **117.70**

Ranking: *Quality* 26 *Value* 64 *Impression* 15 = *Overall* **35th**

Recommendations:
NB: 2000 **Cristom** Pinot Noir Marjorie Vineyard at £55
DM: 1997 **Welgemeend** Estate Red at £26
PW: 2000 **F-X Pichler** Loibner Berg Grüner Veltliner Smaragd at £55

23rd

THE BELL AT SKENFRITH

Skenfrith Monmouthshire NP7 8UH

01600 750235

illiam Hutchings is a true wine enthusiast and this is reflected in this all-embracing wine list. In fact, there are 2 wine lists, as the list for pudding wines and digestifs is separately bound. There are almost 300 wines on the lists, of which nearly 40% are of 3-star quality or higher, and of these 36 wines meet both our quality and price criteria, so there's enough to choose from, as well as some top quality wines at higher prices. Almost a third of the wines listed are in small formats (half-bottles or 50cl), which is extremely conducive to experimentation, especially because over half of them are of 3-star quality or above. Wines by the glass are less impressive. The list is laid out in a somewhat idiosyncratic order but at least there is an index at the front to help find your way round it and there are useful tasting notes for most of the entries to help you along in your choices.

The list starts off with a large selection of Champagne and sparkling wines, with the entry-level Gosset Excellence Brut NV well priced at £25. It's also nice to see that the sparkling wines include the local Monnow Valley Sparkling Seyval Blanc and a sparkling dry Somerset cider, fermented by the *méthode champenoise*, both at £16, although, not having tasted them, we are unable to vouch for the quality. There is a good selection of half-bottles of Champagne with Krug NV reasonably priced at £55. The choice of vintage Champagnes is excellent, with 1996 Dom Pérignon and 1993 Pol Roger Cuvée Sir Winston Churchill both very well priced at £80 and £85 respectively. The most intriguing Champagne, however, is the **1997 Bollinger Vieilles Vignes Françaises Blancs de Noirs**. Only 140 bottles were made, of which only 9 have been allocated to the UK, so this is indeed a rare treat if you are prepared to fork out £295 for the privilege. The list of half-bottles comes next, with Trimbach's Riesling Reserve 2002 at £11 looking good value in the whites. There is even more choice in the reds with a half-bottle of Domaine Tempier's Bandol 2000 at £13 looking good value, too, but even better value is a half-bottle of the super 5-star **2000 Châteauneuf-du-Pape Domaine du Vieux-Télégraphe** at only £19. There are a lot of classy halves at all prices going right up to Château Haut-Brion 1990 at £125.

The white wine list proper then starts. Alte Reben Grüner Veltliner 2003 from Dr. Unger in Austria is in at a very reasonable £13; other wines with a good price/quality ratio are the Gravitas Sauvignon Blanc 2003 from New Zealand at £23, Albariño 2003 from Pazo de Señoránas in Spain at £20 and Chablis 1er Cru Montée de Tonnerre 2003 from Domaine Vauroux at £28. The reds are more numerous. Morgon 2003 from Domaine de la Chanaise (Domaines Piron) in Beaujolais at £19 is excellent value as is the **Cornish Point Drystone Pinot Noir 2002** from Central Otago, New Zealand at £28 and **Domaine Tempier Bandol Cuvée Speciale La Migoua 1999** at £35, the latter 2 being of 4-star quality. Moving up to the big boys, the 1999 Pommard 1er Cru Epenots from Nicolas Potel at £43 looks good value, but after that

Wales

we get into serious money, although Nicolas Potel's 1999 Charmes-Chambertin at £60 is reasonable enough for a *grand cru* wine. Hermitage La Chapelle 1983 at £85 is a good price for the vintage, as is Château Chasse-Spleen 1982 at £72. There are a number of top clarets in mature vintages listed, from the above-mentioned Château Chasse-Spleen, right through to Château Mouton-Rothschild 1986 at £330. In between these prices, Château Cos d'Estournel 1985 at £97, Château Pichon-Longueville-Lalande 1989 at £110, Château Latour 1986 at £170, Château Palmer 1983 at £185, Château Margaux 1985 at £260 and Château Cheval Blanc 1983 at £260, amongst others, gives a wide enough choice. The list finishes with a section called 'Odds and sods' which is essentially a bin-ends list at very cheap prices for the quality. By the time you read this, the bottles on the list sent to us will have probably gone, so there is not much point commenting on them, but this is a section to consider whenever you visit, because we are sure that you will find some bargains there.

There is a separate list for pudding wines and digestifs. Looking good value is a half-bottle of 1999 Domaine Castera Cuvée Privilège from Jurançon in South-West France at £10, De Bortoli Deen Vat 5 Botrytis Semillon 2000 at £11 and Passito di Pantelleria 2001 from Pellegrino at £13. There are some good bottles of Sauternes on the list, but surprisingly no halves; Château Guiraud 1989 is well priced at £49 in a pretty fair vintage and the super 5-star Château Climens 1983 at £75 and Rieussec 1989 at £89 are top drinking material. A bottle of the single-quinta Quinta do Panascal 1988 from Fonseca is good value 3-star drinking at £29 in the port section.

Neville's Best Buy: A half bottle of the super 5-star Châteauneuf-du-Pape 2000 from **Domaine du Vieux-Télégraphe** at £19

Score: *Quality* 68.69   *Value* 27.89   *Impression* 34.00   *Total* **130.58**

Ranking: *Quality* 39   *Value* 34   *Impression* 3 =   *Overall* **23rd**

Recommendations:
NB: 1997 **Bollinger** Vieilles Vignes Françaises Blancs de Noirs at £295
DM: 1999 **Domaine Tempier** Bandol La Migoua at £35
PW: 2002 **Cornish Point** Drystone Pinot Noir at £28

70th

THE CROWN AT WHITEBROOK

Whitebrook Monmouthshire NP25 4TX
01600 860254

nce again, there is good value to be found in rural Wales, although this establishment is perhaps not quite as rural as some, being in the heart of the Wye Valley. There are just over 100 wines on this list; unfortunately, less than 20% meet our quality criteria, but of these around half qualify for our value criteria. If they could list more of the right wines while keeping to their mark up policy, we are sure that there would be a much higher rating for this establishment. There are a reasonable number of half-bottles, but again, very little in the way of 3-star quality or greater, and of 7 wines by the glass nothing is of 3-star quality. The list is arranged quite usefully by grape variety or style, with comprehensive tasting notes.

The white wines kick off with the Chardonnay section, but there is nothing there of quality until you reach the Chablis 1er Cru Les Lys 1998 from Domaine Defaix, although even this is outside our price criteria for the quality at £35.95. There is nothing either in the Pinot Gris section, but in the Sauvignon Blancs, there are 2 worthwhile options from New Zealand, the 3-star Hunter's Winemaker Selection 2002 at £28 and the Cloudy Bay at £30. Unfortunately, there's not much else to go for in the whites, but in the reds, New Zealand scores again with C J Pask's Hawkes Bay Merlot 2000 – good value at £19.75. In the Cabernet Sauvignon section, the **2001 Bowen Estate Coonawarra** example from South Australia is excellent value at £28, and there are a few smart clarets, but at not very interesting prices. There is nothing exciting in the Pinot Noir section, but in the Tempranillos, value can be found with the Viña Salceda Rioja 2000 at £20.25. Gamays don't shine, either, but in the Syrah section, Kaapzicht Shiraz 2001 from Stellenbosch in South Africa is good value at £21.75, as is the **Vieux Mas des Papes 2001**, the second wine of Domaine du Vieux-Télégraphe at £30.85. Finally, in 'Other red grape varieties', there is good value in both the **Rockford Moppa Springs 1999** (Grenache-based) from the Barossa Valley in South Australia at £27.40 and the **Amarone della Valpolicella Classico Superiore Acinatico 2000** from Stefano Accordini at £38.95.

Neville's Best Buy: Cabernet Sauvignon 2001 from **Bowen Estate** in Coonawarra, South Australia at £28

Score: *Quality* 19.26   *Value* 56.25   *Impression* 17.00   *Total* **92.51**

Ranking: *Quality* 100   *Value* 12   *Impression* 61 = *Overall* **70th**

Recommendations:
NB: 1999 **Rockford** Moppa Springs at £27.40
DM: 2001 **Domaine du Vieux-Télégraphe** Vieux Mas des Papes at £30.85
PW: 2000 **Stefano Accordini** Amarone della Valpolicella Classico Superiore Acinatico at £38.95

Find out more about wine and wine producers at *www.winebehindthelabel.com*

Wales

DYLANWAD DA

2 Ffôs-y-Felin Dolgellau Gwynedd LL40 1BS
01341 422870

ompared with most of the lists we have reviewed, this is a minnow, but we are convinced that the undoubted enthusiasm for wine that Dylan Rowlands shows in his introduction will ensure that it will grow in size over the next few years. Let's hope that he will continue to pursue his extraordinarily fair pricing policy (at least, fair for the customer), because this is one of the places where you can drink some real quality wines at a very reasonable price. Only about 25% of the list falls into our quality criteria of 3 stars or above, but of those wines, practically all meet our price criteria, so you can order with confidence, knowing that it won't break the bank. There is also a fair proportion of half-bottles in the list, a quarter of which rank 3 stars or more, but none of the wines by the glass meets our quality criteria. Nevertheless, this is a minor criticism of this customer-friendly list with its informative tasting notes for each wine.

Wales

The list starts off with 'Cellar specials', described as 'an additional selection of quality wines which have been maturing in our cellars and are now ready to drink'. We presume that this implies that there are more goodies to be trotted out over the course of the next few years and we will wait for these with bated breath. Four *cru bourgeois* clarets are offered, with Château Les Ormes de Pez 1996 at £32 the bottle and £18.20 the half seeming to offer the best value. For a step up in quality to 4 stars, Château Grand-Puy-Lacoste 1993 at £33 is only a pound more than the Ormes de Pez, but in an inferior vintage. There follows the super-5 star Châteauneuf-du-Pape Domaine du Vieux-Télégraphe in the good 1995 vintage at an extraordinarily low price of £41.40 the bottle or £21.40 the half. Quality continues with, from Italy, **Barolo Bricco delle Viole 1997** from G D Vajra at £40.60, and Mezzopane 2001, a Sangiovese and Cabernet blend from Poggio San Polo in Montalcino at £28.50. Two stunning 4-star Loire whites follow: **Huët Le Mont Demi-Sec Vouvray 2000** at £19.20 and the Savennières Clos de la Bergerie Roche-aux-Moines 1990 from Nicolas Joly at £30.20. The cellar specials end with Rolly-Gassmann's 3-star Riesling 2001 from Alsace at £17.20.

The main list doesn't offer the same concentration of quality but it is very well priced. If we had to pick out two whites we would go for Peter Jakob Kühn's Riesling Kabinett 2002 from the Rheingau at £15.40 and the Millton Vineyard Chenin Blanc 2001 from Gisborne in New Zealand at £16.80. Our 2 reds would be the **Gigondas 1999 from Domaine Raspail-Ay** at £19.40 and **Ata Rangi Pinot Noir 2001** from Marlborough in New Zealand at £27.80. A half-bottle of Mount Horrocks Cordon Cut Riesling 2004 at £15.20 with the pudding would finish off a memorable meal. It's a pity Dylan doesn't have any accommodation where we could sleep it all off!

Neville's Best Buy: Vouvray Le Mont Demi-Sec 2000 from **Huët** at £19.20

Score: *Quality* 35.08 *Value* 104.17 *Impression* 16.00 *Total* **155.25**

Ranking: *Quality* 85 *Value* 2 *Impression* 73 = *Overall* **7th**

Recommendations:
NB: 2001 **Ata Rangi** Pinot Noir at £27.80
DM: 1999 **Domaine Raspail-Ay** Gigondas at £19.40
PW: 1997 **G D Vajra** Barolo Bricco delle Viole at £40.60

51st

FAIRYHILL

Reynoldston Gower Swansea SA3 1BS

01792 390139

alue here is not as good as in some of the other Welsh establishments, but quality is undoubted with some very fine producers listed. There are just on 400 different wines, of which around half are of 3-star quality or above, but of those, only 16 meet the value criteria which we have set. A pity, because with a little shaving of some of the prices, this list would have had a considerably higher ranking. The list does score well, however, in the number of dry half-bottles available, of which many are of good quality, but in the wine by the glass selection, quality is sacrificed in favour of price. At the beginning of the list are 2 pages headed 'A selection of wines below £20', but we felt that price came before quality. We were somewhat amused to note that of the 23 wines listed here, 21 were at £19.50!

The list proper is conventionally arranged by country and region, starting off with Champagne and sparkling wines and finishing with dessert wines and the list of half-bottles. The Champagne section starts off with some Grande Marque Champagnes at £39.50, but the best value would appear to be the 1996 Dom Pérignon at £95. Among French country wines the **Cuvée Georges et Clem 2001** from Château Le Thou is excellent value at £19.50. Clarets follow and are handily listed by vintage, starting with the youngest available (2001), which includes the 4-star Château Haut Marbuzet at £47.50 (we doubt this is ready to drink yet – the 1999 at the same price looks a better bet), and going right back (but not in every year) to 1955, where you can pick up a bottle of Château Cheval Blanc for £550. In between, the best buys could well be the 5-star Château l'Angélus 1996 at £95 – far better value than the 1997 at £135 – and the equally rated Château Lynch-Bages in the 1978 vintage at £85, which should really be at its best now. In Burgundy, there is a whole page devoted to the wines of Jean-François Coche-Dury, who vies with Comtes Lafon for the Meursault crown, mostly at around the £200 mark. Sadly there is very little value in the white Burgundies, so we have to go for out-and-out quality and would probably plump for the super 5-star Corton-Charlemagne 1996 from Jadot at £120. Very much the same could be said for the red Burgundies, but here the one to go for would be the super 5-star Musigny 1989 from Joseph Drouhin at £95. In the Loire Valley, Henry Natter's Sancerre Blanc 2002 at £25.50 and Rouge 2001 at £26.50 provide 3-star value, while in the Rhône Valley, **André Perret's Condrieu 2001** is on the value cusp at £55 and the one to go for in the reds is the super 5-star Hermitage la Chapelle in the excellent 1989 vintage at £135.

Turning to the rest of the world, **Hollick Coonawarra Chardonnay Reserve 2001** from South Australia is value at £29.50, while in the Australian reds, the best value is in the 5-star Mount Edelstone Shiraz from Henschke at £65 in both the 1999 and the 2000 vintage. There is also value in the Californian section with Ridge Vineyards Lytton Springs Zinfandel 2000 at £45. Italy has some fine reds with Fonterutoli's

Wales

Chianti Classico 2002 at £21.50 although it appears to be the cheaper bottling (the premium one is labelled Castello di Fonterutoli) and from a patchy vintage. New Zealand has the oaked Sauvignon Blanc Marama 2002 from Seresin at £29.50, while in South Africa, the 2002 Sauvignon Blanc and the 2000 Chardonnay from Mulderbosch are both value at £29.50; the Private Collection Shiraz 1999 from Saxenburg is also 3-star value at £26.50. In the Spanish section, the 1999 Condado de Haza from the Ribera del Duero at £27.50 is worth drinking.

There is good value to be found in the full bottles of dessert wines. The 4-star Château La Tour Blanche Sauternes in the excellent 1988 vintage is on offer at £49.50 and the 5-star **Huët Vouvray Moelleux Clos de Bourg** in the equally excellent 1989 vintage is in at £45. There are some quality half-bottles in the list but most of them are pretty pricey for what they are. Henry Natter's 2001 Sancerre Domaine de la Mercy-Dieu at £13.50 looks to be the best value for money, although a half-bottle of Château Latour 1981 might be worth considering at £95.

Neville's Best Buy: The 5-star Vouvray Moelleux Clos de Bourg from **Huët** in the excellent 1989 vintage at £45.

Score: *Quality* 71.12   *Value* 11.02   *Impression* 27.26   *Total* **109.40**

Ranking: *Quality* 35   *Value* 77   *Impression* 7 = *Overall* **51st**

Recommendations:
NB: 2001 **André Perret** Condrieu at £55
DM: 2001 **Château Le Thou** Cuvée Georges et Clem at £19.50
PW: 2001 **Hollick** Coonawarra Chardonnay Reserve at £29.50

Find out more about wine and wine producers at *www.winebehindthelabel.com*

Wales

93rd

MAES-Y-NEUADD

Talsarnau Gwynedd LL47 6YA
01766 780200

his is another fine wine list from rural Wales, but one which perhaps doesn't reach the outstanding value for money shown by some. There are around 180 wines listed of which some 30% meet our quality criteria, but of these, only around one-sixth meet the value criteria as well. Among 10 dry wines by the glass, the **Churton Estate Sauvignon Blanc 2004** from New Zealand at £5 (£19.95 the bottle) delivers 3-star value, and of 29 half-bottles of dry wines, 6 meet our quality criteria. The list is conventionally arranged by country and region, with House wines at the front and dessert wines at the end.

The list starts off promisingly with Australian reds serving up value in the Pinot Noir 2001 from Yering Station in the Yarra Valley at £26. The Cape Mentelle Cabernet/ Merlot is also good value at £29.95, and there is 4-star value in the Wakefield St Andrews Shiraz from Clare Valley at £45. The same cannot be said for the Australian whites or the New Zealand reds, but in New Zealand whites, the Churton Sauvignon Blanc mentioned above is a value wine. In the South African reds, 3-star value is found in **Morgenhof Merlot 2001** at £23.95, and in Spain 2 other wines qualify: Condado de Haza's Tinto Ribera del Duero 2002 at £27.50 and it's big brother, Pesquera Crianza 2002 at £29.50.

Turning to France, there's nothing of great value in the Champagne section, but Bollinger Grande Année 1997 is a reasonable £85. In Alsace, the Tokay-Pinot Gris 2002 from Bruno Sorg is value at £22.50, as is, from Burgundy, the **Savigny-lès-Beaune 1er Cru La Dominode 2000** from Bruno Clair at £27. **Grands Echezeaux 1997** from René Engel is a super 5-star wine at £99 and well worth a look. In white Burgundies, the Chablis Grand Cru Valmur 2003 from Moreau-Naudet is 4-star value at £39. Another 5-star wine, although the price is just off the cusp at £55, is Château de Beaucastel's Châteauneuf-du-Pape 2000 at £55. White Bordeaux has Doisy-Daëne Grand Vin Sec 2000 at £25.95, while in the sweeties, Château Coutet 1997 is not bad value at £69. Clarets are a little on the pricey side, but the super 5-star Château Ducru-Beaucaillou 1983 at £195 for a magnum could be interesting drinking. Vintage ports are not cheap, either, with Dow's 1980 looking the best bet at £69.

Neville's Best Buy: Sauvignon Blanc 2004 from **Churton Estate** in New Zealand at £5 the glass (£19.95 the bottle)

Score: *Quality* 35.15   *Value* 15.88   *Impression* 17.00   *Total* **68.03**

Ranking: *Quality* 84   *Value* 62   *Impression* 61 =   *Overall* **93rd**

Recommendations:
NB: 1997 **René Engel** Grands Echezeaux at £99
DM: 2001 **Morgenhof** Merlot at £23.95
PW: 2000 **Bruno Clair** Savigny-lès-Beaune 1er Cru La Dominode at £27

Find out more about wine and wine producers at *www.winebehindthelabel.com*

Wales

PENHELIG ARMS

Penhelig Arms Hotel Aberdyfi Gwynedd LL35 0LT
01654 767215

---

he enthusiasm of Robert Hughes for his wines shines through the list at this seaside oasis of gastronomy, but what is most remarkable is the gentleness of the prices, which draw customers from many miles away. In fact, the prices are so gentle that it pays to go upmarket here.

The list kicks off with almost a score of House wines available by either the bottle or the glass. However, on the list sent to us (it changes frequently), there was nothing of real quality, so it's best to go straight into the main list where better choices prevail. The list is divided by country, showing both reds and whites from that country in the same section. At the end there is a list of pudding wines available by the glass.

The Australian section has a wealth of class, with Shaw and Smith's M3 Vineyard Chardonnay 2002 from the Adelaide Hills and Plantagenet's Mount Barker Shiraz 2002 from Western Australia, both 4-star quality and both at £20. Charlie Melton's Nine Popes Châteauneuf-du-Pape clone 2000 is a steal at £29.50. There is not the same depth of quality in the Californian section, but Seghesio's entry-level Zinfandel 2001 is reasonable value at £21. The Chilean section lacks premium quality also, but is extremely well priced. New Zealand fares better with Ata Rangi Pinot Noir 2001 good value at £33, and Cloudy Bay Sauvignon Blanc at £26 (the cheapest we found it on any list – see Appendix). Again, there's not a lot of quality in the South African section, but Italy fares better with 3-star selections such as Gavi di Gavi Montessora vineyard 2003 from La Giustiniana at £20 and 4-star **Vespro 2002**, a blend of Montepulciano and Syrah from Contrada Castelletta in the Marche, at just £19.50. The list then winds its way through Wales, Lebanon, Argentina and Germany, before alighting on Spain where you can buy **Pesquera Crianza 2001** for only £18. The selection from Portugal scores heavily with Dirk Niepoort's Redoma Tinto 1997 at £25 and **Quinta do Vale Doña Maria Douro 2000** at £16.

There are some cracking wines from France. For example, Jacky Janodet's Moulin-à-Vent 2002 is good value at £17 and ditto for Guigal's Condrieu 2002 at £35. There's some real quality among the Rhône reds, a toss up between Vieux-Télégraphe 1997 at £29.50 and Chapoutier's Hermitage Monier de la Sizeranne 2000 at £45. Cult Côteaux d'Aix-en-Provence Terra d'Or 1998 is on the list at £48. There is a reasonable selection of Champagnes, with Clicquot and Bollinger both well priced at £35 and Roederer Cristal 1997 is as cheap as you will get in a restaurant at £120. Loire whites do well, with Huët's Le Haut-Lieu Vouvray Sec 1993 at £20 and the 1996 half at £12.50. There is a good selection of Burgundy whites and reds. Standing out for price/quality ratio are the **Jean-Paul Droin Grand Cru Chablis Les Clos 2000** at £35 (with the 1997 available in halves at £17.50) and in reds, it's a toss up between Ghislaine Barthod's Chambolle-Musigny 1er cru Les Cras 1999 at £48 or Tollot-Beaut's Corton-Bressandes Grand Cru 2001 at £55. There is a fair choice of wines

Wales

from Bordeaux, from all corners of the appellation. A half of Château Rabaud-Promis from the excellent 1988 Sauternes vintage makes very fair drinking at £19.50 and Château La Tour Blanche 1989 is not far behind at £22 the half. In the dry reds, a half of Château Fleur-Cardinale Grand Cru Saint-Émilion 1999 at £13.50 looks good, but some of the other selections in half bottles are beginning to look too old. Best to ask the proprietor's advice on these. On the full bottles, Château L'Enclos Pomerol 1998 at £31 looks to be a good drink, as does Château Talbot St-Julien 1995 at £38.

This is a wine list of outstanding value with a good selection of quality wines. Beat a path to the door!

Neville's Best Buy: **Quinta do Vale Doña Maria** Douro 2000 from Portugal at £16

Score: *Quality* 42.77   *Value* 90.37   *Impression* 20.00   *Total* **153.14**

Ranking: *Quality* 71   *Value* 3   *Impression* 34 =   *Overall* **9th**

Recommendations:
NB: 2000 **Jean-Paul Droin** Chablis Grand Cru Les Clos at £35
DM: 2001 **Pesquera** Ribera del Duero Crianza at £18
PW: 2002 **Contrada Castelletta** Vespro at £19.50

41st

PENMAENUCHAF HALL

Penmaenpool Gwynedd LL40 1YB
01341 422129

he philosophy behind the wine list of this hotel in rural Wales is clearly stated in Mark Watson's introduction. In a nutshell, they are striving to present a list that is well balanced, representative of today's wines, reasonably priced, user friendly, manageable and accurate – and by and large, they succeed. There are just under 150 wines listed, of which around 30% reach our quality criteria, and of those, almost half meet our value criteria. There are 23 dry half-bottles listed, but with little in the way of quality, and wines by the glass are few and far between except for an excellent list of sherries. The list is arranged conventionally by country and region with a selection of House wines preceding the main body of the list, some of which are available by the glass. There are tasting notes for most of the wines but they do not always fully describe the flavours. The list that was sent to us featured three wines of the month, with Alois Lageder's Haberlehof Pinot Bianco 2000 from the Alto Adige in Northern Italy looking excellent value at £17.25

In the main list, there is 3-star value in the Alsace section with Bruno Sorg's Gewürztraminer 2002 at £20.25 and the Château Doisy-Daëne Sec 2000 in the white Bordeaux section is also good value at £24.25. At the other end of the scale, the super 5-star **Château Rieussec 1990 Sauternes** (a very good vintage) is in at £69.25, which should be well worth drinking at that price. It's always difficult to find wines that meet our price/quality ratio in the claret section, but here we have three 3-star wines that fit the bill, Château Pâtache d'Aux Haut-Médoc 2000 at £22.75, Château La Tour de By Médoc 1998 at £27.75 and Château Cissac Haut-Médoc 1991 at £26.50, even though it was in a poor vintage, so you may have to ask the proprietor if it is still any good. Of the classed-growth clarets, the 5-star Vieux Château Certan 1996 at £75.75 will probably make better drinking than some of the 4- and 3-star wines on the list at cheaper prices. In the white Burgundy section, Jean Thévenet's Domaine de la Bongrain Mâcon-Villages 2001 at £27.75 is good 3-star value, but the super 5-star Corton-Charlemagne 1993 at £125 may be too much to pay for a poor vintage, despite the overall quality of the estate. It's also nice to see some 3-star red Burgundies meeting the price/quality ratio, too, such as the Gevrey-Chambertin 1999 from Chanson at £28.25 and **Beaune 1er Cru Bressandes 2002** from Henri Germain et Fils at £29.25. There are also 2 wines just over the £50 cusp, but they are both of 5-star quality and for Burgundy, are exceptionally good value: **Vosne-Romanée 1er Cru Clos des Réas 2002** from Michel Gros at £54.50 and Mazy-Chambertin Grand Cru 1998 from Armand Rousseau at £56.25. The latter has the advantage of being a little more mature but it is difficult to choose, maybe order both. In the Rhône Valley reds there is good value in the Gigondas Domaine les Pallières 2001 at £25 and Gilles Barge's Côte-Rôtie Cuvée du Plessy 2000 at £29.95, but the best value in this section is the Hermitage Monier de la Sizeranne 2000 from Chapoutier at £46.75. The white Châteauneuf-du-Pape 2002 from Vieux-Télégraphe at £27.50 is also outstanding

Wales

value. In Spain, Alejandro Fernández's **Pesquera Crianza 2001** from Ribera del Duero at £23.75 is good value, but we found nothing of real interest in Italy, nor in Germany.

The New World sections kick off with wines from Australia, where the Coriole McLaren Vale Shiraz 2002 looks good at £22.25. There is even better value in the New Zealand section in the 3-star Churton Sauvignon Blanc 2004 at £18.50 and the 4-star Ata Rangi Pinot Noir 2001 at £36.50 (if a slightly poorer vintage than usual for this excellent wine). There is nothing that excites us in the American sections (North or South), but there is, from South Africa, the Springfield Estate Work of Time 2001, a Bordeaux blend of 3-star quality at £24.75. The Champagne section has the Beaumont des Crayères 1998 vintage in at an excellently priced £28.50. Finally, the ports are well worth looking at, with Warre's 1980 vintage outstanding value at £45 a bottle, as are the numerous sherries from Hildago with the Jerez Cortado Amontillado at £10 for a half-bottle (£2.50 the glass) and a glass of Pedro Ximenez Viejo at £3.75 a glass.

Neville's Best Buy: Vosne-Romanée 1er Cru Clos des Réas 2002 from **Michel Gros** at £54.50

Score: *Quality* 39.21   *Value* 50.66   *Impression* 22.00   *Total* **111.87**

Ranking: *Quality* 79   *Value* 13   *Impression* 21 =   *Overall* **41st**

Recommendations:
NB: 1990 **Château Rieussec** Sauternes at £69.25
DM: 2001 **Pesquera** Ribera del Duero Crianza at £23.75
PW: 2002 **Henri Germain et Fils** Beaune 1er Cru Bressandes at £29.95

38th

PLAS BODEGROES

Nefyn Road Pwllheli Gwynedd LL53 5TH

01758 612363

nother fine wine list from an establishment in rural Wales. The value and quality is amazing in these places; surely many others throughout the UK can take a leaf out of their books. An additional bonus here is the large percentage of dry half-bottles on the list – almost a quarter of the total – which does make experimentation much easier, although we failed to find any mention of dry wines by the glass on the list. Some 360 wines are listed without tasting notes, except for the 'House selections'. However, each wine is carefully graded – the whites by the degree of dryness to sweetness and the reds by the degree of lightness to fullness, so this helps. About 40% of the wines are of 3-star quality or above and of those, just under a quarter fulfil our value criteria.

'House selections' are taken from the main list and described with some tasting notes. The list is then arranged conventionally by country and region, except for the Champagne and sparkling wines section, of course. There is not a lot of real value to be found in this section – the proprietor recommends the Krug NV, which at £115 is about par for the course. Much better value on the same page are the 5-star white wines from Mas de Daumas Gassac, the 2003 at £39 and the 1991 at £48. In the Loire, **Henry Pellé Menetou-Salon Clos des Blanchais 2002** is good value at £24. White Rhônes have André Perret's 5-star Condrieu Côteaux du Chéry 2002 at £45. In white Burgundies, Jean-Paul Droin's Chablis Grand Cru Les Clos 1998 is value at £48 (£27 the half), whilst in Alsace, two wines from Zind-Humbrecht, Gewürztraminer Wintzenheim 1997 at £33 and Riesling Clos Hauserer 1994 at £48, represent 4-star value. Italian whites include Pieropan's Soave Classico Superiore La Rocca 2002 at £29.50. New World whites kick of with a good value selection from Australia – Plantagenet Riesling 2003 from Western Australia is exceptionally good value at £19, while Vanya Cullen's Chardonnay 1998 at £37 shows what good value the wines from Western Australia are. There is not a lot of interest in the whites from New Zealand or South America, but Testarossa's Private Reserve Chardonnay 2000 from the Napa Valley is good value at £39.50.

Red wines start with a selection of French regional wines, with Domaine de Trévallon 1997 being 5-star quality at only £38. Bordeaux, as usual, doesn't produce any great bargains, but Château Cissac 1995 at £29.50 is worth a punt, although it would probably be wise to fight shy of the 1994 halves listed for this property. In the Classed Growths, Léoville-las-Cases 1981 should still be drinking well for £98 (ask), but Ducru-Beaucaillou 1986 at £112 might be a better bet. In the Graves, Château Haut-Brion 1970 should still be drinking well at £195, as should the 1979 Château Cheval Blanc in Saint-Émilion at £180. Burgundy doesn't produce any bargains, either, but Henri Prudhon's Saint-Aubin 1er Cru Les Frionnes 1998 at £29 is good drinking value, whilst Louis Jadot's Clos de la Roche in the underrated but drinkable vintage of 1997 is worth a try at £85. There is better value to be had in the Rhône, with **Clos des Papes Châteauneuf-du-Pape 1999** outstanding 5-star value at £34 (£18 the half-bottle). The super 5-star Hermitage La Chapelle 1985 at £89 is fair for this good, mature drinking vintage. There are some good

Wales

4-star choices in the Italian section – the Taurasi 1997 from I Feudi dei San Gregorio in Campania at £35 and Talenti's Brunello di Montalcino 1999 at £48. There is also the 5-star Montiano Merlot 1998 from the Falesco Estate in Lazio at £49.50. Spain has some good choices such as Costers del  Siurana's Usatges 1996 at only £22 and La Rioja Alta's Reserva 904 at £42.50 or £82 for a magnum, while Portugal has the 3-star Quinta do Crasto Reserva 2001 from the Douro at £26, although it may be a bit on the young side to drink just yet.

In the New World, **Mount Langi Ghiran Shiraz 2000** from Victoria is 5-star quality at £35 and the best value in the Australian section, but if you are not worried about value, then Penfolds Grange 1985 at £245 is a must. New Zealand has Martinborough Vineyards Pinot Noir 2001 in at £29.50, while the North American section has the 5-star Ridge Geyserville Zinfandel/Carignan 2001 at £39 (£22.50 the half bottle). It also has the **Sine Qua Non Pinot Noir 2001** at the remarkably low price of £85 (for this wine!). The sweet wine selection covers many parts of the world – in France, the best value would seem to be a 50cl bottle of Bonnezeaux SGN in the remarkable 1997 Loire vintage from Domaine du Petit Val at £26, but Château Rieussec Sauternes 1983 at £69 for a whole bottle is also definitely worth a look. Italy has Maculan's Torcolato 1981 from the Veneto at £49, but it might be better to go for one or two halves of the 1997 at £27. (Once again – ask). Ports are remarkably good value with Warre's 1983 and 1970 both snips at £52 and £95 respectively.

Although this list is not as competitively priced as those produced by some of the establishment's neighbours, it has been thoughtfully put together and there are certainly some hidden gems to discover. Some quality wines by the glass would certainly set the list climbing up the rankings.

Neville's Best Buy: **Clos des Papes** Châteauneuf-du-Pape 1999 at £34 (£18 the half bottle)

Score: *Quality* 56.07 *Value* 26.99 *Impression* 31.00 *Total* **114.06**

Ranking: *Quality* 56 *Value* 36 *Impression* 5 = *Overall* **38th**

Recommendations:
NB: 2001 **Sine Qua Non** Pinot Noir at £85
DM: 2002 **Henry Pellé** Menetou-Salon Clos des Blanchais at £24
PW: 2000 **Mount Langi Ghiran** Shiraz at £35

Find out more about wine and wine producers at *www.winebehindthelabel.com*

Wales

94th

HOTEL PORTMEIRION

Portmeirion Gwynedd LL48 6ET
01766 772440

---

he restaurant at the hotel part of this unique resort has an interesting and varied wine list, which perhaps may not have as many quality wines as we might have wished, but does provide some good bargains among those that are listed. There are over 170 wines in all, of which just under 30% reach our quality criteria, and of these, around 25% reach our value criteria as well. Some 20 dry wines come in half-bottle format with some quality amongst them, but the 8 wines by the glass are decidedly geared towards entry-level wines. The list is arranged conventionally by country and region, with tasting notes for most of the wines.

Clarets are a strong point of the list, with the 3-star Château Pâtache d'Aux 1999 being very good value at £23. There are several other 3-star wines just over the £30 cusp, but the 4-star **Château Roc de Cambes 1996**, a benchmark Côtes de Bourg, is really excellent value at £34. Among the super 5-star big boys, it's a toss-up between **Château Ducru-Beaucaillou 1970** at £120 and Château Haut-Brion 1978 at £135. Red Burgundy is nowhere near the clarets in quality and value, but in the white Burgundies, the **Chablis Premier Cru Montée de Tonnerre 2002** from Moreau-Naudet at £25.50 is good value. In the Rhône section, the 5-star Château de Beaucastel 1997 is well priced at £55, while in the Rhône whites, André Perret's Condrieu 2001 is good value at £38.50. There are 2 well priced Alsace wines in the shape of **Lucien Albrecht's Gewürztraminer 2002** at £21.50 and his Riesling Reserve du Domaine 2000 at £24.

Spain has 3-star 1999 Rioja Reserva from the Marqués de Riscal, at £29, but there is nothing exceptional in the Italian section. There are good value Australian reds – the Katnook Estate Cabernet Sauvignon 1999 from Coonawarra at £27 (£14 for a half bottle), and the Yering Station Pinot Noir 2001 from the Yarra Valley in Victoria, also at £27. There is even better value in the Australian whites with the Cape Mentelle Semillon/Sauvignon 2002 from Western Australia at £22, and the Shaw and Smith Sauvignon Blanc 2003 from South Australia, also at £22. Value continues in the New Zealand whites with the Churton Marlborough Sauvignon Blanc 2003 at £18, and the Whitehaven Marlborough Sauvignon Blanc 2003 at £18, too. In the Champagne section, the 5-star Bollinger Grande Année 1996 is very well priced at £65, while in the pudding wines it is a toss-up between a half-bottle of Alois Kracher's Beerenauslese Cuvée 2002 at £21 or a quarter-litre of The Tokaji Aszu 5 Puttonyos 1999 from the Royal Tokaji Company, also at £21

Neville's Best Buy: The 4 star **Château Roc de Cambes** 1996 at £34

Score: *Quality* 30.81 *Value* 17.39 *Impression* 19.00 *Total* **67.20**

Ranking: *Quality* 88 *Value* 57 *Impression* 43 = *Overall* **94th**

Recommendations:
NB: 1970 **Château Ducru-Beaucaillou** at £120
DM: 2002 **Lucien Albrecht** Gewürztraminer at £21.50
*PW:*2002 **Moreau-Naudet** Chablis Premier Cru Montée de Tonnerre at £25.50

Find out more about wine and wine producers at *www.winebehindthelabel.com*

Wales

17th

TYDDYN LLAN

Llandrillo nr Corwen Denbighshire LL21 0ST
01490 440264

here is a growing number of establishments in rural Wales with exciting wine lists and this is the latest of them. What is really impressive is the gentleness of the prices, although they are certainly not the cheapest in the area. The list runs to over 200 bins and is divided quite comprehensively into styles, with 17 different sections to choose from. Within the style sections, the wines are grouped by country, rather than price. Additionally, there is a reasonable selection of half-bottles and 18 wines by the glass.

'Section 1 – Bubbly'. There is nothing outstanding in the non-Champagne part of this section, but the short list of Champagnes is impressive, starting with the 3-star entry-level Jacquart Mosaïque NV at £32 and running right up to the super 5-star Roederer Cristal 1995 at £144. The 'Light dry whites' section just misses our 3-star quality criteria, but then none of the wines is listed at more than £20. 'Dry and pungent whites' has Cline Cellars Marsanne 1999 from Sonoma at £28.50 and the 'Off-dry to medium whites' features the intriguing Conundrum Blend 2001 produced by Caymus Vineyards in the Napa Valley at £33.50 and a half-bottle of Castello di Ama's Vin Santo 1997 at £21.50. Domaine Mollet-Maudry's expressive **Pouilly-Fumé Les Sables 2003** at £25 stands out in the 'Fruity, fragrant and aromatic' section, while Luna Vineyard's Pinot Grigio 2000 from the Napa Valley at £29.50 scores for value in the 'Fruity or spicy full-bodied whites'. The 'Fine rich dry to medium dry whites' have the judiciously oaked Pouilly-Fuissé from Domaine des Gerbeaux at £29.00 – particularly good value for a top Mâconnais Burgundy. The 'Full-bodied dry to medium dry' whites goes heavyweight with Robert Chevillon's Nuits-Saint-Georges Blanc 1997 at £37.50 and Henri Germain's Chassagne-Montrachet 1er Cru Morgeot 1999 at £53.50 looking to be the best value. 'Section 9 – Sweet wines', boasts a 50cl bottle of **Patrick Baudouin Côteaux du Layon SGN Maria Juby 1997**, a hand-picked selection of botrytis-affected grapes producing an intensely sweet wine. Very small production – hence the price tag of £55, but it's scarcity value you are paying for there as well as 5-star quality.

On to the reds – 'Section 10 – Light, dry reds' has Julia's Vineyard Pinot Noir 1997 from Cambria Vineyards in California at £29.50 and in the 'Light fruity reds' section, Paradise Enough Vineyard from South Gippsland in Victoria has the 2000 Pinot Noir listed at £23. Stepping up a notch, there is the intriguing blend of Grenache, Syrah and Zinfandel from Sean Thackrey called Pleiades X (no vintage) at £39. Quality abounds in the 'Medium-bodied dry reds', with Faugères Rouge Tradition 2001 from Domaine Léon Barral at only £21 being the star buy. The top attraction in the 'Medium-bodied fruity red' section is the Glenmore Cabernet Sauvignon 2000 at only £25 from Margaret River, once again proving the wonderful value for money you get from Western Australia. 'Big scale dry reds' bristle with top wines from Piedmont, with the **1997 Roberto Voerzio Vignaserra** blend of Barbera and Nebbiolo at £32

Wales

and Claudio Alario's Barolo Riva 1999 at £52.50. 'Section 15 – Big scale fruity reds' is a powerhouse of quality, from the 4-star Keith Tulloch's Kester Shiraz 2000 from the Hunter Valley at £27.50, through the 5-star **Alban Vineyards Lorraine Syrah 1997** at £43.50, to other 5-star greats such as La Spinetta's Barbaresco Starderi 1999 at £83 and Joseph Phelps's Bordeaux blend Insignia in the cult 1997 vintage at £118. There are 4 older vintages of Insignia in the 'Smooth and mature red wines' section at prices ranging from £100 to £124. This section presents a host of top quality older wines from around the globe, but the French selection stands out with Beaucastel 1988 (a good Rhône vintage) at £75, Vosne-Romanée Les Beaumonts 1990 from Joseph Drouhin at £70 from Burgundy and a host of clarets, among which the 1978 Château Gruaud-Larose at £80 looks particularly good value. But the smooth and mature reds are not confined to the superstars. Virgin Hills Red 1993 from Victoria at £29.50, Joseph Phelps' Syrah 1995 at £35, La Rioja Alta, Gran Reserva 904, 1994 at £45 and Château Cissac 1990 at £54 are all very fine wines at good prices.

The last section – '17 – Dry rosé wines' – does not have anything greater than 2-star wines, but then how many rosé wines score 3 stars or more (except Champagnes)? André Dézat's Sancerre Rosé 2003 at £21.50 and the Cabernet in Rosa 2003 from Vigneto delle Terre Rosse, near Bologna, at £21, are both worth drinking.

The list finishes up with a short selection of red and white dry half-bottles, where good pickings include Blockheadia Ringnosii Sauvignon Blanc 1999 from the Napa Valley at £15.50 the half-bottle in white and Château d'Angludet 2001 at £19 in red, but for the more upmarket drinkers, a foray into Chianti Classico Vigneto Bellavista 1995 from Castello di Ama at £50 and Stag's Leap Wine Cellars SLV Estate Cabernet Sauvignon 1998 at £44 would be more rewarding. The inclusion of comprehensive tasting notes for all but the most famous producers is a useful adjunct to the listing arrangement by style and obviates the need to employ a sommelier. The savings in this respect have obviously been passed on to the consumer to the benefit of all concerned.

Neville's Best Buy: **Alban Vineyards** Lorraine Syrah 1997 at £43.50

Score: *Quality* 72.33   *Value* 41.13   *Impression* 26.00   *Total* **139.46**

Ranking: *Quality* 32   *Value* 21   *Impression* 11   =   *Overall* **17th**

Recommendations:
NB: 1997 **Patrick Baudouin** Côteaux du Layon SGN Maria Juby at £55
DM: 2003 **Domaine Mollet-Maudry** Pouilly-Fumé Les Sables at £25
PW: 1997 **Roberto Voerzio** Vignaserra at £32

Find out more about wine and wine producers at *www.winebehindthelabel.com*

YE OLDE BULL'S HEAD INN

Castle Street Beaumaris Isle of Anglesey LL58 8AP
01248 810329

---

f you are getting the ferry from Holyhead to Dublin, this is an ideal and very civilised stopover, barely a half an hour from the ferry terminal. The wine list is fairly short (121 bins) with pretty much half the wines of 3-star quality or above. Of these, more than half the wines meet our price criteria, which accounts for the high score that this establishment has achieved. The list is conventionally divided into regions and there is no concession to dessert wines, which are listed under whichever region they come from, together with the dry wines.

The House wines, 2 white and 2 red, are nice, but not special, so you will have to look to the main body of the list if you want anything of real quality. The list starts off with Bordeaux reds and whites, including a bottle of Château Rabaud-Promis 1986, a good vintage for Sauternes, and well worth the £37.50 being asked for it. A number of the clarets are from the not very impressive 1993 vintage, although the names of the châteaux are impressive enough. There is Ducru-Beaucaillou in that vintage at £55 and Château Margaux at £130, but if you are looking for a better vintage, then try Cos Labory 1990 at £37.50, or Pichon-Longueville-Baron 1986 at £75.50. There follows a small list of quality Beaujolais, with the Moulin-à-Vent 2002 from Domaine Les Fines Graves looking best at £17.95. In Burgundy proper it's best to go for Dujac's

Wales

Morey-Saint-Denis 1998 at £35 in the reds and Sauzet's Puligny-Montrachet 1er Cru Les Perrières 1999 at £57 in the whites. There is a Chablis Grand Cru Les Clos from Jean-Paul Droin at £42, but it's from the poor 1994 vintage, so you will need to check if it isn't past its best. Loire Valley wines has Cailbourdin's Pouilly-Fumé 2002 at £18.95 and Saumur-Champigny 2001 from Château du Hureau at £16.50, both very well priced. There is also a Sancerre Rosé 1999 from François Cotat at £22.50. The Rhône selection has the 5-star **Châteauneuf-du-Pape 1998 from Clos des Papes** at £27.50 – very well priced indeed – whilst the white Saint-Joseph 1999 from André Perret is also good value at £18.75. In the Champagne section, Vilmart Grand Reserve Brut NV is good value at £29.50, whilst Veuve Clicquot 1996 is not badly priced at £55. Italy is a different story, with some terrific value for money wines, notably Foradori's Granato 1996, 4-star quality at £26.50, and Santadi's Terre Brune 1999, 5-star quality at £37.50. The wines from La Spinetta are well priced, too, with the Barbera Ca' di Pian 2000 at £25 and the splendid **Monferrato Rosso Pin 2000** (from Nebbiolo, Barbera and Cabernet Sauvignon) at just £36. Spain has Bodegas Alión 1999 at £33.50 and the white Rioja 1997 from Marqués de Murrieta at £19.50 as top value wines.

It's when we get to the New World selections, however, that the list come into its own. There is great value in the Australian section with Vasse Felix's Cabernet Sauvignon/Merlot 2001 from the Margaret River at £23.50 and Henschke's 5-star Mount Edelstone Shiraz 1999 at £43.50 in the reds and the evocatively named Paradise Enough Chardonnay 2000 from remote South Gippsland, Victoria at £23 in the whites. There's a trio of great value reds from California – Cline Cellars Small Berry Vineyard Mourvèdre 1998 at £27.50, **Joseph Phelps Napa Valley Syrah 1995** at £28.50 and Sanford Winery Santa Barbara Pinot Noir 1999 at £32.50. New Zealand is well represented, too, with **2000 Stonyridge Larose**, a top Cabernet-based blend, from Waiheke Island, at £47.50 in the reds and Pegasus Bay Chardonnay 2002 from Canterbury at £22.50 in the whites.

The selection of half-bottles has a number of quality wines, notably Clos du Marquis 1986 (the second wine of Château Léoville-las-Cases) at £19.50, Château Rabaud-Promis 1er Cru Sauternes 1983 at £21.50 and Viña Ardanza Rioja 1996 at £16.95. There are some hidden gems in this list at extraordinarily reasonable prices and a decent amount of wines with some bottle age to make a most enjoyable drinking experience.

Neville's Best Buy: **Joseph Phelps** Napa Valley Syrah 1995 at £28.50

Score: *Quality* 68.64 *Value* 72.32 *Impression* 14.00 *Total* **154.95**

Ranking: *Quality* 40 *Value* 9 *Impression* 80 = *Overall* **8th**

Recommendations:
NB: 2000 **Stonyridge** Larose at £47.50
DM: 1998 **Clos des Papes** Châteauneuf-du-Pape at £27.50
PW: 2000 **La Spinetta** Monferrato Rosso Pin at £36

Find out more about wine and wine producers at *www.winebehindthelabel.com*

98th

CAYENNE

7 Ascot House Shaftesbury Square Belfast BT2 7DB
028 9033 1532

---

his is one of Belfast's best restaurants and has an interesting wine list, listed by grape variety and style but with no tasting notes. There are just over 130 wines on the list of which just under 20% are of 3-star quality or more and of these around a fifth qualify to reach our price criteria. Just 8 half-bottles of dry wines are listed and 11 wines by the glass are really geared to the lower price spectrum.

In Champagne the 4-star **Charles Heidsieck Mis en Cave 2000** at £42 (£8.50 a glass) beats anything else for value. The Sauvignon Blanc section has the 3-star Hunter's Marlborough Sauvignon Blanc 2003 at £27.75, while in the Riesling section the **Ostertag Riesling d' Epfig 2002** is good value at £24.75. In 'Some other aromatics', **Brokenwood Semillon 2003** from the Hunter Valley in Australia at £28.50 is also good 3-star value (if young for drinking now), but most of the other white wines do not reach higher than 2-star quality and some of those are not cheap, either.

It's pretty much the same story in the reds. The 'Cabernet-based' and the 'Merlot/Malbec' sections do not have a single wine of 3-star quality or above, neither does Pinot Noir, but in the Shiraz section **Errázuriz Max Reserva Syrah 2001** from Chile is £27.95 and Howard Park Scotsdale Shiraz 2001 is also 3-star quality but outside the corral at £37.50. In 'Southern French grapes', Les Clos de Paulilles Collioure 2001 is just off the value cusp at £31.50, while the Saint-Joseph 2002 from Domaine Courbis at £36.95 is a bit further adrift (and why this wine is not in the Shiraz section is a bit of a mystery to us). At the end of the list is a page of fine wines, most of which are very fine indeed at very fine prices but if we had to make a choice, we would plump for the 4-star Rochioli Russian River Chardonnay 2001 at £51 in the whites and the Hermitage Monier de la Sizeranne 1996 from Chapoutier in the Rhône at £50 in the reds, although the 4-star Hermitage 1991 from Guigal is not far behind at £59.50, since it is in a far superior vintage. Château Pichon-Lalande 1988 at £95 should not be ignored either.

Neville's Best Buy: **Charles Heidsieck** Champagne Mis en Cave 2000 at £42 (£8.50 a glass)

Score: *Quality* 26.09 *Value* 22.02 *Impression* 11.00 *Total* **59.11**

Ranking: *Quality* 92 *Value* 45 *Impression* 94 = *Overall* **98th**

Recommendations:
NB: 2002 **Ostertag** Riesling d' Epfig at £24.75
DM: 2001 **Errázuriz** Max Reserva Syrah at £27.95
PW: 2003 **Brokenwood** Semillon at £28.50

Find out more about wine and wine producers at *www.winebehindthelabel.com*

Northern Ireland

100th

ROSCOFF

7-11 Linenhall Street Belfast BT2 8AA

028 9031 1150

This was at one time Paul Rankin's flagship restaurant in Belfast, but it seems from the wine lists that have been sent to us that the upmarket restaurant business has been transferred to Cayenne (qv) and that Roscoff has been turned into a brasserie. It also seems that much of the old wine list has remained, because it looks to be too good for a brasserie. Conventionally arranged by country and region, about 30% of the 130 strong-list is of 3-star quality or above, but of these wines, only 5 make the price criteria. There are few half-bottles of dry wines and the 8 wines by the glass which, except for one Champagne, are not of any real interest.

In the Champagne section, Charles Heidsieck's Brut Mis en Cave 2000 is 4-star value at £47.50 (£9.50 a glass), but some of the prestige cuvées are pretty pricey. There is nothing in the white Burgundy or Loire sections to intrigue us, but in the odd grouping of 'Alsace, Rhône and regional' wines, the **Coteaux du Languedoc Les Rocailles 2002** from Château de Capitoul at £31.50 is probably worth trying. There are some interesting 2-star wines in the rest of the whites, too.

In the red wine section, **Château de Capitoul's 2002 Les Rocailles** red is good value at £28.75, as is the **Errázuriz Max Reserva Cabernet Sauvignon 2003** from Chile at £25.25. There are also 2 upmarket wines from Chile – Sena 1999 at £60 and Viñedo Chadwick 2000 at £75 – both 4-star quality and both blends of Cabernet Sauvignon, Merlot and Carmenère with lashings of new oak and comparable in quality, if not in style, to, say, the Côte-Rôtie 2001 from Yves Cuilleron at £72.50 and the Brunello di Montalcino 1999 from Il Poggione at £69.50. There are 2 cracking Shiraz wines from South Australia, both 5-star quality – **Peter Lehmann Stonewall Shiraz 1998** at £75 and Hardy's Eileen Hardy Shiraz 1998 at £120. In the dessert wine section it's a toss up between the **Peter Lehmann Botrytis Semillon 2002** at £19.50 a half-bottle (£4.00 a glass) and Anselmi's 4-star I Capitelli 2002 at £32 a half-bottle, while in the fine selection of ports there is the 3-star Late Bottled Vintage 1998 from Quinta de la Rosa at £39.95 (£4.50 a glass) and the super 5-star Dow's Vintage 1983 at £80 (£8 a glass).

Neville's Best Buy: **Errázuriz** Max Reserva Cabernet Sauvignon 2003 from Chile at £25.25

Score: *Quality* 24.65 *Value* 16.07 *Impression* 16.00 *Total* **56.72**

Ranking: *Quality* 87 *Value* 79 *Impression* 97 = *Overall* **100th**

Recommendations:

NB: 1998 **Peter Lehmann** Stonewall Shiraz at £75
DM: 2002 **Ch. de Capitoul** Coteaux du Languedoc Les Rocailles at £28.75
PW: 2002 **Peter Lehmann** Botrytis Semillon (half-bottle) at £19.50

Find out more about wine and wine producers at *www.winebehindthelabel.com*

Northern Ireland

49th

SHANKS

his is the highest rated list from Northern Ireland. It has a goodly number of quality wines – over 50% are of 3-star quality or above – of which around a third meet our value criteria as well. Prices, perhaps, are not as gentle as they could be, but this may be due in part to the high cost of transporting them. Nevertheless, there are a number of fine bargains among the 200-plus wines and there are also a decent number of quality halves.

The list starts off with the House wines but there is nothing here to excite. Champagnes follow and, while all the wines listed are from top quality houses, there is little of any value. Bollinger Grande Année 1996 is 5-star quality but £100 is a pretty stiff price to pay for it. White Bordeaux has Château Tour de Mirambeau 2003 listed at a very respectable £17, whilst in the Rhône Valley, the white Saint-Joseph Le Paradis Saint-Pierre 2000 from Pierre Coursodon is right on the value limit at £30. There are a lot of quality wines in the white Burgundy section, many from Vincent Girardin, with the 4-star Chassagne-Montrachet 1er Cru Morgeots 2001 standing out at £59. Germany offers good value with Zeltinger Sonnenuhr Riesling Auslese 1999 from Selbach at £23, while from Italy, the 4-star Chardonnay-based Cervaro 2002 from Antinori at £49 is also value for money. Spain, too, has a value wine listed in the shape of the Albariño 2003 from Pazo de Señoráns at £26. Australia, naturally, has some wines with a good price/quality ratio, the keenest being the 2001 Coonawarra Chardonnay from Ian Hollick at £21. There are some good whites from California; as usual, value is hard to find, but Rochioli's Russian River Sauvignon Blanc 2003 just makes the cut at £30. New Zealand has Hunter's Oaked and Unoaked Sauvignon Blanc at good prices – the unoaked 2003 at £22 and the oaked 2001 at £24 – and the lone South African white listed, Rustenberg Chardonnay 2001, is also 3-star value at £24.

Clarets kick off the red wines and none of them gets in under our price/quality criteria. However, what does look particularly good value is the super 5-star Château La Mission Haut-Brion from the legendary 1982 vintage at £225. The same value problem applies to the Burgundies, but here you would be best to go for the 3-star Santenay 1er Cru Les Gravières 2000 from Vincent Girardin at £39, which certainly has a better price/quality ratio than some of the 4-star wines on the list. Georges Duboeuf's Morgon Jean Descombes 2002 is worth a punt at £21, while from the Languedoc Les Nobles Pierres Pic Saint-Loup 2000 from Château de Lascaux at £24 is also well worth drinking. In the comprehensive red Rhône section, the Châteauneuf-du-Pape 2002 from Château La Nerthe stands out at £48, but it's probably a bit too young to drink. There is good 4-star value in the 1997 Bandol from Château de Pibarnon at £32, while from the Loire, the Chinon Les Varennes du Grand Clos 2000 from Charles Joguet is 3-star value at £28. There are some big hitters from Italy, but the 1999 Barolo from Luigi Pira looks best value at £49. The same can be said of the Spanish reds with the Pesquera Tinto Crianza 2002 taking the honours here at £29. From South Africa, Rustenberg's John X Merriman 2002 Bordeaux blend is sound value at £28. In the Australian section, Western Australia's Chatsfield Cabernet Franc 2000 is good value at £21 and Penfolds Grange 1993 at £140 and 1992 at £165 is not overpriced either. In between these, Charlie Melton's 4-star Nine Popes 2000 is in at £40. There is a strong list of Californian reds with the wines from Ridge taking the honours – the 5-star Geyserville Zinfandel 2001 coming in for best value at £48. In New Zealand the Mount Edward Central Otago Pinot Noir 2003 stands out at £49.

Best value of the dry half-bottles is Vincent Girardin's Santenay Clos de la Confrérie 2002 at £19, while in the page of dessert wines there are greater choices, with full bottles of Banyuls Rimage Mise Tardive 2002 from Les Clos de Paulilles at £25 and Château Filhot Sauternes 1997 at £55; and a 50cl bottle of Les Cyprès de Climens 2001 at £38 should also be worth drinking.

Score: *Quality* 69.20   *Value* 29.14   *Impression* 12.00   *Total* **110.34**

Ranking: *Quality* 38   *Value* 33   *Impression* 92 =   *Overall* **49th**

Between the compilation of this report and the publication of the book, Shanks Restaurant has closed due to the tragic death of chef/proprietor Robbie Millar. We leave this appraisal of his wine list in as a memorial to one of Northern Ireland's outstanding restaurants. Unfortunately you will no longer be able to try it out for yourself

---

APPENDIX: PRICES COMPARED

1: Dom Pérignon 1996

We thought that it might be interesting to compare prices for some of the most frequently seen wines on the lists submitted to us. We found that the wine that was listed most often was Dom Pérignon 1996: 51 out of the 100 establishments had this wine (and a further 15 had it in a different vintage, mostly 1995, but these have been ignored as we wanted to strictly compare like with like). Below we set out the price charged for this wine by all the restaurants that stocked it.

Prices ranged from £79.50 to £220.00, but before you jump to the wrong conclusion, you do have to take into consideration that not all these establishments will have paid the same price for the wine. The larger hotels and hotel groups do have the economies of scale and are more likely to have bought the wine direct from Moët & Chandon at a lower price than a regional restaurant might have paid to buy it from a regional wholesaler who would have added a mark up. Prestige restaurants, which some producers target as 'must be seen in' establishments, may have also had the benefit of a special discount not normally given to others as an inducement to list the wine. Nonetheless, it seems inconceivable that the cheapest listing has been purchased at less than 40% of the most expensive!

1	HOTEL DU VIN, TUNBRIDGE WELLS	£79.50
2	THE BELL AT SKENFRITH	£80.00
3	DARROCH LEARG	£85.00
4	THE WILDEBEEST ARMS	£89.95
5	PEAT INN	£90.00
6	FAIRY HILL	£95.00
7	THE LIME TREE	£95.00
8	LINTHWAITE HOUSE HOTEL	£96.00
9	COMBE HOUSE	£105.00
10	LES MIRABELLES	£105.00
11	ETAIN	£110.00
12	OPERA HOUSE	£110.00
13	THE CHESTER GROSVENOR, ARKLE	£110.00
14	THYME	£110.00
15	HOTEL DU VIN, HARROGATE	£115.00
16	LEWTRENCHARD MANOR	£115.00
17	TYDDYN LLAN	£120.00
18	BRADLEYS	£120.00
19	BRIAN MAULE	£120.00
20	ENOTECA TURI	£120.00
21	HOLBECK GHYLL	£120.00

22	SHARROW BAY	£120.00
23	SIR CHARLES NAPIER	£120.00
24	THE OLD VICARAGE, RIDGEWAY	£120.00
25	36 ON THE QUAY	£125.00
26	60 HOPE STREET	£130.00
27	WITCHERY BY THE CASTLE	£130.00
28	THE MANSION HOUSE, POOLE	£134.00
29	BLEEDING HEART	£135.00
30	RANSOME'S DOCK	£135.00
31	CROOKED BILLET	£140.00
32	THE WINDMILL	£140.00
33	BENTLEY KEMPINSKI 1880	£145.00
34	HOTEL DU VIN, BIRMINGHAM	£145.00
35	NOVELLI AT AUBERGE DU LAC	£145.00
36	HAMBLETON HALL	£147.00
37	KENSINGTON PLACE	£150.00
38	LONGUEVILLE MANOR	£150.00
39	SHANKS	£150.00
40	GREAT EASTERN HOTEL, AURORA	£155.00
41	MAES-Y-NEUADD	£155.00
42	UBIQUITOUS CHIP	£158.95
43	GORDON RAMSAY	£160.00
44	LOWRY HOTEL	£160.00
45	THE DON	£165.00
46	FIFTH FLOOR HARVEY NICHOLS	£170.00
47	OXO TOWER	£170.00
48	ROSCOFF	£175.00
49	YORKE ARMS, RAMSGILL	£175.00
50	COTSWOLD HOUSE	£180.00
51	MC CLEMENTS	£220.00

2: Cloudy Bay Sauvignon Blanc 2004

A total of 38 of the 100 establishments had this wine listed and a further 10 had it in other vintages (mainly 2003). Again, the cheapest listing was around 40% of the most expensive. Of course, it may have gone through more than one middleman before it reaches the restaurant, but it could be argued that in some cases margins have been deliberately increased as a 'punishment' for those customers who can't be bothered to look through the carefully and lovingly constructed wine list and just go for the most recognizable name!

1	PENHELIG ARMS	£26.00
2	OLD BRIDGE, HUNTINGDON	£27.00
3	DARROCH LEARG	£28.00
4	THE GRANGE, BRAMPTON	£28.00

5	WHITE MOSS HOUSE	£29.00
6	BURLINGTON RESTAURANT, DEVONSHIRE ARMS	£29.50
7	CHAMPIGNON SAUVAGE	£30.00
8	LITTLE BARWICK HOUSE	£30.50
9	THE ALBANNACH	£31.00
10	LES MIRABELLES	£31.90
11	CORSE LAWN	£32.50
12	CHAMPANY INN	£33.00
13	HOTEL DU VIN, BIRMINGHAM	£33.00
14	GRAVETYE MANOR	£34.00
15	LEWTRENCHARD MANOR	£34.00
16	THE MANSION HOUSE POOLE	£34.50
17	UBIQUITOUS CHIP	£34.50
18	FAIRY HILL	£35.00
19	LINTHWAITE HOUSE HOTEL	£35.00
20	SHARROW BAY	£35.00
21	THE STAR INN, HAROME	£35.00
22	YE OLDE BULL'S HEAD	£35.00
23	MAES-Y-NEUADD	£37.00
24	SWINTON PARK	£37.00
25	JSW	£38.00
26	FIFTH FLOOR HARVEY NICHOLS	£38.50
27	PLAS BODEGROES	£39.00
28	ETAIN	£39.50
29	SUMMER ISLES HOTEL	£39.50
30	WITCHERY BY THE CASTLE	£40.00
31	LONGUEVILLE MANOR	£45.00
32	PORTMEIRION HOTEL	£45.00
33	NORTHCOTE MANOR	£45.25
34	SIR CHARLES NAPIER	£48.00
35	36 ON THE QUAY	£49.00
36	THE THREE CHIMNEYS	£49.95
37	COTSWOLD HOUSE	£60.00
38	NOVELLI AT AUBERGE DU LAC	£67.00

INDEX

INDEX

INDEX

NOTES

NOTES

NOTES

NOTES

NOTES